Advance praise for How Stories Heal

"Founder of the revolutionary SPN method Robert J. Nash has created a detailed guide on how to bear witness to our lives by writing our own scholarly stories. His belief that the world of academe has suffered from depersonalization—and that higher learning more effectively takes place when students and teachers are able to explore and communicate their unique experiences as they relate to the human experience in its entirety—has led to the development of this postmodern system of academic writing. Sydnee Viray shares Nash's conviction that by writing our stories using SPN, we can create existential meaning for our lives. Her involvement not only adds a feminine perspective, but a second clear voice which highlights non-judgment and compassion.

A radical departure from the dusty tomes typically associated with higher education, as well as the soulless material students are traditionally taught to write, SPN gives students, instead, the tools to thoroughly explicate their lives, share what they have learned, and apply that learning to universal philosophy. As a dedicated writer of my own stories, I hear from people every day who struggle with the 'how' of telling theirs. SPN offers us the chance to articulate our own idiosyncratic struggles, release pain, and find peace and passion throughout the process."

—Erica Leibrandt, featured writer for *Elephant Journal*,
YA 200 yoga instructor, and memoirist

"It's high time we honored our personal stories not as peripheral to but as pillars of research and scholarship. At once secular and sacred, academic and intensely personal, *How Stories Heal* brings to mind the work of philosopher Martin Buber, who wrote '...we live in the currents of universal reciprocity.' Nash and Viray have assembled a collection of stories that is equal parts memoir, methodology, and mirror, embodying and teaching the very truths they set out to convey. Putting 'meaning-making' into the process of learning, of becoming fully human, is something we owe ourselves and each other, as students and educators. This book is a gift not only to the academy, but perhaps more importantly, beyond it."

—Jena Strong, Associate Director, Career Options Resource Center,
Hampshire College; author of two collections of poetry and prose,
Don't Miss This and *The Inside of Out*

How Stories Heal

To Jozef,

You are an extremely talented personal narrative writer. I am so deeply appreciative for all your support of my work with students over the past 25 years. I look forward with excitement to reading your upcoming book!

Robert J. Nash

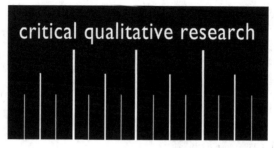

critical qualitative research

CRITICAL ISSUES FOR LEARNING AND TEACHING

Shirley R. Steinberg and Gaile S. Cannella
General Editors

Vol. 11

The Critical Qualitative Research series
is part of the Peter Lang Education list.
Every volume is peer reviewed and meets
the highest quality standards for content and production.

PETER LANG
New York • Washington, D.C./Baltimore • Bern
Frankfurt • Berlin • Brussels • Vienna • Oxford

Robert J. Nash & Sydnee Viray

How Stories Heal

Writing Our Way to Meaning & Wholeness in the Academy

PETER LANG
New York • Washington, D.C./Baltimore • Bern
Frankfurt • Berlin • Brussels • Vienna • Oxford

Library of Congress Cataloging-in-Publication Data

Nash, Robert J.
How stories heal: writing our way to meaning and wholeness in the academy /
Robert J. Nash, Sydnee Viray.
pages cm. — (Critical qualitative research; Vol. 11)
Includes bibliographical references.
1. English language—Rhetoric—Study and teaching. 2. Academic writing—Study and
teaching. 3. Narration (Rhetoric)—Psychological aspects. 4. Creative writing—
Therapeutic use. 5. Healing—Literary collections. 6. Autobiography—Authorship.
I. Viray, Sydnee. II. Title.
PE1404.N376   808'.0420711—dc23   2013045675
ISBN 978-1-4331-2483-9 (hardcover)
ISBN 978-1-4331-2482-2 (paperback)
ISBN 978-1-4539-1301-7 (e-book)
ISSN 1947-5993

Bibliographic information published by **Die Deutsche Nationalbibliothek.**
Die Deutsche Nationalbibliothek lists this publication in the "Deutsche
Nationalbibliografie"; detailed bibliographic data is available
on the Internet at http://dnb.d-nb.de/.

The paper in this book meets the guidelines for permanence and durability
of the Committee on Production Guidelines for Book Longevity
of the Council of Library Resources.

© 2014 Peter Lang Publishing, Inc., New York
29 Broadway, 18th floor, New York, NY 10006
www.peterlang.com

Printed in the United States of America

Contents

**Part I. The *Wisdom* of Scholarly Personal Narrative—
Writing from the Head to the Heart...and Back Again**

Part II. The Emotional Impact of Scholarly Personal Narrative— Writing from the Gut

Part III. The Transformative Power of Scholarly Personal Narrative— Writing about Change from the Field

Acknowledgments

First, I wish to thank Sydnee Viray, my talented and fearless SPN co-author and superb intellectual ironist, for once more taking on such a formidable book-writing project with me. You are truly an SPN exemplar of the highest order as well as an invaluable personal support for a later-life professor like myself.

Second, I am indebted to those writers who contributed pieces to this book. This includes (in alphabetical order) Wind Paz-Amor, Jarett Chizick, Madelyn Nash, and Jen Prue. Thank you each for your willingness to write from both your heart and your head.

Third, I am professionally grateful to the following colleagues at the University of Vermont for their willingness to support a new type of scholarly methodology and, also, to serve on a number of SPN comps, thesis, and dissertation committees. I list these colleagues in alphabetical order: Judith Aiken, Penny Bishop, DeMethra L. Bradley, Holly-Lynn Busier, Judith Cohen, Deb Hunter, Christopher Koliba, Colleen MacKinnon, Wolfgang Mieder, Jen Prue, Charles Rathbone, Cynthia Reyes, Jill Tarule, Shelley Vermilya, Stuart Whitney, and, of course, the Dean of the College of Education and Social Services at the University of Vermont, Fayneese Miller. I also want to thank Richard Greggory Johnson III, a professor at the University of San Francisco, for his undying loyalty and encouragement.

Fourth, I cannot thank enough all the students through the years who have chosen to write their way to healing, meaning, and wholeness in their SPN course assignments, as well as in their final comps, thesis, and dissertation manuscripts. The number of such students is now in the thousands. Please know one and all that I admire your ability, energy, wisdom, and inspiration.

Fifth, I cannot say enough about all the students who have gone through my Interdisciplinary Graduate program over the past 45 years. You have taken on the formidable challenges of SPN writing, even when it was not fashionable to do so in a Public Ivy University. Trust me when I say that without your extraordinary talent, grit, and determination throughout the past four decades, we would not have been able to legitimize SPN as a valid research methodology—not just at the University of Vermont but throughout the country and abroad.

Finally, I offer enduring gratitude to my always-supportive, and brilliantly discerning, wife of 51 years, Madelyn A. Nash. You are an ideal combination of both head and heart, and I can honestly say that I would never have been able to produce over 100 scholarly articles and 14 books without your loving presence, and patience, in my life.

—Robert J. Nash

. . . .

"The only important thing in a book is the meaning that it has for you."
—W. Somerset Maugham

I would like to acknowledge my esteemed coauthor, Dr. Robert J. Nash. He has been a rock of support and a lantern of guidance as I navigate my journey as a scholarly writer. Though we mostly wrote this book in separate physical spaces, he was always with me via phone, video calls, or through emails. It was his voice that championed me as I dove deep, leaned in and on, and re-discovered the mysteries of my own healing and meaning making journey. For this I am honored to label him as a dear friend.

My acknowledgment would be empty if I neglected all of the souls that I have met who are survivors and especially those who have listened to my stories, my revisited conversations of self-recovery, and who have found me to be their nonjudgmental witness to their excursions toward healing.

I would like to especially acknowledge all those who are about to read this book who are on a journey to find meaning and wholeness in the walls of the academy, we wrote this to you. To remind you that you are not alone on your path toward wholeness as a scholar, writer, and most importantly an individual who has a story to share. Dare to find the meaning that this book could have for you as you progress toward healing, meaning, and wholeness.

Thank you to all of the editors at Peter Lang Publishing and to our endorsers who have read the manuscript to give their honest reflections of our work.

—Sydnee Viray

Part 1

The *Wisdom* of Scholarly Personal Narrative
Writing from the Head to the Heart…and Back Again

In the chapters that follow in Part I, Robert explains the whats, hows, and whys of Scholarly Personal Narrative Writing. Some of the chapters are more personal than others—by intention. Robert's goal is two-sided: to illustrate the more technical principles and techniques of SPN writing by telling his own story and by drawing briefly on the stories of others. The wisdom of SPN lies in the recognition that writing from the head to the heart…and back again requires a unique set of technical skills that enable both the writer, and the reader, to arrive at the ultimate goals of self-understanding and self-transformation. These skills include a willingness to dig deeply in order to discover the truths that lie buried in our pasts and presents, an ability to thematize and universalize these insights for readers, and a profound, almost unyielding commitment to the belief that writing one's way to healing, meaning, and wholeness is not only possible—it is necessary. All of this leads to *wisdom*.

Writing Our Lives as an Act of Personal Witness

ROBERT J. NASH & SYDNEE VIRAY

· ·

A Letter from Jared: "Please Help Me!"

Dear Professor Nash,

I am so sorry that I have been out of touch the last year since my gradua-tion. This is not a happy email. I have been lost in every sense of the word. I am unhappy with my work situation, even though I make more than enough money to satisfy my needs. In fact, I hate my boring job, even though for the first time in my life, I've achieved financial freedom. A lot of my friends have moved away from Vermont in order to find work, settle down into a lasting relationship, and add stability to their lives. My best friend is joining the Army because he thinks that the uniform and the medals will give his life a mean-ing that it hasn't had since he graduated. I feel lonely and down all the time. I am beginning to wonder if I should go back to school and pursue a graduate degree. I certainly can't go home, because New York city is another world for me right now, and my parents just divorced…angrily. In fact, I never had much of a relationship with my family—a father who was a drunk and a drug addict, and a disillusioned mother who was always in denial and who spent most of her time hidden away in her bedroom. But, if I return to school, what should I study? I am just not happy with who I have become, and I am struggling to dig deep and get back into fighting shape to deal with the next several years of my quarterlife. As we so often talked about in your personal narrative writing class, I need some meaning big-time right now. I'm living, but I'm living like a dead man, if you know what I mean. I'm wasting my zombie life away lazing around on the couch, eating crap and getting fat, playing stupid electronic games on my dumb phone, hooking up with anyone and everyone at the dreary drinking bars downtown, and then, before I know it, the hookup chicks disappear from my life. Poof. Gone. I graduated cum laude with a business degree. I thought I was set. But I'm not. I have no idea who I am, why I am, or where I am. I'm seeing two different therapists each week, but I end up bullshitting them. Anti-depressants make me feel even flatter than I am without them. So, Great Professor of Scholarly Personal Narrative Writing: what should I do? I really, really need to be back in one of your courses. I am so ready, particularly at this juncture, to make sense of my life. I need to write. I need to tell my stories. What is it you used to say: each of us needs to write our way into meaning and wholeness. Why wasn't there some place on campus for me to go to write about all this stuff throughout the four years when I was a student? I only did this in your writing course. Truth to tell, I didn't take most of your stuff seriously. It just didn't seem like real academic work for me to write about me. Well, Kind Writing Professor—I do now. Believe me—I do now. Please help me.

Jared

"Writing as an Act of Personal Witness" —Ruth Behar

The book you are about to read—*How Stories Heal: Writing Our Way to Meaning and Wholeness in the Academy*—is a natural sequel, and, therefore, a companion volume, to our publication in 2013—*Our Stories Matter: Liberating the Voices of Marginalized Students Through Scholarly Personal Narrative Writing* (both published by Peter Lang). Our intention is to write this book sequel for a less specific audience than our earlier volume which focused on the importance of marginalized, disenfranchised students' developing the writing skills to narrate their individual stories of liberation. We want this new book to be a complement to our previous volume. It will expand on some of the themes in our earlier book, but it will break considerably newer and much more inclusive ground.

We also anticipate a much larger reading audience, including both marginalized and non-marginalized people. How so? Our overall theme in this book is a universal one, regardless of our specific identities, psyches, and backgrounds. We believe that all of us must confront the human challenge to make *meaning* of our lives. All of us, at various points in our day-to-day living, find ourselves undertaking the journey to become *whole* human beings. So, too, each of us has had to undergo difficult periods of psychological *healing* during the ordinary and extraordinary storms and stresses we encounter in the process of trying to live our lives with integrity, joy, love, purpose, hope, and courage.

Jared, our letter writer who begins this chapter, is exhibit A of someone who finds value in writing his way to meaning and wholeness. As an undergraduate, Jared took a Scholarly Personal Narrative (SPN) writing course with Robert. He came to the university from the inner city, having won a full four-year scholarship because of his academic success in high school. While undertaking the challenging transition from New York City to Burlington, Vermont, Jared, an early quarterlife, African-American, rap-music lyricist, learned to write in an SPN style about where he had been, where he was now, and where he wanted to go in his life. Jared suffers from incurable Sickle Cell Anemia. He is slowly losing his vision. He suffers from periods of interminable nose bleeds. When he graduated with his honors business degree, he felt he had arrived. Finally! But he hadn't. He was still dealing with unsettled quarterlife issues. His nine-hour-a-day, well-paying, but highly routinized job had put a freeze on writing his way to healing and understanding—the single creative activity he enjoyed most while in college.

Jared's candid letter to Robert was a desperate plea to help him return to school, to write his story, to connect with others, and to make sense of the aimlessness and emptiness that was plaguing him each and every day. He was falling into self-destructive despair, into a state of mind- and heart-numbing ennui. Robert and Sydnee have met countless Jareds in their SPN writing course each year. No matter how different their life's contingencies appear to be, these students all share one need in common: They have reached a point in their life cycles when they must create a purpose to live for, a passion to die for, a love to care for, and a joy to strive for. They crave the opportunity, and the support, to author their personal stories of success and failure, despair and hope.

For these students, there is no alternative to Ruth Behar's words in the epigraph that opens this section: Each of us needs to write the story of our lives as "an act of personal witness." What Behar (1993), a noted anthropology scholar, who is also a MacArthur Genius Award Winner, means by this is to the point: Scholars need to stop the "depersonalizing trend" in research that results in massive collections of so-called "objective data" regarding the "other" but nothing at all about the "self" who is collecting the data. A scholar who writes as an act of personal witness attempts to "desegregate the boundaries between the self and the other." Personal witness means to write "vulnerably." It is all about identifying, and acknowledging, the central role of the writer's personal experience in any type of scholarship. In Behar's words: "…it requires a keen understanding of what aspects of the self are the most important filters through which one perceives the world and, more importantly, the topic being studied." Is there any better way than this to create meaning, to heal, and to be whole? Behar's entire book *The Vulnerable Observer: Anthropology That Breaks Your Heart* is a wonderful example of a renowned anthropological scholar's "bearing personal witness" to the story of her own, vulnerable writer's self.

For the both of us, we can genuinely assert that we have yet to meet anyone, either inside or outside our classrooms and college offices, who is impervious to what we consider to be *the* major survival human need: *making meaning and becoming a whole person by telling their stories.* In fact, for Hayden White, a literary historian, the word "narrative" derives from the ancient Sanskrit "gna," a root term that means "know," "tell," and even, by extension, "survive." Moreover, this is an innate evolutionary drive, according to such experts as H. Porter Abbott, Jerome Bruner, and Paul J. Eakin (see Abbott, 2002). For some evolutionary theorists, there are few human practices that have as much adaptive value as the human instinct to tell, and to hear, stories about meaning-making.

Some of our students and colleagues, of course, confront this need to tell their stories earlier, some later; some do it consciously, some unconsciously; some experience this need intensely, some less intensely. But all of us, sooner or later, must come to terms with something that Nietzsche, the great philosopher of meaning-making, once said: "He who has a 'why' to live can bear almost any 'how.'" In fact, it was this maxim that helped Viktor E. Frankl (2006), a Jew, to survive three terrible years of suffering in the Nazi death camps during the Holocaust. What sustained him each and every miserable day, in his own words, was his particular "why" insight: "The meaning of my life is to help others find the meaning of theirs" (p. 165). And this is the personal story that Frankl went on to write in several books after his release from the World War II concentration camps.

We can honestly say that we have not met a single human being over decades of dealing with students, colleagues, friends, and loved ones who is impervious to the human need to tell stories and to hear the stories of others. Stories provide the opportunity to write our way to meaning and wholeness in the academy. As we enter the 21st century in higher education, we believe it is a necessity for us to innovate our approaches to research and teaching by encouraging our students, and our colleagues, to write their personal stories. Therefore, we have taken Viktor Frankl's meaning-insight to heart ourselves, and moved meaning-making one step further: We want to help others to *write* their way into meaning, healing, and wholeness. In fact, this is the primary purpose of Scholarly Personal Narrative writing as we teach it. SPN is a new form of non-fiction, essay writing, and we are convinced that it is every bit as rigorous, and as vigorous, as other types of academically-certified, quantitative and qualitative research. In a real sense, then, we hope that this book enlarges, enriches, and deepens the more conventional meaning of academic scholarship.

Both of us co-teach a course in this newer genre of SPN scholarship (created by Robert two decades ago). Each semester large numbers of graduate and undergraduate students flock to our elective writing course in order to make sense of the quarterlife and mid-life turbulence that saps the energy out of any sense of meaning and purpose in their lives. Hundreds of our students from a variety of disciplinary majors and minors, and from professional schools as well, have told us that the opportunity we give them to write personally and narratively is "transformative" and "healing" for them. What they are saying is that no longer are they required to remain in one prescriptive writing style. The vast majority of these students tell us that they have never been asked to narrate their own stories before the fact, and then to make scholarly, more universalizable, sense of these stories after the fact. Most of our students comment that before taking our course they had no idea how to write an essay as a scholarly personal narrative. They had been taught by "scholars" to see the world from the outside-in rather than from the inside-out. They had been taught that subjectivity is always less "rigorous" than objectivity. The consequence of this is that so many of our students seem to have lost the "vigor" of self-discovery in the pursuit of "rigor" in scholarship detached from the self.

We believe that this gap in our students' education at all levels is tragic. We currently live in an age of memoir-writing. People love to tell their stories and to hear the stories of others. At this point in time, academe has not caught up to the world outside the ivy walls. For most university scholars, writing for a general public smacks of "mere journalism." Worse, if scholars strive to make their writing comprehensible for an audience beyond the university, then they run the risk of being charged with compromising the intellectual prestige of their disciplines. Moreover, say the critics, personal narrative writing doesn't win grants. Neither, the critics remind us, does it get faculty renewed contracts, tenure, promotion, or distinguished professorships. There is a supreme irony here: in the pursuit of conventional rewards, many faculty lose connection to their own personal histories. Consequently, a few faculty attempt to reconnect their professional and personal lives by waiting until much later in their careers to write more personally. For example, Amy Chua (2011), the holder of the John M. Duff Professorship at Yale University Law School, has published a best-selling memoir *Battle Hymn of the Tiger Mother*. Her book tells the provocative, down-to-earth story of how her strict Chinese upbringing influenced her own parenting style regarding the mistakes she made and the successes she had with her two daughters.

Here is a simple fact: the printed, and online, books and articles that sell best nowadays are true-to-life personal narratives that appeal to a much larger public readership. Naomi Schaefer Riley (2011), an award-winning, higher education journalist, reports that a university press–published book in the social sciences or humanities is doing well if it sells a mere 300 copies, and most of these are purchased by university libraries for inflated sums of money to cover the cost of printing. Likewise, a research-based article (according to economist Richard Vedder [2004], two million scholarly articles are published every year) in a refereed academic journal averages about a dozen readers at most. The truth is that most faculty publish for only one reason: to avoid perishing—to secure tenure and promotion. Once these goals are reached, only a relatively small percentage of faculty bother to publish anything afterwards (the estimate has been as low as 10%). We believe that if university scholars could report their findings in accessible, engaging prose, and even tell a few personal stories along the way, then they might get more feedback from readers. And reader-response (whether positive or negative) can be a great motivator for a faculty member to continue writing and publishing.

It is time for academics to face this fact: nothing is more appealing to readers (especially to our students) than to experience an author's personal stories with meaning-making implications that can touch all lives. No matter the age or stage, the personal or collective identity, everyone we know (whether professorial, professional, or pre-professional; whether quarterlife, mid-life, or later-life) is dealing with meaning-making issues that will challenge them, and others, throughout their lifetimes. These are universal themes that are endemic to the human condition. These themes encompass understanding, and implementing, several life-sustaining hopes and dreams for the future. They include the following: constructing a moral and ethical life-plan; choosing the right religion and spirituality to give strength and hope during the difficult times; creating mutually beneficial core relationships that are lasting and loving; exploring intersecting identities that do not box or separate but, instead, result in making connections with others; knowing the differences between education and credentialism, as well as the difference between having a career and living a vocation; getting actively involved in civic engagement projects; learning how to deal with loss, pain, disappointment, and a sense of meaninglessness and purposelessness; and creating, and practicing, key strategies that will pay off in living a whole, healthy, joyful, and balanced life.

We are convinced that our book will satisfy a huge need in higher education and scholarship, particularly for those students who are writing theses and dissertations; and, also, for those junior and senior faculty who are looking to construct alternative forms of scholarship for publication. We believe that we have reached an exciting time in the academy. The time has come—particularly when STEM research methodologies are further disconnecting scholars from a more general audience—for each of the disciplines to look for the value in personal narrative writing. We refer to this type of writing as the "turn to the subjective I" or to "me-search research." Actually, there is hope. Gerald Graff (2003), a leading literary scholar and former President of the Modern Language Association, lists the names of several respected scholars who are striving to combine the language of the personal vernacular with the technical terminology of their academic disciplines. We support this both-and approach to innovative scholarship. They are attempting to turn scholarly inaccessibility into public accessibility. He calls this mixture of writing styles a "bridge discourse" that could conceivably transform the meaning of scholarly writing in the academy. We call this type of writing a "connection discourse": connecting the "I" of the scholar to the "It" of the scholarship.

We intend to write a book that is down-to-earth, clear, and accessible to non-scholars, as well as to scholars, who represent a variety of professions and disciplines. Our voices will be impassioned, but, most of all, our writing will be honest, direct, and self-disclosing. This will be a book about SPN writing actually written in an SPN style. Not only will we explain the way to write meaning-making, scholarly personal narratives; we, ourselves, will write as scholarly personal narrative authors. In other words, we will work hard to exemplify what we explicate. While we have the greatest amount of respect for the scholarly disciplines (both of us have been trained in the disciplines—Robert in English, philosophy, cultural anthropology, and religious studies, and Sydnee in psychology, economics, and social work), we will attempt to deliver our ideas without having to filter them through the sometimes impenetrable argot (case in point?) of the scholarly disciplines. We will write as public intellectuals and as down-to-earth practitioner-scholars.

We want to write a book for all our readers that features a kind of philosophical, meaning-making curative rooted in our own personal stories, as well as in the wisdom of some of the greatest thinkers and writers of all time. We will also include, when appropriate, a few examples of SPN stories of meaning-making and wholeness that some of our students have written to help in their own life-healing. As authors, we both agree with Epicurus that, to a great extent, educators everywhere need to deal with the "suffering of the mind" as well as the mind's greatest intellectual accomplishments. Also, we support the wisdom of the Roman Stoic, Marcus Aurelius: "the happiness of one's life depends upon the quality of one's thoughts." We will write a book that encourages all students everywhere to examine the quality of their thinking (so that some might become "thought leaders" both inside and outside the university) along with the quality of their everyday living.

How and Why We Will Write Our Book: A Summary

What follows, then, is a summary of how, and why, we will write our book:

- We will write our book as an SPN. The book will draw from a variety of genres in autobiographical and narrative writing, creative literature, philosophy, ethics, the various wisdom and religio-spiritual traditions, narrative medicine, and educational theory. Our overall purpose will be to show how these genres can be useful in furthering the emotional, spiritual, and intellectual development of students everywhere. Our approach will be interdisciplinary, practical, philosophical, and, we hope, healing. Our basic assumption is that one of the most powerful ways to make meaning is to write our way to wholeness and understanding by telling our stories and by helping our readers to draw larger lessons from them.

- We will write our book directly to practitioners and to students at various levels of professional training and formal education. We will write primarily out of the context of our personal, as well as our professional, lives. We will work hard to make our writing accessible and clear. We will intentionally keep our scholarly references to a minimum, but we will never lose sight of the value of the wisdom of others (both everyday persons we know as well as the thinkers who are famous) who, themselves, have much to offer us by way of meaning-making. We will write with candor. We will tell aggregated personal stories about others, and about ourselves. We will aim for the reader's heart as well as for the head. We will go for the smile as well as for the grimace. We will seek the eureka-flash of understanding, as well as acknowledging, and respecting, the unavoidable mysteries of meaning-making and healing.

- We will also address the internal, ethical-personal dilemmas of uncovering stories buried deep in our families' stories and ourselves. We will discuss how we set up our classroom environments to create a supportive person-to-person community of learning that allows for peers share openly and honestly with one another. This type of classroom community puts the student/author at the center of their own learning. We touch on the ethics regarding the element of self-disclosure, and its implications for relevant others, in Scholarly Personal Narrative writing.

- We will try to convey in each of our chapters the profound love we have for our subject matter, for our students, for our colleagues, and for all the people we serve. We will write in a spirit of joyfulness and hope, even though some of what we discuss might be sad and troubling. We will make it a point never to sink to a level of cynicism or critique for critique's sake. We will compose our stories as ongoing journeys to find and make meaning—both ours and our students'. We will try to exemplify the courage we believe it takes to write our way into meaning, healing, and transformation. This will entail that we speak our own truths with frankness, even when these might make some readers uncomfortable. We will also strive to achieve a tone throughout our book that is generous, humble, wise, and not without a sense of humor.

- Finally, we will never forget that we, too, are learners. We, too, will be using our book to write our own ways into meaning. We, too, have stories to tell, stories to evoke from others, and stories that, when used effectively, can provide a framework for understanding the more universal stories of the human condition. In the pages ahead, you will be reading actual SPN pieces that we (and a few others) have written. Be prepared for a no-holds-barred series of candid self-disclosures that we hope exemplify and explicate the main intention of our book: To show that stories heal, that meaning matters, that wholeness is possible, and that SPN writing can be both scholarly and self-transforming.

We will include in each chapter actual examples of a particular piece of SPN writing on the chapter theme. Most of these examples will come from our own writings, and some from our students' writings. We will refer to these writing samples in order to illustrate, and explain, the power of SPN in writing our way to meaning, wholeness, and healing. Always, we will draw larger lessons from both our own writing and the students' writings by pointing to insights from relevant experts on meaning-making, healing, and wholeness as well as experts on personal narrative writing. We will end each chapter with a conclusion.

Who and What We Are

Finally, in many ways we are an unlikely pair of co-authors. Sydnee is a Filipina American immigrant, a late quarterlifer, a community-activist social worker, and a financial affairs administrator. Robert is a working-class late-lifer, a humanities scholar, a tenured full professor in a college of education and social services, a prolific writer, and an officially designated University of Vermont Scholar in the Social Sciences and Humanities. Both of us, however, are interdisciplinarians. Both of us are scholar-practitioners. Both of us appreciate scholarship that is self-disclosing, lyrical, philosophical, thematically universalizable, and cathartic. And both of us are highly aware of how controversial this type of writing is in Carnegie Research-I Universities. Most important, however, both of us know from first-hand experience that SPN writing is extraordinarily difficult because we have written in this genre ourselves.

Most of the conventional research and scholarship that faculty undertake in professional schools and in the social and natural sciences is empirically-based, either of a scientific, qualitative, or quantitative bent. We know a great deal about empirical scholarship because each of us has undertaken such research. Sydnee's academic background is based in the social sciences, and Robert has advised several theses and dissertations in one or more of the empirical scholarship genres. As we have gotten to know one another these last few years, and despite our disciplinary and professional differences, it didn't take long for us to realize we had much in common.

We both describe ourselves as scholar-practitioners. We are both pragmatists. Sydnee is an ironist. Robert is a postmodernist. We both love to teach and to write. We enjoy asking the "big questions," as well as the "little questions," about creating existential meaning. We love non-conventional forms of scholarly writing. The most wonderful discovery for both of us as our collaborative relationship has evolved, though, is to realize that, in our own unique ways, we are both philosophers. We mention this delightful discovery because, by definition, a philosopher is someone who loves the *pursuit* of wisdom even more than the actual *attainment* of it. A philosopher is a seeker not a finder; a practitioner of the interrogative, not the declarative or the imperative. A philosopher is, by definition, both a lover of ideas, and a lover of those who profess to love ideas. Each of us tends to project an intellectual spirit that is at once restless and yet grounded. Both of us in our own ways live our life as if we are on a continual quest for meaning by asking the deeper philosophical questions having to do with wholeness, meaning, and healing.

Even though in some ways we are *yin* and *yang*, we are both independent and interdependent. We are both secular and spiritual. We are both inveterate readers in a variety of genres, including technical scientific material, philosophy, poetry, and the social sciences. In our pedagogy, we encourage our students to engage in heart-felt discussion and sharing. We are both intuitive and intentional. We respect both thinking *and* feeling in a seminar. We make it a point to see our students as mutually inclusive "heads" *and* "hearts."

Our shared regard for personal narrative writing is what drew the both of us to this particular project. In a nutshell, SPN is a special way of thinking, and writing, about the world of professional practice. This kind of writing begins with the personhood of the author and radiates outward. It places subjectivity on a par with objectivity. It is both concrete and abstract; particular and universal. SPN writing leads with the author's personal take on the world of ideas and experiences by encouraging writers to see themselves as the pivotal variables in their texts—without whom there would be no texts. SPN locates the author's life and experiences as central to a scholarly analysis or a research study.

In the last few decades, SPN types of scholarship have found a home in such disciplines as cultural pluralism studies, women's studies, narrative theology, postmodern philosophy, and composition and rhetoric studies. What has sometimes been referred to as "autobiographical scholarship" or "personal scholarship" is an effort on the part of many feminist writers and postmodern authors to re-vision their scholarly inquiries. SPN writing looks to the lived life of the writer-scholar as the major source of questions, perspectives, and methods. Socrates said that the "unexamined life is not worth living." We believe that the "unlived life is not worth examining."

Whatever the academic discipline, the two of us believe that SPN is a scholarly methodology that effectively blends stories, interpretation, theory, and universalizable themes. In the words of Diane P. Freedman and Olivia Frey (1993), this kind of scholarship has the potential of producing "beautiful, evocative writing that connects with readers and can serve as a trusted, enlightening source" (p. 20). This is what we hope will happen for all our readers in the SPN writing style that shapes our book.

Because we believe that, at some level, all writing is personal, we want to talk about the work we do with our students and colleagues. We will strive to do this in a candid, up-front, self-disclosing, writing format. For the purposes of this particular, co-authored project, we believe that SPN writing is not merely another interesting research option for two professional collaborators to engage in. Rather, we feel that it is one way (not the *only* way), at this particular time in our lives, that we can communicate to others the raw personal and professional truths of our own encounters with writing our way into meaning and wholeness.

A Postscript

What follows is a reflection written by Jared, whose letter opens this chapter. He wrote this reflection while he was taking the SPN course in 2009. Even then, as a first-year 18-year-old undergraduate, his writing presaged issues that even now continue to concern him in his current life. He was the only first-year student in that SPN class, and one of just three undergraduates. All the rest were graduate- and post-graduate students. Jared felt he lacked credibility because of his age, his race, his limited life-experience, and his low socio-economic status. He had talked with Robert about feeling insecure and "dismissed" by some others in the class. He badly wanted what he called "academic 'cred'." And, so, after meeting with Robert, he composed this personal reflection. (It is important for the reader to remember that Jared had already lived a lifetime in his 18 short years—homeless, battered, incurably diseased, addicted, and, yet, a courageous, adaptive survivor with a high I.Q.; most definitely a victor not a victim.) Finally, what makes the following piece so poignant is that, in contrast with Jared's opening letter to Robert, the 18-year-old Jared's reflection reveals the answer to the earlier 24-year-old Jared's existential questions.

"Please Don't Be Scared of Me"
(Jared)

I walked though campus thinking about the feedback I had received from Robert in my Scholarly Personal Narrative writing course. "Maybe your intellect intimidates people. Maybe the people you're asking for help don't see the world as you see it, and it probably makes them feel less sure of themselves because they can't believe that someone like you, that someone of your age, can actually think that deeply about life." Someone like me? What does that mean? I spent my walk home thinking of what that could mean and why people would really be afraid of me—a young man who thought about the Bible, death, history, love, meaning, and philosophy. So what if I was only 18 years old? Why would people actually fear someone who lives and loves to think? Why would they put down my work, my writing, and my rap music? Why don't they look me in the face and say I intimidate them? I mean, like Robert says about himself, 'I am a cool realist.' I can take it. Why can't they see me that way? To be honest, I don't know what they think of me, but it can't be good, can it?

My walk home actually turned into an unplanned walk downtown. There I was, walking past my usual hangout, "Mr. Mike's," watching college kids drink their beers and eat their pizza as they sat there with all of their friends laughing and joking. I looked into the window and thought of how close they all were.

Were any of them intimidated by one another? I thought about why I felt this way, not just in Robert's class but everywhere else; why I felt like no one could understand who I am or what I believe, and why I used prescription drugs to make sense of my own fear and my own questions. And then it hit me...

I realized then that I was off balance, and maybe it wasn't the fact that people were intimidated or fearful of me. Maybe the reason why I felt this way was because I was afraid of myself, and I was limiting myself to the expectations of the world around me. I had "refused to go gently into this good night," one of Robert's favorite quotes. I had refused to go gently into anything I tried to do or create mainly because I was scared of who I was becoming. All this time I had been looking for some sort of recognition, some sort of answer from other people, and the whole time what I really wanted was to remove the auto-tune program off my voice and let the real me be heard. I wanted to stand in front of this world and say "No auto-tune, but you can feel the pain. It all comes spilling out like I hit a vein" ("Fear" by Drake). I wanted to just let it all out but I couldn't, because I had masked my own fear and projected it into others.

I realized—during what was supposed to be a five-minute walk (but turned into an hour of realization)—that I wanted people to understand who I was and accept me for me. I wanted people in the SPN class to read my work and feel every little word and line. I wanted them to see the me underneath the loser who got messed up all the time. But what I realized on that walk is that was all they were going to see, mainly because the reason I did drugs and I "popped bottles was because I bottled my emotions" ("Fear" by Drake). But who was going to know that really? I didn't even know it, and if I were told that before this moment I wouldn't believe it. I guess all the questions I was asking were never going to get answers. Why? Because it wasn't that people were intimidated my me, but that I was intimidated by myself.

· ·

Chapter 2

Writing Our Way into Healing, Meaning, and Wholeness
A Personal Example

ROBERT J. NASH

Five years ago a strange state of mind began to grow upon me: I had moments of perplexity, of a stoppage, as it were, of life, as if I did not know how I was to live, what I was to do.... These stoppages of life always presented themselves to me with the same question: "Why?" and "What for?"... These questions demanded an answer with greater and greater persistence and, like dots, grouped themselves into one black spot.

—*Leo Tolstoy*

I will introduce the concepts of healing, meaning, and wholeness by sharing with all my readers the most personal piece of writing I have ever done. It has never been published before. For me, this chapter is a risky self-disclosure because the "Robert" in this narrative is not the "Robert" that my colleagues and students have ever seen. I thought long and hard about writing this essay, and I decided that it is time for me to put my SPN money where my SPN mouth is. Moreover, I can think of no better way to talk about healing, meaning, and wholeness than by talking about my own personal challenges to achieve these outcomes. In fact, during the summer of 2013 when I wrote this retrospective piece about my past, present, and future life, I was able to more clearly write my way into meaning, healing, and wholeness.

At the end of my personal essay, I will further explore the philosophical and psychological implications of these three terms. But I will always refer back to the personal particulars in my essay to exemplify and explicate—or better still to make real—these larger themes. In Chapter 3, I share a piece of writing that this essay inspired and without which I never would have revisited an event

I had repressed for years. In Chapters 4, 5, and 6, I will identify, and explain, the more technical fundamentals of SPN writing. In Chapter 5, I will also issue myself a report card on how well, and how poorly, I think I used the SPN "tools" of authorship in a chapter I wrote for a book in 2002.

. . . .

My SPN Essay: "What Does My Life Mean? The Most Urgent Question of All"

I believe that a crisis of meaning surrounds us, professionals and students alike. Paraphrasing Tolstoy, at the beginning of the 21st century, far too many of us stand on "crumbling ground." The escalating threats of terrorism throughout the world, fluctuating stock markets and tenuous global economies, massive downsizing in the corporations, military interventions and occupations throughout the globe, religious and nationalistic fanaticisms, the creeping loss of civil liberties, the ideological turn toward simplistic political answers to complex questions—all of these, and more, represent the third millennium's "crumbling ground," its "dark nights of despair." These nights affect all of us. I know that they affect me and my students.

I have seen in my own work as an educator that life appears to be without meaning to many individuals—at all stages and ages of development. During these times, each of us "stands close to the precipice, and we see nothing but ruin," said Tolstoy (2009, p. 40). Camus remarked that the "question of life's meaning is the most urgent question of all." In fact, for him, it's the only philosophical question worth asking. Therefore, I ask, and explore for myself, this pivotal question here in a very personal way.

Spiraling Downward: A Personal Case in Point

As a child in a Catholic grammar school, I often challenged my parents' taken-for-granted atheism with the same fervor as a village atheist questioning a believer's taken-for-granted theism. "How come you don't go to church like my friends' parents?" I asked. "Are you heathens?" "Why don't we pray before eating?" "How come you never say the rosary or go to confession?" "Why do you always criticize priests and nuns, and people who go to church, for being hypocrites?" "What is it you believe, anyway?" "Is the reason that the nuns don't like me because you hate God?"

I realize now that I was just taunting my parents in order to be cruel, as a payback to make them miserable for sending me to Catholic school for the "discipline" and not for the "religion," as they often reminded me. Little did they know that I hated Catholic school. I hated the nuns in their forbidding black and white habits, their faint smell of talcum powder, the way they meted out corporal punishment by thrashing the backs of our hands with steel, razor-edged rulers until our knuckles bled. Most of all, though, I hated the nuns' arrogance, and smugness, whenever they told me, word for word, what God expected of me. And I'd better watch out, or I'd burn in hell for all eternity. And what would hurt worse than the flames scorching my body was the absence of God's face in my life forever. So I'd better say a rosary, go to confession, and get right with my Creator.

"Hypocrite" was a word I learned from my parents when I was in the first grade, and it became the most common putdown I heard during all the time I lived with them. I remember to this day how often I cringed whenever my mother and father dismissed someone I respected with the disdainful epithet, "hypocrite." I am ashamed to say that one of the primary reasons why I embrace non-belief today is because of the dramatic disconnects I see between what believers profess and how believers act. I say "ashamed" because if ever that unlikely day were to come that I would be presented with irrefutable evidence to believe, I would still be looking for the contradictions in believers' lives to justify my nonbelief. Obviously this is not a recipe for happiness.

As a young pre-teen, I alienated many nuns and priests in my Catholic grade school, St. Gregory's, in Boston, by continually questioning their pronouncements on how I had to live my life if I were to be redeemed by God's grace. "How do you know?" I once asked the pastor of my parish who was also the principal of my elementary school. For this act of insubordination, he kept me after school for one month so that I couldn't walk home with my friends. I remember that I reeked of his cigar smoke when I got home, and my mother made me take a bath in the afternoon to get rid of the stench in my hair.

My eighth-grade teacher, Sister Mary Joseph, told me that my "contrary nature" would get me into "trouble with God for the rest of [my] natural and supernatural life." Although I wasn't completely sure what a "contrary nature" was, this gloomy prediction was enough for me to happily excommunicate myself from the God club, without waiting for the Pope in Rome to lay this on me. I just couldn't imagine an eternal afterlife without at least a few people feeling "contrary" and trying to spice up the continuing dialogue with God and His angels with a few provocative questions designed to piss them off; to put to the test their peaceful, beatific visions, so to speak; to see if they were, in fact, hypocrites. Wouldn't eternity be more than a little dull without the opportunity to verbally joust with one another?

Being true to form, throughout high school, I was the persistent contrarian, ever on the lookout to deny the validity of someone's particular political or philosophical claim to a glorious truth that would set me, and others, free. Sister Mary Joseph's prediction was right: I was becoming a contrary pain in the ass. I attacked the political absolutes of *all* my friends and classmates who were Republicans, Democrats, and Libertarians with the same single-minded relish with which each of them attacked one another. Gradually, however, my contrarian's game got boring, and I grew tired of looking for hypocrites in the haystacks. I won most of the battles but lost my friends.

I also lost interest in seeking after some permanently satisfying, larger purpose to my life because it always seemed to be of no avail; and so I settled for the smaller, transient pleasures of sports, after-school jobs, and girls—beautiful, smart, sweet-smelling, willing girls. In fact, though, I was as unsuccessful in finding any happiness in these activities as I was in finding a lasting meaning in philosophy, religion, or politics. I was especially inept with girls, even the ones who weren't so sweet-smelling or smart. I was a blue-collar, working-class kid, the brash son of uneducated orphans, who was, as one of these girls called me, a "loser without any class." I was a pathetic, sexist blunderer, even before I knew what a sexist was.

In college and graduate school, I made the decision, after studying literature, philosophy, and, particularly, existentialism, to create my own meaning in the world, and to hell with anyone else's meaning. No longer did I ask "What is the meaning of existence?" Rather, now I began to ask: "What is the purpose of *my* existence?" This question seemed more manageable to me; a question with potential answers rather than unsolvable mysteries. It also put me in charge of my own destiny in the universe. This was a destiny of my own making; a destiny beyond the reach of mythical gods and the messianic men and women who alone claimed to represent the will of these gods; and a destiny beyond the reach of all those authoritarian institutions, sacred books, and dogmas that were said to contain the unchangeable, divine words of these gods.

Finally, I was free, or so I thought. Now I could ask with Rilke: "What will you do God, if I die? I am your jug, what if I shatter? I am your drink, what if I spoil? I am your robe and your profession. Losing me, you lose your meaning. I *am* your meaning!" In other words, without me there was no God. Without me and my meanings, God was without meaning. God depended on me, not the other way around. God was an outcome, and not the source, of my meaning. No story of meaning on my part, no God. I created the God I wanted, not vice versa. I liked this. I was a freethinking storyteller who shaped his own container of meanings and purposes in a book called "life," with its risks and opportunities, its tragedies and comedies, all under my complete control. And this is the way I constructed, and lived out, my life as an academician for the next twenty years.

But in my fiftieth year, after fathering two wonderful, successful daughters who went on to receive doctorates in their chosen fields, reaching the pinnacle of my career as a respected professor, teacher, and scholar, and sustaining a rich, long-term relationship with Maddie, my beloved partner, it all came crashing down around me. Somehow, I had lost the will to go on crafting the story of my life. I was empty. Nothing seemed worth doing or thinking. I had no meaning.

Running marathons at a very competitive regional level—a necessary, but physically agonizing, 12-year distraction from my inner turmoil—exhausted me. I quit running one day cold turkey due to a series of nagging, overuse injuries, and I haven't run one step since. Publishing well-received, scholarly articles grew stale and tedious. I simply lost the belly for it. My teaching became more of a chore than a passion. The thought of spending one more year in a "public ivy" university sent me into a depression that was virtually immobilizing.

To cover up, I went on the attack, even more than when I was in my 30s. I was no longer a philosopher who loved wisdom or people, if I ever was. I used my intellect to logic-chop and hammer my students into submission in the seminar room, and to do the same to my colleagues in the professional conference room. I slept in a lot and developed major urinary tract infections, along with enervating, vomitous reactions to the score of antibiotics I took. I was hurting. I was reeling.

I wanted to die in those emergency rooms where I was frequently rushed because of my uncontrollable retching, provoked as much by my grinding fears that my life had no meaning as by the powerful medicines I was taking. I lived from one intravenous drip to another, waiting desperately for the blessed relief from those dry heaves that the anti-nausea medicine brought me. But the relief was always short-lived, and the pitiful cycle of suffering started all over again. I was a mess.

I had achieved much in the eyes of the academy, but I felt like a brittle shell without a solid center; outside I looked like a "painted white sepulcher," inside I was "filled with dead men's bones," as Jesus, in the Christian Bible, described his detested Pharisees. I had nothing to hold on to, no framework of background beliefs to shape my life; no soaring hope or faith that might surpass my critical understanding; no moral compass to guide me through the swamps of the political jungle called the American university. Charles Taylor (1992), the communitarian philosopher, claims that every individual needs a "moral ontology," a commitment to some end that makes life worth living and loving. I had neither the commitment, nor the will, to live *or* to love. I was angry most of the time, and sad.

I fell into a state of mind that oscillated between a foreboding dread and a heightened anxiety, emotions triggered by anything and everything new that came into my life without warning, and that seemed to pose a threat to my security. Psychotherapy didn't touch this terrible downward spiral, and I tried several different types: behavioral conditioning, family systems, existential, cognitive-behavioral, Rogerian, pastoral, and Eastern. Talking about my life to a variety of sensitive, well-meaning therapists only made my condition worse. I lied to all of them, and to myself, because I did not want to face my worst fears; and, in the deepest recesses of my brain, I thought they were all self-serving hypocrites anyway. And so I tried to beat them at their own games by bullshitting them.

My Existential Anxiety: Should I Live or Should I Die?

Like Tolstoy (2009, p. 40), in his fiftieth year, I found myself in a very dangerous place. Here are Tolstoy's words as he contemplated suicide:

> The question, which in my fiftieth year had brought me to the notion of suicide, was the simplest of all questions, lying in the soul of every man from the undeveloped child to wisest sage: "What will come from my whole life?" Otherwise expressed—"Why should I live? Why should I wish for anything? Why should I do anything?" Again, in other words: "Is there any meaning in my life which will not be destroyed by the inevitable death awaiting me?"

While out for a very early walk one dark and cold winter morning, I asked myself these very same questions under a tree in a deserted Vermont woods. I had been up all night convulsively vomiting, trying without success to urinate, and my physical and mental states were weakened. I was racked by soulache, heartache, stomachache, and headache. Worse, I found myself wondering how many of the highest dosage of sleeping pills that I was carrying in my pocket would kill me if I were to swallow them all at once. It would be nice to die here in these quiet, secluded, snowy woods, I thought. Peace would finally be mine. And, in the end, who would really care? At the least, I would never again have to live one more minute suffering from the existential anxiety that turned my life into a hell of fear, apprehension, and despondency.

Would my family of origin care? This was doubtful, because we had been irremediably fractured for decades. My mother, an orphan, never had a role model for a parent, so she tried to learn how to parent as she went along. She raised her six sons largely by holding grudges (some lasting for years), and by subjecting all of us to constant verbal cruelty and threats if we ever crossed her. She was vindictive and punishing, and she played off all her sons against one another. Years before she passed, she disowned two of my brothers whom she utterly disdained while they were growing up. They had strong minds of their own, and, at every turn, they resisted being guilted by her. She refused to allow them to attend my father's funeral service.

My father, also an orphan, was interested primarily in pleasing my mother. He dreaded her rage, her self-righteousness, and her insatiable hunger for vengeance, and so he gave her the babies she craved as a way to win her favor. He did not want to take on the role of a father, however, because he desperately needed his wife to be his surrogate "mother," as well as his intimate partner. For my father, his sons functioned primarily as competitors for his wife's precious attention, and her inattention toward him left him feeling lonely and unsupported.

Such were my parents: needy, isolated from the rest of the world, loners who never learned to trust, or build relationships with, others. (For decades, this is how I lived my own life, and, to some extent, I still resist the urge to distrust.) They were responsible providers and caretakers, to be sure, and for this I am grateful; but they were also incapable of unconditional love and support. Each of us left our parents' home forever at, or before, the age of 17. When my father passed away decades later, only three sons were in attendance at his memorial service. When my mother recently died of a series of strokes in a nursing home, only I and my wife, and one of our daughters and her children—as well as one brother and his son—were at the funeral service. Also, in the small room was an undertaker, and a priest who sprinkled some "holy water" on the casket and, in a barely audible monotone, read one or two rote passages from his Bible. After finishing his designated priestly task in two or three minutes, he promptly collected his payment from the undertaker and left. Sadly, in his "homily," he forgot my mother's name. When the priest left, my wife, Maddie, took it upon herself to share some positive memories of her relationship with my parents.

As I slumped on the cold, damp, winter ground that early morning, I thought of my aging parents and my estranged brothers—some of whom I hadn't spoken to in decades. I also wondered that if I had tried harder to make an emotional connection with my parents and my brothers—if I had been more forgiving and present to each of them—then perhaps I might have had someone to talk with about my soul's despair, my nagging sense of meaninglessness, and my intense inner turmoil. But the sad reality was that I had no consoling parents I could go to, because I had emotionally "disowned" them years ago in order to avoid the overwhelming anxiety they stirred up within me. Worse, I was convinced that if they had been in my life, they would never have made the effort to understand me. They were simply incapable of caring about any one of their sons because they, themselves, had never been cared for when they were growing up. They just didn't know how to care! In the cold, dark woods that day, I felt a deep sadness for the loss of my family of origin, and guilty for not taking on the reconciler-role expected of an eldest son in some cultures.

Lying on the ground with my sleeping pills at the ready, I decided that the greatest caretaker in my life was Maddie, my partner of several decades. I knew that she would care, and care profoundly. So would my children. Perhaps even a student or two would care; some wonderfully, sensitive student who was able to see past my self-constructed, gruff, "scholarly" exterior in order to find the insecure loner who resided within and who only wanted to love and be loved, foibles and all. There were a few students at the university who had reached out to me during the first two decades I was there. But I chose never to get emotionally close to a single one of them for fear of looking weak and dependent.

I also had to face the dismal truth that there would be no "close" friends outside the university who would miss me, because I—always the independent loner—rarely bothered to create a close relationship with anyone but my wife. Even the few colleagues I chose to hang out with on occasion, I kept at arms' length, because, deep down, I felt anxious around them. They looked to me more as a mentor than a friend, and mentorship just felt like too much responsibility for me to bear. I was experiencing enough inner turmoil of my own that the thought of being an exemplar for others terrified me. I couldn't deal with the pressure. One of these older colleagues, with whom I built a nationally renowned graduate program, died from spinal cancer after a decade of friendship. The other colleague went on to become renowned as a political activist, and, while I admired him greatly, I had neither the time nor enthusiasm he had for his important political causes. We slowly grew apart, and, today, in his retirement, we have no relationship at all.

Outside of these few colleagues, I honestly didn't think a single faculty member at the university would care if I disappeared from the face of the earth that very morning, because I had never taken the time to reach out and befriend one. I was always too busy competing with my colleagues for scarce material resources, for the promotions, tenure, sabbaticals, and awards that we all ached for. Because I was a first-generation high school graduate who attended a community college, and who was, also, the alum of an open-admissions undergraduate teachers college, I always felt inferior to them. The vast majority of my colleagues were graduates of some of the most prestigious universities in the United States. I worked very, very hard to be better than them in every way, and I openly flaunted my early tenure, and promotion to full professor before the age of 34—a direct result of my compulsively prolific publishing record. No wonder my colleagues had very little to do with me. I wouldn't have wanted anything to do with me either. I was driven, political (with a small, manipulative "p"), spiteful, and hyper-competitive.

It was at that dismal moment of choice, lying on the ground shivering in the snow, that I decided to turn my life around. I struggled mightily on that chilly winter morning to get outside of myself in order to get a clearer glimpse of the "myself" who was sprawled on the ground. And what I saw I didn't like. I looked like a damned fool lying there. What was I trying to prove? Was this all that my pathetic little life had come to in my fifth decade—throwing up in the bushes, in between trying to squeeze out a few drops of urine mixed with blood, and practically passing out in the process? Thinking dark thoughts and wallowing in despair? Sobbing like a fool totally out of control of his life?

No more, I decided on that morning, would I ever sit alone under a tree in the middle of an icy, cold nowhere contemplating what Camus called the most important philosophical question of all: *Should I live or die?* No longer would I obsess over those existential end-stage questions that had no final answers, and if they had, I would probably never accept them anyway: Is non-being really better than being? Will I vanish without a trace if I "off" myself right here, right now? Will death be my enemy or my friend? Is this, in the end, what it all comes down to—meaninglessness, isolation, and despair?

No, from now on, the practical question for me would be this one: How can I deal with the basic absurdity and contingency of my life in such a way that I can be happy and productive, and, in the process, be loving and giving to others, while also being good to myself? How can I accept with courage and grace what Machiavelli once described as the inescapable, recurring narrative of everyone's life? This is a story written in chapters on the challenges of necessity, choice, and chance. How can I enlarge my chapter on choice while also coming to terms with the chapters on necessity and chance that bind my life in inescapable ways? What can I believe in, fall back upon, feel secure about, and then let the chips fall where they may? And so I began, from that moment on, to choose my life.

Major surgery for my chronic urinary tract infections was first on my reconstruction agenda. Extensive time with an anxiety-specialist psychologist and a depression-specialist psychiatrist was next. One talked me down, the other prescribed me up. This combination of mind medicine and brain medication was unbeatable and very successful.

Finally, I underwent an intensive, self-designed, reading program in postmodern literary theory and philosophy, personal narrative writing, existential psychology, feminist theory, Eastern religious studies, and moral and ethical philosophy, all calculated to get me to ask both the "big questions" *and* the "little questions." During sabbaticals, I also went on to acquire additional graduate degrees in some of these fields. Like Descartes, I wanted to know if there was anything I could ever be sure of by way of making meaning. Was there any value, any knowledge, any natural or supernatural reality that existed outside of my peculiar intellectual, moral, emotional, and experiential takes on the world? Was it all subjective or was it all objective, or was it various shades of each?

Instead of agonizing over the unanswerability of such big questions, as I once did, I decided to settle on asking the little questions, one at a time, although the big questions are still fun for me to explore. My seminars, today, are full of little and big inquiries, and my students quickly warm to the task, particularly when I leave all my questions open-ended and full of genuine wonder. I am evolving into a postmodern, existential, secular pragmatist, with strong spiritual roots in Zen Buddhism and Taoism, although I am not a practitioner of either system's "religious" teachings. I borrow a little wisdom from here and a little from there, whenever I need to. One of my students who is a French teacher calls me a "meaning *bricoleur*," someone who patches together a bit of this and a bit of that. I guess I am.

This has been my project for the last 20 years of my teaching career. I have never been happier, either personally or professionally. All the courses that I teach, and the writing and speaking that I do, as well as the wonderful, graduate student friendships that take up so much of my time nowadays, concern themselves almost exclusively with helping my students to make sense of their personal and professional lives. What I am becoming is a professional meaning-maker who assists others in making their meanings. In the process, I end up making, and remaking, mine, time and time again. I am lucky beyond words. My life has meaning, and it endures, even while it changes. This is the meaning that makes the most sense to me right now.

So What Is the Meaning of It All?

Students frequently come to me seeking the meaning of their lives. I look at them with bewilderment and helplessness, but more so with empathy and solidarity. I don't even know the meaning of *my* life, except that I was born, I live, love, loathe, and learn, and I will die. Along the way I will experience many delights and many defeats. I often wonder if there is anything more to my life, or to theirs, than this "eternal recurrence," the Hindu view that time repeats itself cyclically *ad infinitum*. Approximately 100 billion human beings, since the beginning of human time, have lived this repetitive cycle. Nobody escapes it. Few are remembered for long. Will I be remembered even years after my death, let alone decades or centuries? Or will I merely melt into one enormous statistic as billions of others have before me? And why is this important to me anyway?

An old philosophy professor of mine, steeped in Nietzsche, Schopenhauer, Buddhism, and Hinduism, used to make the following comments over and over again, whenever we were arrogant enough to think we'd come up with a sensational new insight about the meaning of life: "Such as it always was. Such as it always is. And such as it always will be. So what? Now what?" We did not know, then, that he was restating Schopenhauer: "The true philosophy of history lies in perceiving that, in all the endless changes and motley complexity of events, it is only the self-same unchangeable being which is before us."

Nevertheless, my professor's familiar riposte always brought us up short. Even though it pissed us off, it also forced us to look deeper within ourselves to accept our responsibility to make meaning of our lives, no matter how repetitive and predictable life can be. Some of these 100 billion people, of course, lived life better, some lived it worse. Some died living, some lived dying. Some lived for the next life, some lived for the now. Some lived without a concern for meaning, some found it impossible to live without meaning. The meaning of life's ceaseless ebb and flow is not for me to assert for my students, but only mine to declare for myself. And so I look back at them in response to their question, and ask in my teacherly way: "You tell me. What *does* your life mean? What do you *want* it to mean?"

Cycles of Meaning Making

And this is what they say:

Younger adults respond along these lines: "Only I can live my life for myself. Nobody else can tell me who I am and what I must live for. From this moment on, I'm the one who has to make sense of my life. And I've got almost forever to do it, because I'm young and healthy, and I feel immortal. Even though this independence is scary, I'm looking forward to being on my own, without anyone telling me what to do." Seneca's *praebere se fato* ("choose yourself") is the imperative of this stage of meaning making.

Young adults (the "quarterlifers") offer this account of their meaning making: "I have a responsibility to become what I am, because someday I must die. I now understand that my life is not forever. But what is it I can do that is worthwhile? Who should I love? When should I make lifelong commitments? What should I believe? Others are depending on me to fulfill my promise as an adult. Just what are my duties to myself and my duties to others, though, and what should I do when these are in conflict? Is it really possible for me to live a life of personal integrity when every choice I make stands to harm or to help others?" All of these questions can be summed up in the quarterlifers' dominant unspoken question: *Quid hoc vita vult?* ("What does this life mean?")

Middle adults are still in the process of constructing meaning, but now it takes on a sharper, existential edge. It's more tuned in to the limitations of finite existence and bounded choice-making; as well as to what the Greeks called *fortuna* ("chance" or "luck"). No longer is the middle adult a superman or superwoman. Happiness, at best, is a fleeting thing, and the years are as passing seasons. During this cycle of making meaning, middle adults ask: "Is there any enduring meaning in my life? I've done everything I'm supposed to do. I'm in a satisfying relationship, I've worked hard, and I've raised wonderful children. To the outside world, I'm an unmitigated success. But why is it that inside I feel so unsettled, so restless? I've still got decades of my life to live, if I'm lucky." *Ubi vadeo ab hic?* ("Where do I go from here?")

Older adults tend to express some version of Goethe's assertion, "Age takes hold of us by surprise." Often, when I listen to older adults talk about the meaning of their lives, I am reminded of a Woody Allen line: "I'm not afraid of death. I just don't want to be there when it happens." Older adults' more sober reflections, however, often take this tack: "Life occurred almost when I wasn't looking, and, lo and behold, I'm old. Now what? I've still got so much left to do, but I'm realizing my time is running out. How can I avoid slipping into despair? Do people still love and respect me even though I am not as active a risk-taker as I used to be? What in the world do I have in common with people who are younger, more creative, and vital than I am, including my own children? Do I look too eccentric and settled to them, completely out of touch? What could I possibly give to them?" A comment that older adults sometimes make, each in their own way, is this: *Vitam perdidi, operose nihil agendo?* "Have I wasted my life busily doing nothing?"

I am one of these older adults, and I am more and more becoming a creature of rituals and routines. In the words of Victor Hugo, I am trying to "recover the ground beneath my feet." But I don't want to become a "rock that is massive, haughty, and immobile" in my older age. Instead, I strive for *gelassenheit*, or "letting be." How often do I find myself delivering to students, and to other loved ones, these clichés: "Live and let live. Practice some generosity toward others, especially toward those whose choices, ideas, and lifestyles, you dislike. Let go, and let be. Enjoy. In the end, it's all a matter of taste and temperament, anyway."

These bromides are nothing but the outward manifestation of my particular, generative cycle in the process of creating meaning. They are also the outgrowth of my understanding that, developmentally, we're all more alike than not, even though our individual stories are very different. Few of us want our stories "stolen" from us. We want to tell our stories in our own ways and have others tell theirs as well.

As an educator, I believe that what binds us all together is the universality of our questions, and the commonality of our psycho-biological needs. What separates us, though, are the unique, age- and cycle-related stories we fashion in order to deal with our particular cries for meaning. But this separation needn't resign us to a life of isolation and loneliness.

And so, at the first class meeting of the semester, I often say to my students, whether they be adolescents, young, middle, or older adults: "Chances are I'm not going to change your mind about anything and vice versa, nor do I really want to. In my opinion, keeping company with you in order to change you is energy misspent. It might even be immoral. At the very least, it's damned presumptuous. Who the hell am I to know what's good for you?

"So let's make a pact with one another—a mutual non-imposition treaty, if you will. Let's assume that you and I are all about discovering and making meanings that will sustain us in the days and years ahead. Let's also agree that your meanings may not work for me and vice versa. Therefore, don't tread on me, and I won't tread on you. Don't foist your successful formula for finding the keys to your existence on me, and I'll promise to return the favor. Meanwhile, whenever it's necessary, let's agree to huddle together within the protective cocoon of our mutual humanity for the comfort and affirmation we need when things go dismally wrong, or for that matter, ecstatically right. You share your meanings with me, and I'll do the same with you. Beyond this, we cannot, indeed, dare not, go."

My SPN Afterthoughts—What I Learned: Writing My Way to Healing, Meaning, and Wholeness

So, what are my take-aways from writing the above SPN on the meaning of my life? Here, in summary, is what I have reaffirmed for myself regarding what helps me to **heal**, what gives my life **meaning**, and what makes me **whole**. Here, too, are what I believe to be the universal implications of these qualities for all the students who take our course in SPN writing.

Healing

What exactly does it mean to heal psychologically and philosophically? Healing is more than simply a popular buzz-word in the health-and-wellness field in higher education. Neither does it necessarily mean recovering from some major psychological trauma. The fact is that everyone is in the process of "healing" (restoring, revitalizing, renewing our physical, mental, and spiritual health) in some way—because, at least metaphorically, most of us have been exhausted, wounded, injured, broken, or hurt in some fashion. When I wrote my essay above, I wasn't injured or wounded in the way that accident victims might be. Neither was I recovering from a serious disease or chronic illness. And neither was I so mentally damaged that I required hospitalization or other types of institutional commitment. While composing this essay, I wanted to heal my still-troubled psyche by exploring where I am now regarding the meaning of my life. This question, for me, has continued to be the most urgent question of all during the last few decades. I want to understand where I have been, where I am currently, and where I wish to be in the years that I have left to live my life. Never again do I want to go into the woods, lie vomiting under a tree, sob uncontrollably, and prepare myself to die.

Writing this essay helped me to understand more clearly why I was on the verge of ending my life at a time when, at least superficially, it looked to the world that I had everything that I wanted. Why was I experiencing the kind of existential anxiety that Tolstoy (in the epigraph at the beginning of this chapter), himself, experienced at age 50? How much of this anxiety was the *product* of my physical issues, and how much was the *cause* of my physical problems? I re-learned from writing this essay that no matter how one's outer life appears to others, one's inner life may or may not correspond to the outward impression. I was able to revisit a question I have asked for decades: Is existential anxiety a state of mind that all of us recycle throughout our lives because of life's ups and downs; because of the inscrutable mysteries that haunt us at some times and that energize us at other times?

I also reinforced my belief that healing is inseparable from such larger themes as wholeness, meaning, and spirituality. Healing is physical, psychological, and spiritual. Healing is all about the restoration of psychological and philosophical health and well-being. Healing is a complex process of understanding the intricate, and inescapable, connections between my body, mind, and spirit. This process holds the promise of increasing the breadth and depth of my zest, joy, and happiness. This, in the end, is what makes my life worthwhile. Healing revitalizes the human psyche. Healing results in different, more creative ways to see, and therefore, to live my life. Healing puts my life, and its inevitable uncertainties, into a larger, more understandable perspective. Healing is all about adaptation, flexibility, and resilience—three qualities of living that I'm working to cultivate each and every day. Healing is about both surviving and prospering. Healing is my way of pausing to reexamine what is of utmost importance to me in my day-to-day struggle to exist with integrity, dignity, style, and grace. And, lo and behold, healing, as I understand it, is what all my colleagues, family, friends, loved ones, and students pursue as well. In fact, healing is a lifelong agenda because this is what it means to be fully human, and to be fully *healthy* (the adjective for the verb *to heal*).

Meaning

Writing this essay gave me another opportunity to affirm the undeniable meaning in my teaching—as long as I keep it narrative-based, open-ended, and relational. No matter what subject I teach, I always try to evoke the personal stories of my students. The personal stories hold the key to the meaning of academic content for my students. Without my students' personal stories, subject matter withers and dies immediately after the exams. Worse, students themselves wither and die, little by little, each and every day they sit dazed and quizzical before us in our seminars and lecture halls. Many students wonder why they just can't memorize the textbook or the lecture notes, and let it go at that, without having to suffer the four-to-six-year ordeal of parking their bodies in an impersonal lecture hall—trying to stay awake and look interested. Many sneak frequent peeks at their Smart Phones and email inboxes. Some know how to text and tweet without looking at the keys. And some spend more time on their Facebook page than on reading, writing, or listening to the lectures and staring vapidly at the PowerPoint presentations.

We tell our stories to prove that we've lived, that we're still alive, and that we intend to live into some unknown future. Without our stories, our lives are without form or content. So too with subject matter. When all the technical trappings are removed, an academic discipline is really a particular group's storied view of the world, and the story changes often. Find the story of the subject matter (whether it's a social science, a humanity, or a science), and you've located the core of the academic discipline. You've also brought it to life. In writing this personal essay, I was telling my lifelong story of anxiety, fear, dread, and worry.

Rarely, if ever, have I told this story to anyone. I was ashamed of it. I was baffled by it. I refused to acknowledge the iron grip it had on me. I was living in what I call "narrative denial." And so I spent the first two decades of my faculty career living a covering-up story. I put on the face of invulnerability. I refused to let anyone get close to me. Furthermore, writing this essay helped me to revisit my family upbringing with all of its dysfunction. No wonder I lived so much of my own life in narrative denial; this was, and is, my way of coping with unwanted memories of my past. I wrote the story of my upbringing—not to shame, blame, or defame—but to try to make sense of some of the glaring contradictions in the way I live my life today. In so many ways, I am both my mother and father. I reflect both their strengths and their weaknesses. Writing this essay has helped me to understand my past with more compassion and insight. I simply would not be the "me" that I am at this time without the influence of the "they" who were my family of origin. Like them, I am a complex, contradictory container of meanings. But, really, who isn't?

In writing my way into meaning-making in my essay, I am convinced more than ever that sooner or later we all must face the "real questions." In Sartre's language, each of us is "condemned to make meaning." There is no escape, no easy way out, no blessed exit from our responsibility to live the authentic life, and to create, and re-create, ourselves with every choice we make each and every day. I made the choice lying on the ground under the tree in that winter woods to live. I made the choice to change my life. I made the choice to take control of my life by actively authoring it each and every day. One way I do this is by raising the central meaning questions in my teaching whenever, and wherever, and every chance I get. I do this because what I have learned from my own meaning-making is that amidst those periods of our worst anguish, only faith and hope remain. And so I teach with hope. I live with faith (trust). My intent is to help students to create stories of meaning that will sustain them through the hard times when they find themselves in Tolstoy's "cold, dark, meaningless place." I am convinced that freedom is always there for the taking. We have the power to make meaning of our anguish as well as our joy. In fact, we can turn the former into the latter. This is my pedagogical agenda, and it will continue to be right up until the moment I pass. There is no turning back.

Wholeness

Few of my students realize that the word *integrity* (*L. integra*) means *whole*. To be a person of integrity is to live life whole; to be consistent; to resolve contradictions; to be respectful of differences by looking for commonalities; and to accept onself, imperfections and all. I began to heal when I realized how important it was for me to live my life whole; to live it with integrity. This awareness became vivid for me in writing my SPN above. I realized once again that there are many different ways of being whole in the world. I don't have to reproduce anyone's particular wholeness template. I can be who and what I am in my own way. I do not have to replicate the life of anyone else in order to experience self-worth, or to win the approval, indeed the acclaim, of others. I will live my life on my own terms. Over the last few decades, this has become my own preferred way of being a professor and of teaching, writing, advising, and serving others. This is what, for me, it means to live a whole life.

I think the reason why all my elective courses fill up is that students know I have no pet ideological agendas to impress upon them. I say this, not boast-fully, but with a personal insight I've only lately arrived at by trying to be more personal and honest in my writing. The courses I teach contain the most con-troversial and potentially volatile subject matter in my college, and all of them are electives. These courses run the gamut from religion, to ethics, to scholarly personal narrative writing, to philosophy of meaning-making, and to social justice controversies. Why is it, I am asked by colleagues, that undergraduate and graduate students flock to these courses in a professional school? After all, none of them is very "practical." None will get students certified or licensed.

Here, then, is my latest insight about why students register for all my con-troversial, seemingly impractical, courses. They want a teacher who really tries to live life whole. My hope is that students see me as an educator with integ-rity because I care about them. I am loyal to them. I have no Absolute Truths to sell them. I honor them. I spend large amounts of time with them. And I encourage them to become their own persons. Along the way, I am a lover of wisdom, a dispenser of joy, a meaning-maker, and a person with the courage to accept his imperfections without being anxious or defensive all the time. As I begin my 46th year of teaching in higher education, I am moving ever closer to accepting that, yes, I am a person of integrity, even though I might be more than a bit unconventional.

In summary, then, this, for me, is what wholeness is all about. It's about the courage to live my own truth. It's about professing a commitment to treating others always with respect and dignity. It's about knowing when to compro-mise on moral principles and when not to. It's about being patient, humble, and generous. It's about honoring another's life story, even though it might be drastically different from mine. It's about living a life, and practicing a profes-sion, that is whole and consistent. It's about being willing to speak out, maybe even act as a whistleblower, whenever my profession is tempted to behave in a way that is discordant with its highest moral aspirations. But, most of all, for me, wholeness is the willingness to be open, available to all truths, and to see their complementarity with my own.

My integrity is neither imperialistic nor absolutistic. Rather, it's humble in its profession of faith, pluralistic in its view of truth, and, yet, passionate in the conviction that the best way to serve people is with the utmost care and compassion, along with the utmost competence and accountability. And it means that if I call myself a professional or a professor, then I need to *profess* a strong, authentic belief in something, no matter how controversial. This latter, in fact, might be the most challenging integrity-task of all, especially in higher education where compromise, politics, and self-serving displays of collegiality are the expectations of the day. Without these, few rewards are forthcoming.

●

Chapter 3

If Stories Heal, Then What Exactly Is a Story?
And How Do I Find My Writer's Voice?

ROBERT J. NASH

Our very definition as human beings is very much bound up with the stories we tell about our own lives and the world in which we live. We cannot, in our dreams, our daydreams, our ambitious fantasies, avoid the imaginative imposition of form on life.
—*Peter Brooks*

What "exactly" is a story? Who really knows…"exactly"? What is a story to you may not be a story to me. What I can say with some degree of assurance, however, is that a story serves many functions both for humanity at large and for the person in particular. A story helps us to make connections of the disparate events, and people, that appear in our lives. A story creates order out of chaos. A story entertains. A story teaches. A story elevates. A story inspires. A story, in Peter Brooks' language in the epigraph above (1985), defines us as human beings. Who am I? I am "very much bound up with" all the stories I tell and that are told about me. I am my dreams, my daydreams, and my fantasies (p. 19). I am also my nightmares, my tragedies, and my terrible, repressed memories. I often say to my students who want to be teachers, evoke the stories of your students and you've reached them in a way they will never forget. Even more, tell them your own stories, and you have made friends for life. Stories humanize us. They bring us down to earth and make us accessible.

I believe that each of us conceals a nagging need to tell some kind of truth about our lives. And each of us, at some point, wants to move from "conceals" to "reveals." When, and if, we are ready, then the best way to convey a truth is to tell a story. A story is always profoundly personal and unique to some degree, never replicated in exactly the same form by anyone else. Your truth may be very different from mine, and vice versa. But if I can hear your truth within the context of your own personal story, I might be better able to find its corollary in my own story. I hope that the very personal story I told in Chapter 2 finds its unique corollary in each of my readers' lives.

What I tried to highlight in my story is the existential anxiety that each of us experiences throughout our lives, whenever we think about our inevitable finitude. For me, what I am calling "existential anxiety" is a universal state of being. Who among my readers has not experienced the death of someone close or even far away? And, in the process, who has not, at the very least, thought about their own inevitable non-existence, before they got caught up once again with the everyday humdrum of their lives? Ernest Becker once wrote a Pulitzer-Prize winning book titled *The Denial of Death* (1973). I maintain that the denial of our human finitude is impossible, no matter how much we want to run away from it, because all around us we get daily reminders of how ephemeral our lives can be.

Although we have been taught by the world's religions to strive for the infinite and the eternal, of necessity we must always deal with the finite, day-to-day reminders that we are mortal. We suffer. We have setbacks. We despair. We don't always feel respected or loved. We fail to realize our hopes and dreams, and when we do, we soon learn that these are but passing clouds in the firmament. Success, while satisfying, is momentary. The fear of failure continually haunts us. Happiness, based on pleasure-seeking, is elusive and short-lived. Joy, based on an upbeat, mindful attitude toward life in general, is far more valuable, but, at times, even more difficult to sustain. However, as I tried to say in my story, transience, while precarious and worrisome, also offers each of us the opportunity to fully live our lives in the present. We grow to understand that each day is precious. Each day offers us the opportunity to construct ourselves in such a way as to heal, create meaning, and live life whole. I think of myself as a narrative-activist: The story I tell, as well as the way I tell my story, is the way I want to live my life.

I can never say this enough: Everyone has a story to tell, and everyone has the potential and the power to tell a story. Moreover, everyone can write a story. How so? Anyone who has ever managed a childhood, intimate relationship, education, job, or parenthood can tell a story. Anyone who has ever been a sibling, teacher, student, friend, or boss can tell a story. Anyone who has ever suffered or rejoiced can tell a story. Anyone who has ever been betrayed by someone, or has been the betrayer, can tell a story. Anyone who has strong (or even weak) political, moral, or religious convictions can tell a story. All of this is simply to say that anyone can tell a story by virtue of having lived a normal life.

Here's the upshot of what I'm trying to say: If you can tell a story that is honest, trustworthy, revealing, and close to the core of your own experience, then you can most certainly write one. And if you write your story in your own voice, then, in the words of Richard Rhodes, your story will "enlarge the world." But, first, you must discover the courage to tell your personal story with passion, insight, and vulnerability. In my own case, I drew upon whatever residue of courage exists within me to tell the story you've just read in Chapter 2. I am here to say that it is the most honest and self-disclosing writing I have ever done. And, voila! In the story-telling process, I created a self that I'm willing to live with and even love…at least for now.

How Do You Find Your Narrative Voice?

Here are six votes of confidence for finding your unique, story-teller's voice:

First, be confident that underneath all the protective layers of the self that you present to the world is a storyteller. As a storyteller, you will need to know how to develop colorful characters who engage readers at a number of levels. Readers need to care about the characters in your personal essay, and this includes, especially caring about *you*, the author. You, after all, are the central character in your story. You are the primary conduit for all the healing, meaning, and wholeness that your story will convey.

Second, be confident that you can, indeed, create engaging characters in your writing. You will learn through practice how to describe your primary characters in detail, with all their idiosyncracies. You will find the words to make them real if you work at it. This won't always be easy, of course, but if you take the trouble to think carefully about each of the key persons in your story—why each is truly unique, maybe even a bit eccentric—you will find a way to make them stand out. And, because *you* will be the central character in your writing, you will find the courage, as you go along, to make yourself a memorable character. This will necessitate that you pull few punches in your narrative self-depiction. You are not bigger than life itself; actually, you are no bigger or smaller than the life you are actually living, the life you are crafting for yourself each and every day.

Third, be confident that you don't have to be some kind of *artistic* genius to write your story. Some writers are more visual than others. Some writers see images or word-pictures when they write. Some find it easy to create metaphors. You may be more of a literal thinker who relies on logic, analysis, and unpacking difficult ideas for readers. You may be a better essayist than you are a memoirist, poet, or fiction writer. Whatever your innate writing penchants, you will learn to go with your strengths as an SPN writer. The key is to tell your truth as honestly and clearly as you can, and if you are more of a "craft" person than an artist in your story-telling, be proud of this gift. But don't forget to take some risks, and venture into the realm of artistry, at least every now and then.

Fourth, be confident that you can draw in your readers. This means that you will need to learn how to set the stage at the beginning of your story that will entice, even seduce, readers. You will need to know how to create "teaser-hooks" that will capture their attention. You will have to be aware of your "narrative arc" at all times. You will need to introduce your story's "plot line" somewhere at the beginning, and refer back to it frequently during the course of your writing. This will be the best way to keep your readers on track. At the very least, your readers need to be willing to begin the journey with you. And, along the way, you will have to introduce conflicts, challenges, and other "high-stakes hooks" that will keep readers' attention.

Fifth, be confident that every story you have lived in has reached some kind of a climax, or a series of climaxes. And some of these climaxes have also reached resolution. Keep this basic truth in front of you as you write: No reader starts a story looking to stop in the middle. The old Aristotelian adage that the best story is one with a beginning, middle, and end still holds true. All readers need the motivation to continue reading a story. Your story is no exception. And, remember, too, that each and every story has its own natural *denouement*. The word is French, and it means "to untie knots." A denouement is the winding down of a story where all the narrative knots are untied for the reader… or at least most of them are. Readers need to feel some kind of satisfaction as they come to the end of your story. The implication for all of us as storytellers is not to avoid tying "knots" in our stories, but to be aware that too many "untied knots" leave readers in suspense and craving some kind of resolution. Remember this, however: writers can work hard to untie these knots while also realizing that our personal narrative stories never really end…they stop for awhile—only to be continued later. Our stories go on and on until that inevitable day when our mortal bodies and minds die; and, even then, our stories live on in the people who mean the most to us.

Sixth, be confident that you will eventually be able to identify those truths in your life that keep you together during the times when you feel as if you are coming apart. Ask yourself this question—What is really important to me at this particular time in my life? Remember that your story-telling in SPN writing is never an end in itself. Rather, it is a means to an end. You will learn, as time goes on, to reveal as much of your inner self as you choose, in order to deliver the payload to your readers—the generalizable themes, truths, and insights. But while story-telling may not be its own end, it is the non-negotiable, delivery system carrying the truths that may set readers free, at least momentarily, as they get immersed in your writing.

Putting the Theory into Practice

What follows is the last entry in my Chapter 2 story "What Does My Life Mean?" that I have omitted up to now. It is both the climax and the denouement. I decided after writing the previous chapter to revisit my father's funeral to deliver an *ex post facto* eulogy very different from the one I actually delivered. Crafting this 2013 eulogy has given me an opportunity to re-create my father's 2007 funeral narrative in such a way that it enables me to re-write, and to re-think, the story of my father's dying...and living. Remember, as you read this story, that I am writing it from the story I am living in six years later. I would not have been able to re-eulogize my father if I had not written the aforementioned Chapter 2. While I never delivered the *ex post facto* eulogy below (I did deliver one in 2007 that was a shell of what I might have said), I wish I had. I truly wish I had. Etymologically, a *eulogy* is a statment of praise. At this point in my life, I am glad to be able to craft a retrospective eulogy that commends my father for all our readers. There has been healing for me in writing this. While the storyline in what follows is a funeral eulogy, I never once felt sadness or moroseness as I wrote it. In fact, I felt a sense of liberation. Finally, I had made the long-overdue decision to revisit an event that I had repressed for years.

. . . .

"My Father Died in 2007": My 2013 Eulogy

My father died six years ago. The last time I saw him alive he was lying unconscious in an intensive care unit after 7 1/2 gruelling hours of surgery. A 90-year old man who in his final months had been falling down a lot, suffering an immobilizing dizziness and nausea, and losing a precipitous amount of weight because of severe appetite loss—my father was told that he needed immediate surgery if he was to survive with any quality of life. When the doctors cut into his body with their scalpels, they found what an MRI had earlier predicted: a rapidly metastasizing lymphoma cancer that had eaten up much of his insides. So, they proceeded to cut out some vital, internal organs, sew him up, pronounce the operation a "success," and then they left him to die—hideously, painfully, eerily comatose until the very end. We never saw those surgeons again; they disappeared.

It took my father six terrible weeks to die. His once-200-pound, sculpted, athlete's body looked more and more like a skeletal cadaver during that time. On the day of his death, he weighed slightly over 100 pounds. I am convinced that this so-called "necessary" surgery served only to prolong my father's death rather than to extend his life. A 24-hour-a-day morphine drip and feeding tube, pumped intravenously into a barely living, comatose cadaver, does not constitute a quality of life, at least in my non-medical opinion.

And, so, the call from a brother came right after a class I was teaching. "Robert, dad died. The wake and funeral will take place on Wednesday and Thursday of this week. He will be given a military funeral because, as you know, he was a World War II veteran. Could you come to New Hampshire and give the eulogy—as his oldest son?" A eulogy? I panicked. The dictionary says a eulogy is a statement of praise delivered as a blessing by somebody who knows the deceased well. I didn't know my father. I had no personal relationship with him at all, and never had, in fact. Our family was, and is, notoriously dysfunctional. What could I possibly say that could come from my heart? A blessing? As a non-believer, like both my atheist parents, how could I deliver a blessing? How, in good conscience, could I articulate powerful, emotional words that would comfort, maybe inspire, others—his wife (my mother), his sons (my brothers, two of whom never bothered to show up at the funeral for their own good reasons), their wives and sons, and his friends, when I myself was experiencing no strong emotions at all, except relief that he was no longer suffering so unbearably?

I never got to know my father very well, because he was an extremely private man who was unable, and unwilling, to express his feelings to others. What he had left to give his family after 18-hour work days—during the days as a beat-walking cop and then, at night and on weekends, as a longshoreman, every Monday through Sunday—was an unrelenting deference to my mother in a 70-year marriage. My most vivid memory of him while I was growing up, before I left home at the age of seventeen, was watching him work himself to the bone seven days a week, dragging his tired body to the dinner table too exhausted to talk, and then trudging off to bed after a quick soak in the tub so that he could begin the cycle all over again, day after day, week after week, month after month, year after year.

I teach a few courses at my university that include conversation about cultural pluralism. Whenever I am asked in the diversity-sensitive academy where I work what *my* dominant identity is, I answer that, even though I am a success in the eyes of the world, I still think of myself as an older, poor, blue-collar, working class white man, the child of two orphans without even a high-school education. Early identity imprinting, in many ways, is non-erasable. I was raised in four-story tenement houses, trailer parks, and housing projects, one after another after another. I have no clue at all as to my ethnic past or present. I am a person without ethnic, religious, or cultural identity; a man without a history longer than my parental family of origin: no grandparents, aunts, or uncles; not a single vestige of an extended family. Do I regret this? Not a bit. Of course, I readily acknowledge that I have long since passed into a comfortable and secure, over-educated (four graduate degrees), middle-class status. But I will always think of myself as a working-class product of a number of poor, inner-city Boston neighborhoods, second-rate public schools, hand-me-down clothes, and "rent-a-wreck" cars. Today, I am told that I am a respected university professor who should be proud of his professional achievements, but I have never, even for one single instant, forgotten the blue-collar roots that have so profoundly shaped my narrative identity today. And I have never denied these roots, nor will I ever. Who exactly am I, then?

Who I am today is the first-born son (after the death of a first-born son, and one of six brothers) of an orphaned man and orphaned woman who lived their lives without a trace of a sense of entitlement or privilege. Social class membership is the major identity indicator, I believe, of who a person is, who that person will ultimately become, and how that person will go about fashioning a survival narrative, personality, and public face. I believe this because I have lived it. I am convinced of this because I am reminded of its truth every single day of my life. In so many ways, I am a fish out of water here at my "public ivy" university. There were no private schools, prestigious universities, or golden legacy spoons placed in my mouth, as there were for so many of my professorial colleagues. Whenever my colleagues and I are together, even today the social class chasm is immense, nearly unbridgeable, even though it might be subtle. What and where we eat, what we do in our leisure time, the topics we converse about, and the clothes we wear and houses we live in, are so different as to render us virtual strangers to one another. At the very least, we are uncomfortable in one another's presence, once the formal, more superficial collegial business of university life has been taken care of.

My father, grossly undereducated, and tragically abused by several sets of foster parents, was left on his own in life at the tender age of fourteen. He rarely told his six sons stories of his dismal past, except to drop tantalizing, yet very sad, little morsels every once in awhile when we were whining about some wrong being done to us at school or elsewhere. When he was a teenager, my father often lived in the deep woods, or on the back doorsteps of a church or priest's rectory, or even inside the church, or in a deserted and dilapidated

Maine or New Hampshire barn. He hunkered down for the night wherever he could find a safe, anonymous place to sleep without calling attention to himself, and thereby risking arrest as a vagrant. He scrounged food wherever he could, frequently from dumpsters, and he gladly took on any job that didn't require an ounce of formal education.

My dad was a *survivor*. He took, and passed, with the highest score in the city, the Boston police exam when he was in his early 30s, lying to his superiors that he had a high school diploma, which he "lost." He was also a *victor* at a time when so many people I knew, and know now, thought of themselves as *victims*. He knew he had developed the crucial survival skills in the rough-and-tumble world he inhabited as a scorned youth to be able to beat the world at its own "success" game. He knew that to be successful in the middle-class arena you had to work hard, set achievable goals, raise a family, be ambitious, and stop complaining. You see, these qualities—endurance, resilience, persistence, work ethic, patience, competitiveness, grit, and drive—are the primary working-class, blue-collar ideals. Moreover, what I learned from my father was a result of the *example* of personal sustainability he set, instead of any high-sounding, morality lectures he refused to give; neither did he give into the justifiable whining over his past life and present situation that he could have indulged in, but resolved never to do in the years I knew him.

I saw my father throughout his life work hard to become "intellectually aware" and "self-educated." He would pore over dozens of reference books after those interminably long days of working. He would memorize the big words in dictionaries. He was able to crack *The New York Times* Sunday crossword puzzle in less than an hour. The size of his reading vocabulary was stunning, even though his pronunciation of those multi-syllabic words left much to be desired. You see, he had nobody in his workaday world who was capable of helping him to correctly pronounce those jawbreaking words he loved so much. I know, now, that my own love of language was influenced by my father's example. I also know that my reverence for books, especially non-fiction, came from him. He always wanted to write and never did. And, so, I decided that one day I would work at a job where I could became a writer and not have to work nearly as hard as he did. I wanted to work with my head and not with my hands or back. I wanted to inspire not perspire.

My father was also a bullshit detector of the highest order. His favorite term for people he couldn't stand was "hypocrite." How often he snarled this word about someone! A hypocrite, to him, was a person who was a pretender, someone who claimed to be something but really wasn't. His advice to all of his sons was: "You're really no better than anyone else, so stop thinking you're some big shot, and don't be a damned hypocrite. You get what you put out, and if what you get back is shit, then stop giving out shit." My father found all pretenders—those "snobs" who claimed to be one thing but did another, whether they were religious leaders, politicians, bosses, or professors—to be intolerable phonies. I have long known why I feel the same way to this day, why I have so few peer-friends in the academy (although the ones I do have are wonderful because most share my blue-collar background), for example, and why I would rather hang out with certain of my working-class, graduate students, along with those folks who form the working-class infrastructure of restaurants and retail stores—all those people who wait hand and foot on middle-class folks like me. These folks seem real to me, with very little affectation, pretension, or expectation—despite their compulsory "have a nice day" goodbyes. They work hard, they play hard, they love and hate hard, they make no excuses, and that's it.

My father never once got his name in the newspaper, or wrote a book, or published an article, or keynoted an important conference, or won even a single, small token of recognition for living his life without complaint and always with integrity. I've done all these things in my own life, except not complain, but I've never taken an inch of my successes for granted. I work very hard to keep myself in realistic perspective, because I am the son of a blue-collar man. I have made it to the top of my profession, or so others tell me, by living out those qualities of moral character and social class that my father thought to be so important. My father lived his life small, not tall but small, and in the process, he left a tall legacy. Even though he was a virtual stranger in so many ways to me, as well as to his other sons, my father was a *hero*. He made the cliché of "overcoming adversity" an actuality because of his persistent drive to make something of himself, regardless of his nightmarish past. I will be forever grateful for having him in my life, albeit the impact of his presence always seemed more from afar than near.

And so I say *requiescat in pace* James Russell Nash. You are a man I wish I had gotten to know personally far better than I did. But our paths diverged very early in our lives, and they didn't cross much after that point, for one reason or another. Having said this, though, I am convinced that you did the best you could, and so did I. What I can promise you, however, is that I will try to be worthy of the wonderful example you've set for me and all your sons. I want you to know that I am fully aware of where I came from, and I will never, ever forget it. What's more, I am proud of it. I will strive until my dying days to live a life as authentic, as hungry to know, and as loyal and faithful to the values that I hold, as you did. Once again, dad, *Requiescat in pace*. And thank you for reminding me that no matter how estranged two people might be during the course of their lives, it is possible to reconcile…even if the reconciliation oc-curs long after the death and funeral of one of them. Most important, though, I have had reinforced for me the truth that reconciliation can take place only in the spirit of forgiveness, compassion, and gratitude.

· ·

Chapter 4

Starting Out…and Finishing
The First Class Meeting—
and the Last—on How to Write SPNs

ROBERT J. NASH

There is no greater agony than bearing an untold story inside you.

—*Maya Angelou*

Personal narrative writers must manufacture a text, imposing narrative order on a jumble of half-remembered events. With that feat of manipulation they arrive at a truth that is theirs alone, not quite like that of anybody else who was present at the same events.

—*William Zinsser*

Stories in all their forms satisfy our deepest selves; that far from being an amusement or an aesthetic patina on our daily lives, narrative is fundamental to our bodies, minds, communities, and souls…the narrative urge is central!

—*Joanne Trautmann Banks*

Life can only be understood backwards, but it must be lived forwards.

—*Soren Kierkegaard*

Welcome to Our Writing Class: The First Meeting

Come with us as we walk into the first Scholarly Personal Narrative writing class of the semester. It is 4pm, and we will be together for the next 15 weeks for three hours each Wednesday. About 20 students are sitting in rows anxiously, some impatiently, waiting for class to begin and looking around the room to see if they know anyone. The first comment Robert makes is this: "Please move the chairs into a circle. This will be the seating arrangment for the entire semester. This is a class that will feature interaction and transaction, not professor-induced stupefaction." Few students laugh at this forced verbal jocularity. Most look at one another, and then at us, and then a few look at their watches and cell phones to check how much time is left before they can leave. The usual late stragglers make their way into the room. A few apologize, citing traffic jams and going to the wrong buildings. A few look lost upon first seeing a circle of people sitting so close to one another (the room is small), and wonder aloud if this is the right room for the SPN course. As co-instructors, we wear an inviting smile, say "hello" warmly to the students who might already know us, and make sure that the strangers do not feel left out of the "inner circle of SPN true believers."

Some of the students immediately open their laptops making sure they have an online connection. A few finish cell phone conversations and texting, and then turn off their phones. After awhile, the initial noise dies down, the shuffling about ceases, and students await our opening remarks. We then ask them to introduce themselves, not by the usual name, rank, and serial number, but by who they are in the deepest sense. We ask them to tell us a brief "story" about themselves that will situate them personally for one another at this initial meeting. We emphasize that this story should include their "real" reasons for being in the class, and the rule is to avoid cliches and the obligatory "make-the-professor-feel-good" rhetoric.

We want to know why, deep-down, they decided to sign up for an extensive and intensive, elective writing course in a genre that is a stranger (even, for some faculty, an actual "enemy") to the academy and that will require a lot of self-discipline, creativity, focus, leaving comfort zones, and plain hard work throughout the semester. We want to know what the lure of personal narrative writing might be to them. One introductory prompt we often ask is: "Please tell us in a *six-word memoir* who, why, where, when, and what you are." Then we ask them to "unpack" (explain to the rest of us) their brief memoir in language that is down-to-earth, personal, and that tells a little story. (The idea of a *Six-Word Memoir* was first launched by *Smith Magazine* in 2006. At the end of this chapter, we will include some examples of Six-Word Memoirs.)

On another occasion, we might ask our students to write a one-paragraph, or longer, *"This I believe..."* statement. We stress that this short "reflective credo" can be about any topic under (or even over) the sun. We assure our students that no belief will be considered too controversial, argumentative, or ideological, as long as it's honest, authentic, and heartfelt. "A *passionately* held belief is even better," we say. We reassure them that we will all listen, learn, and, if necessary, laugh, and, yes, maybe we'll even even love what the belief is and/

or how it is worded. We stipulate, however, that loathing is strictly out of order, unless the loather is willing to write a counter- "This I Do *Not* Believe…" statement that comes from a warm heart as well as from a cool head, and from the subjective emotions as well as from the objective intellect. We acknowledge up front that the purpose of doing this writing on the first evening of class is to get a genuine sense of what is near and dear to each one of us that might contradict what our outward appearances say about us. (The idea of a minimum 500-word *"This I Believe…"* Statement was first featured on National Public Radio [NPR] in the early 1950s. It is alive and well on the air even today. At the end of this chapter, we present a 1000-word "This I Believe Statement…" written by Robert.)

On this first evening of the course, we learn that in attendance are several undergraduates and graduate students, a couple of college administrators and adjunct faculty, and a few non-degree-seeking people of all ages from the outside community. What they all have in common is the desire to write their ongoing stories of meaning and healing in an attempt to become whole human beings. At some level, they understand the truth of Kierkegaard's observation in our opening epigraph: "Life can only be understood backwards, but it must be lived forwards." The best way to live a life forward, with meaning, healing, and purpose, is to understand a life lived backwards; and writing one's life both forwards and backwards is a sure prescription for greater self-understanding.

One undergraduate student wants to write an SPN honors thesis on the topic of mourning, based on the sudden suicidal loss of her younger teenage sister who was also her best friend. Another is trying to make sense of the cultural differences she is facing as an International Asian student, particularly in the areas of politics and religion. Another undergraduate has a writing goal to document her experiences going through a near-death illness a few years ago, and trying to draw out some larger learnings that might help others in a similar situation. And still another student wants to tell his story of being a first-generation college student who was raised in poverty and who, even with generous need-based financial aid, will still end up owing almost $100,000 when he graduates. Finally, one of the undergraduate seniors wants to write an honor's thesis about his own personal experience as a philosophy major and why he believes the study of philosophy is still important in a professionally driven, scientific-technological work-world. As he says: "I want to think of my future work as a lifelong vocation, not just a career or a job. To do this, I need to develop a philosophical understanding of what my life means and how I can make life meaningful for others."

Some of the graduate students in the seminar want to learn how to write an SPN thesis or dissertation. One of these students is a school superintendent; another an elementary school principal. Two of the graduate students are high-level university administrators. One doctoral student is a military officer, another a professor of education in a state college. Another student is a hospital administrator, one is a nurse, and one is a lawyer. Some of these students have been encouraged by their advisors to take the course; but, sadly, a few have been discouraged by advisors who consider personal narrative writing to be "soft" and the "easy way out." Some faculty, because of colleague socialization and disciplinary training, refuse to see the truth in Joanne Trautmann Banks's (1986) epigraph that opens this chapter: "Stories in all their forms satisfy our deepest selves; that far from being an amusement or an aesthetic patina on our daily lives, narrative is fundamental to our bodies, minds, communities, and souls...the narrative urge is central!" (p. 93).

But each one of these graduate students is willing to give this unorthodox genre of scholarly writing a chance, because, each in their own ways, agrees with the epigraph at the beginning of this chapter by Maya Angelou (2009): "There is no greater agony than bearing an untold story inside you." Many of these students have already decided on a thesis or dissertation topic; others will use the course to explore topical possibilities. At the end of this chapter, we will provide some brief examples of these topics excerpted from SPN graduate manuscripts completed during the course. Throughout the book, we, as authors, will also include examples of our own SPN writings.

Our Course Syllabus

Now, the introductions are over. We've learned some personal things about one another. Students are beginning to feel a bit more comfortable in what, for some, is a very strange, very user-friendly, academic environment. As instructors, we've done our best to express our own excitement about Scholarly Personal Narrative writing and what we, ourselves, hope to get out of the semester we will all be together. We tell them that each of us will actually be undertaking a writing project of our own. Finished, as well, is a little meditation exercise we've done with our students (which we will do at the beginning of each future class) in order to help them relax, stay in the here-and-now, and establish the right frame of mindfulness for thinking creatively and sharing personally. And, then, comes a barrage of the inevitable questions: "Is there a syllabus for the course? What are the reading and writing requirements? How will we be graded? What if we've never done this kind of writing before—how will we be compared to those in the seminar who have? What if we don't know what we want to write about?" It is at this point that we pass out our syllabus in hard copy—the only document from us, their instructors, that our students will receive during the entire term that will not be an email attachment.

What follows is a copy of the syllabus that all our students receive on opening night. We make it a point to write our syllabus as a personal letter to each and every person in the class. We do this for several reasons, but the main one is to rid our syllabus of unnecessary academic jargon and to personalize the content as much as we can. Feedback from our students on this type of syllabus format is always positive, if for no other reason than that students feel spoken to as real persons rather than as mere generators of credit hours (paying consumers) for the instructors. (The following syllabus is a variation of one that Robert has used for several years. This syllabus appears also in Nash & Bradley, *Me-Search and Re-Search,* 2011, in a somewhat different form. Dr. Bradley has been a co-teacher, co-author, and co-presenter with Robert on SPN as an emergent research methodology. She also wrote an SPN thesis and dissertation.)

. . . .

Scholarly Personal Narrative Course Syllabus

Dear SPN Students,

Welcome to all of you. Let's spend this first evening getting to know one another.

First, let us say a few introductory words. Our lives, our cultures are made up of many overlapping stories and experiences. If we listen to the media we may hear all the negative stories being pushed on us and may begin to believe that everything is bad. Everything. *The New York Times* reports on August 28th, 2012: "Churning Storm Nears Hurricane Strength"; "Court Rules Israel Wasn't at Fault in US Activist's Death" ; "Afghan Beheadings Could Signal Confusion in Taliban Ranks". But as Chimamanda Ngozi Adichie, a Nigerian states, "The single story creates stereotypes, and the problem with stereotypes is not that they are untrue, but that they are incomplete. They make one story become the only story." So, SPN friend and student, we ask you who are in this course to do perhaps what could be the most courageous act of all—we ask you to write, to write your own story. And not just one. We ask you to write as many stories as you can muster. And we, your instructors, are here, to teach, guide, and to support you in your individual writing endeavors. We are here to give you the freedom to wrench the stories from your gut and your intellect, and to encourage you to grow into an understanding that your stories are important both for you and for others. We will help you the best we can, while maintaining that ultimately it is all up to you to start, sustain, and finish your writing project.

How vain it is to sit down to write when you have not stood up to live.
                                            —*Henry David Thoreau*

If, at this time before our course begins, you know that you will be so busy living life that you have no time to sit down to do the readings or do a lot of writing, then you will have to ask yourself a question: is this the semester when I should be "standing up to live" rather than "sitting down to write?" If your answer is yes, then please consider putting off taking this course until next fall. To be a good writer requires that in addition to living, you also need to do much sitting. Richard Rhodes, the winner of two Pulitzer Prizes for his books, says that the most important part of the anatomy for a writer is not the hand, head, heart, or eyes…it is the butt. Without putting "butt to chair" on a regular basis, writing will not get done. "Butt to chair" is the basic posture for all writers. So, if you think that your activities for this upcoming semester are likely to take away all your time for writing/reading, then please drop the course. We will not ask you any questions or hold anything against you. In fact, we will respect and admire you for your good sense, honesty, and self-insight. We are sure that Henry David Thoreau would be proud of you too, if what he says above is any indication.

And, now, a brief word on requirements this semester, because we know from experience that this is one of your immediate questions whenever you take a course. You will have one major piece of writing to accomplish this term. Yes, you read this right! Only one manuscript for us to read, evaluate, provide feedback, and help you to improve. But be forewarned, even before you read the syllabus further. Your grade will be based mainly on your narrative *self*-evaluation, and we expect this self-narrative to be substantial. Of course, we will add our own grade to your self-assigned grade, and then we will split the difference. More on requirements later in this syllabus.

We do have some non-negotiables, however. We ask that you show up for class each week *only if you've done the assigned writings and readings*. If not, do yourself, and us, a favor and stay home, at work, or wherever. Have some fun. Relax. Do what you need to do to be happy. But don't show up here if this is the last, or even the second-last, place you want to be. We want fully participating, enthusiastic, amply-prepared students to join us each and every week. No SPN free-loaders allowed.

We know that each one of you is in this *elective* writing seminar for your own compelling personal and professional purposes. Each set of needs here will be very different, as you will see after this evening's introductions. How you want to use us, your instructors, and one another, is completely up to you. It's your course, and we're here to serve you. Your instructors will be in attendance with great enthusiasm each and every week, barring significant sickness, injury, or previously planned, out-of-town business. If on any given course evening, nothing productive is happening, even after strenuous efforts on our, and your, parts to get things going, we will say a happy good night, and bid you a fond adieu. We hope you will do the same. We ask only that instead of taking off to go home or to a downtown bar, you find a secluded place to do some writing.

We have selected what we think are some great readings this semester. We think of these readings as gifts to you. We also want you to do some writing each and every week. We will read everything that you want us to. We do not want to deal with hard copies of anything, though. We ask that you attach all your writing to an email as a Word. document, and we will respond to each piece, if you want us to. Be mindful always that, for us, your instructors, reading and writing, and reading your writing, are among our greatest pleasures.

We are passionate about all this material, but we don't intend to proselytize anyone, or to impose obligations on anyone. We just want to know that every single one of you is here each week because *you* want to, and not because *we* want you to. We think of this seminar as an ongoing, intense, very respectful, safe, and enjoyable workshop in writing. Thus, our work style will be a work-shopping style throughout the semester. We will be doing lots of small- and large-group meetings together. We will be giving one another continual feed-back on writing samples.

Scholarly Personal Narrative (SPN) writing is the brainstorm of Robert J. Nash, one of your co-instructors. It is a genre still in process, so we will pretty much be making it up as we go along. There are no "rubrics." There are no "con-ventions." There are no "absolute rules." There are no unwavering "standards." There are no absolute criteria for Validity or Truth. There is only writing, and adventuring, and taking risks, and finding one's voice, and telling stories, and looking for universalizable themes and ideas, and, oh yes, in case you haven't gotten the message yet…writing, writing, writing. One of Nash's SPN books, an assigned reading this semester, is the first book in the country to talk about this type of scholarly writing for pre-professionals, educators, and human service professionals. Its title is *Liberating Scholarly Writing: The Power of Personal Narra-tive*, and was published by Teachers College Press, Columbia University, in 2004.

Doesn't all of this sound like fun? If not, our strong suggestion to you is to find another course. If you need direction, stipulations, structure, and tight evaluation in a course, you won't get these here. So, if you stay, you'll be miser-able. We won't be telling you what you need to do. Only *you* will be telling you what *you* need to do. If, though, you want to write a thesis, a comps/orals paper, a dissertation, an article, a book, or whatever, and you're willing to take some chances, then we can help you. The group can help you. But we can do this only if you know what you want, and you are able, and willing, to help yourself. If you are a self-starter, then this is your course. If you are a low-maintenance student, then this is your course. If you are someone who loves to write on your own terms, then this is your course.

If you decide to remain, we welcome you with enthusiasm. If you decide to leave, we say goodbye with understanding. If you need more help with your decision, we will assist you without judging you. For those of you who decide to "stay the course," here is what we will be expecting of you:

- Work on a specific writing project (final comps paper, thesis, dissertation, proposal, book, blog, article,chapter, memoir, set of writings, etc.).

- Compose an official writing contract, due the 4th class meeting. This is the contract for which we will hold you accountable and offer our support when needed.

- Perform all the reading in a self-reflective, practical-application manner. You will be responsible to find the real-world applications in the readings for your own writing. You will share some of these insights each and every week both in the large and small groups.

- Write a *minimum* 10,000-word manuscript due by the end of the term (no exceptions allowed). We will see your manuscript in thirds (see Important Calendar Information section). Please do not ask about *page* length (this syllabus, for example, is about 3500 words), because, as you know, you can make your manuscripts any length you wish, depending on font size and type, spacing, title pages, and other "padding" variables, etc. Publishers, in case you might be interested, are concerned only about word count, as are we.

- Learn how to reference and document in Chicago style—*not* APA. Chicago uses superscripts, embedded literature reviews, (annotated) endnotes (not footnotes), and eliminates lengthy, technical explications of methodology in the document. Chicago style is most fitting for SPN writing.

- Edit your own papers for typos, misspellings, grammatical errors, etc. This is your responsibility to make sure your editing is as meticulous as possible. We are not editors. We will comment on the quality of your S, P, and N in your content, as well as on your manuscript formatting and structuring. If you ask, we will give you the names of past, gifted SPN students who are also excellent editors, if you decide you need them. They charge an hourly rate.

- You will write, and then you will write some more—every single week, both in and out of class. Brief written reflections will be required each week on an assigned topic. In this course, there will be no waiting until the last weekend of the semester (or of the month) to slap something together, the way we have all learned to do in academia. (Each of us usually justifies this last-minute, panicky, adrenaline-driven surge by saying something like "I work best under pressure with strict deadlines." Unfortunately, this might be why we have thousands of disillusioned ABTs [All But the Thesis] and ABDs [All But the Dissertation] who have dropped out of graduate programs all over the country and are working in jobs they dislike.) We will schedule longer SPN writing-project check-ins every third week or so. You will also do in-class free-writes, depending on the SPN thematic focus each week.

• Share your writing each week with the rest of us—both in small groups and/or in the large group as well. If you are shy about sharing your writing publicly, then perhaps we can help you to do this. We will always ask for volunteers in the big group—but when none are forthcoming, we reserve the right to call on people.

• Attend as many classes as possible! Weekly attendance is crucial! This is the best way for us to get to know you and for you to know us and one another; as well as to learn how to do excellent SPN writing projects. We just ask you to let us know if you will be unable to attend a class session.

• You will realize that if the course is working well or poorly, then it is because the students *and* instructors, you *and* we, are working well or poorly. We are all in this together, and we have freely chosen to be here in this non-required course; thus, as a group, we share equal responsibility for our successes, as well as our failures.

• At the end of the term, assign yourself a grade that will be calculated as 50% of your final grade. We will assign the other 50% of the final grade. We will be looking for consistent weekly attendance; starting, sustaining, and finishing in your semester-long writing output; and a willingness to be actively involved in class each and every week. (It won't hurt for you to be enthusiastic each week.)

• Hopefully, you will choose to have some fun, share some ideas, open up a bit, and work hard to create a writing community built on trust, mutual assistance, generosity, and lots of humility.

I invite you to imagine the act of writing less as a special talent and more as a purposeful craft. Think of writing as carpentry, and think of the techniques I offer you as tools—not rules. With practice you will devise your own tools; you will

become handy with these tools over time; they will become part of your process,
natural and automatic!

—Roy Peter Clark

In the spirit of Clark's epigraph, here is a collection of tools (not rules) that will serve to introduce you to the craft of SPN writing. As the semester goes on, and you practice the craft of writing every chance you get, you will add your own SPN tools and enlarge your own toolbox. In so doing, you will help us to enlarge our own sets of tools as well. We thank you in advance for this gift.

What Is Scholarly Personal Narrative (SPN)?

- First and foremost, it is not everyone's preference to write or to read, nor should it be. It is a commonplace in the humanities but a stranger in professional schools as well as in the social sciences and sciences.

- It is but one tool in the scholar's toolbox, functional for some, dysfunctional or nonfunctional for others.

- It tells a good story and/or many good stories.

- It features a clear point of view, an organizing theme, and/or a coherent argument.

- It starts with the "I" and proceeds outward to the "you" and the "they." The author's distinct and honest voice is key. The author's ideas are only as strong as the voice that delivers them. By the same token, absent the ideas, the personal voice can sometimes be seen as self-indulgent or overly confessional.

- It uses personal stories to deliver the message.

- It strives for an ideal mix of particularity and generalizability, concreteness and abstractness, practice and theory. SPN writing has four major components: it starts with the identification of key *themes*; then it connects these themes to the writer's personal stories in order to exemplify and explicate the points being made; then it draws on relevant, pre-existing *research and scholarship* in order to ground and enrich the personal narrative; and, finally, it ends up with *universalizable ideas and applications* that connect with all readers in some way. In a book on SPN writing they wrote in 2011, Robert and Dr. DeMethra L. Bradley call these four SPN components in order—pre-search, me-search, re-search, and we-search.

- It does not present the author as some omniscient, third-person authority. The author's voice is personal, clear, fallible, and honest. It is also humble and open-ended.

- It generously cites other authors' works and ideas. We call these references "proof-texts."

- It shows some passion. It is not a detached, "objective" examination of a topic. It is a thoughtful, first-person attempt to make a point or teach a lesson by drawing on the author's own life experiences to provide context.

- It tries to help the reader to see the world a little differently, from the author's personal point of view.

- It is editorially and technically meticulous.

- It is more an exercise in creative writing than it is writing to fit a particular research formula, rubric, or template.

- It takes personal risks.

- It begins with the self-confidence that the author has a personal story worth telling and a point worth making.

- It always keeps front and center the interests of the audience who will read the work. Why would the reader want to spend time reading the author's words? So what?

- It understands the difference between "academic rigor" and "rigor mortis."

The best writing partner is the one who listens, and encourages, and affirms, and only afterwards talks about what works and what doesn't. A good writing partner feels no moral or aesthetic compulsion to rip your writing to shreds. When you are having a bad day of writing you don't need a lot of advice. You just need a little love. If your critic is too strident or adamant, ditch the sucker. Look around, take your time, and you will find that person who can fill you up when you are empty.
—Anne Lamott

Whatever you can do, Or dream you can do, Begin it. Boldness has genius, power, and magic in it. Begin it now. Now!
—Goethe

So why do we write? We write so that when we look back and see the moment when we were totally clear, completely brilliant and astoundingly wise, there is proof— proof right there on the god-damned page. And we can read our words and say "I actually wrote that!" And if we did it once—we can do it again.
—Nancy Slonim Aronie

Required Readings in Alphabetical Order

Christina Baldwin, *Storycatcher: Making Sense of Our Lives through the Power and Practice of Story*

Roy P. Clark, *Writing Tools: 50 Essential Strategies for Every Writer*

Anne Lamott, *Bird by Bird: Some Instructions for Writing and Life*

Robert J. Nash, *Liberating Scholarly Writing: The Power of Personal Narrative*

Robert J. Nash and DeMethra LaSha Bradley, *Me-Search and Re-search: A Guide for Writing Scholarly Personal Narrative Manuscripts*

Robert J. Nash and Sydnee Viray, *Our Stories Matter: Liberating Marginalized Voices Using Scholarly Personal Narrative*

Our Preliminary Gift to You—Some Inspiring Writing Maxims

You will know you are a writer when the pain of not writing is greater than the pain of writing.

—*Robert J. Nash*

Writing became such a process of discovery that I couldn't wait to get to work in the morning: I wanted to know what I was going to say.

—*Sharon O'Brien*

If the doctor told me I had six minutes to live, I'd type a little faster.

—*Isaac Asimov*

No one means all he says, and yet very few say all they mean, for words are slippery and thought is viscous.

—*Henry Brooks Adams*

Every writer I know has trouble writing.

—*Joseph Heller*

I asked Ring Lardner the other day how he writes his short stories, and he said he wrote a few widely separated words or phrases on a piece of paper and then went back and filled in the spaces.

—*Harold Ross*

You write to communicate to the hearts and minds of others what's burning inside you. And you edit to let the fire show through the smoke.

—*Arthur Polotnik*

There is no royal path to good writing; and such paths that do exist do not lead through neat critical gardens, various as they are, but through the jungles of self, the world, and of craft.

—*Jessamyn West*

There is a terrible lie pervasive in the universe that when writers finally become famous they will inhabit a paradise where criticism no longer wounds, where writing materializes with little or no effort, and where our muses sing us to sleep each evening with lilting lullabys of inspiration and love

—*Mark Matousek & Robert J. Nash*

Writing classes are like marriages; they require unconditional, non-judgmental support, honesty and commitment, flexibility, and a good sense of humor. In a writing class, you'll probably have a better chance than most marriages because there won't be money or children involved.

—*Nancy Slonim Aronie*

Deliver me from writers who say the way they live doesn't matter. I'm not sure a bad person can write a good book. If art doesn't make us better, then what on earth is it for.

—*Alice Walker*

And, so, dear SPN writers-to-be, we come to the *end* of our letter-syllabus to you, here at the *beginning* of our course together. We promise (to the best of our ability) to be here for you throughout the semester. Just email us when and if you might need us for one thing or another. Remember that we are here to help you to become the best writers you can be during this course. And we will be writing, right along with you ☺

Sincerely,
Robert J. Nash & Sydnee Viray

How Our Students Respond to the Syllabus

After reading the syllabus, and asking for clarification regarding some of the more technical terms we use throughout, our students then get down to business. We often ask them to construct a short, five-minute, free-write letter back to us ("Dear Robert and Sydnee,") with any "lingering, perhaps even burning, questions and concerns" they would like us to respond to as a result of reading our somewhat unconventional syllabus. Then we take some time before leaving class on that first evening to respond to these "lingering, burning" issues. Most students appreciate our honesty in spelling out our course expectations in the syllabus letter. Most appreciate the bulleted specificity and detail regarding the tools required for SPN writing. Almost all appreciate the conversational rules of engagement and feedback that we describe. Some are especially grateful for the gift of our maxims, and even take the time to unpack a few of these in their own maxim-laden language (a kind of *quid pro quo* maxim exchange).

There are always the inevitable few students, however, who will apologize for deciding that our course is just not what they need at this time in their lives, and that they will be dropping it. One major concern in these cases is the 10,000-word minimum final writing project. This is a huge expectation for those students who are taking several other courses, and who have never written such a lengthy paper for a course. They wonder about their competence, and time, to complete such an assignment. Another important concern is the requirement to write personally. For some students, self-disclosure is very threatening; for others, it doesn't seem "academic" enough. And for still others, it is an impossible request because they've never learned how to do it either in their undergraduate or graduate courses. They yearn for bite-sized, research-writing formulas, clearly stated right-and-wrong standards from us, their instructors, and line-by-line editing from both of us on each and every page they write.

Zinsser's (2001) words in our opening epigraph come across to these students as literally terrifying: "Personal narrative writers must manufacture a text, imposing narrative order on a jumble of half-remembered events. With that feat of manipulation they arrive at a truth that is theirs alone, not quite like that of anybody else who was present at the same events" (p. 33). How to even begin to do this (to "impose a narrative order" on the chaos of their lives) seems to be a total mystery. Sadly for them, but gladly for us, we will not be able to provide the step-by-step, do-this-our-way oversight they so desperately need at this time in their lives. It is our strongest pedagogical (and existential) belief that only the writer is able to author a life in order to "arrive at a truth that is theirs alone." We will gladly be SPN cheerleaders, clarifiers, inspirers, and exemplars (in our own writing), but we will not assume the role of the expert SPN overseer. This is just not our preferred pedagogical story.

After that first meeting, however, almost all of the students will return each week to start, sustain, and finish the semester. And, lo and behold, each and every one of them will produce an extensive, and intensive, SPN document that they will cherish for the rest of their lives. How do we know this? Robert has run into students he had in class decades ago, and, almost without exception, they will tell him that their final SPN manuscripts were the only college writings they have saved to share with friends, loved ones, and families. This has been the writing they are most proud of. And, as one student said, "when I crossed the 10,000-word, SPN finish line in your course, it was more satisfying than crossing the finish line of the 10 marathons that I've run since I graduated."

Fast Forward…to the End of the Course

Okay, now it is early December, and the course is over. Our group has become more than a collection of writers; it is now a community of friends. There have been lots of false, even painful, starts in beginning work on manuscripts. For some, the greatest pain has been to persevere in the writing in order to reach the finish line. But, at the 15-week point in the course, all have managed to start, sustain, and finish a significant SPN document. There has been considerable bonding among our colony of SPN writers. Why? Because a mutually respectful sharing of honest, vulnerable, insightful stories about one's life begets these same stories from everyone else; and, voila!, we discover that we have more in common with others than we ever could have thought.

Story-telling is contagious. Its lure is unavoidable. Each and every one of us in the class is a story-bearing, story-hearing creature. We are our stories. We make no sense of ourselves without our stories. In fact, absent our stories there is no self. The self (like a soul) is a construct that will never show up in an MRI or a Cat Scan. The self, in Nietzsche's word, is a "fiction" that each of us contructs by telling stories that explain us to ourselves and to others. We are each "distributed selves" (in Bruner's memorable phrase) in the sense that the self we show to the world (and to ourselves) is a product of the multiple stories that we inhabit at any given time. And each of these stories is the result of an interrelated, unlimited set of experiences, contexts, circumstances, and relationships. I am who I am depending on the story I'm choosing to live in at any given time. What we've learned together this semester is that it is sheer bliss to be able to write both the brokenness and the fullness of our selves into meaning and wholeness by telling our stories.

And suddenly, it seems, 15 weeks have flown, or crawled, by, depending on a student's felt-level of exhilaration or exhaustion at the end of three busy, writing-filled months. The end has come. Weekly writing assignments are no longer on the must-do agenda. Deadlines are, yes, dead. The chance to go public in class for the first or last time by reading aloud a sensitive piece of writing has passed. The three, 3000-word check-ins have come and gone, and with them the grinding pressure (or the wonderful opportunity, depending on how one looks at it) to produce something worthy. The weekly, small-group writers' support teams are a thing of the past. Gone forever is the opportunity to get instructors' feedback on the writing. Gone, as well, are the responses to our feedback—ranging from a student's saying it was "extremely helpful," to another's "I need more from each of you," or, maybe the worst, "I still don't think I'll ever be the kind of writer I want to be. This stuff is just too tough. I realize that my life sucks, but it sucks even more that I'm just not ready to write about it."

What will be most memorably absent from our lives, however—and perhaps these final images will never disappear for any of us—are the sad (sometimes tearful) goodbyes to one another at the end of the course, and the tangible loss students experience of a genuine, non-threatening, supportive writing commuity. As more than one student has remarked: "How is it that, at times, I've felt closer to this group each week than to anyone else in my life? It has been my family away from home, or better still, the family I never had." For us, the answer lies in the aforementioned Maya Angelou quotation. If "bearing an untold story inside us is the greatest agony" of all, then the greatest ecstasy must be to be able, finally, to release that story to others (in written form) as a gift freely given and as a gift freely received with kindness, generosity, and affection. How do I know that I exist? I exist, because I am able to tell my story and have it heard, and affirmed, by others. With apologies to Descartes, we assert: *Narro, ergo cogito, ergo sum* ("I narrate, therefore I think, therefore I am").

Comments from Students' SPN Manuscripts

And, so, in ending our course, and this chapter, we will include excerpts from half a dozen of our students' final papers regarding what some of them valued most about learning how to write in a "strange" genre called SPN:

· ·

My inspirational mentor, Audre Lorde, once said: "I write for those women who do not speak, for those who do not have a voice because they were so terrified, because we are taught to respect fear more than ourselves. We've been taught that silence would save us, but it won't." This narrative is written for single mothers who cannot write for themselves. Single-mother voices often go unnoticed in higher education, and so I write. I do not consider myself a writer, in fact writing this manuscript has been one of the most terrifying projects I have ever done. And this is the first time I have told my story. My story is one of fear and triumph. I decided to write my comprehensive exam in the form of Scholarly Personal Narrative (SPN) because SPN allows me to focus on my "me"—my journey as a single mother to the ivory towers. However, I would be naive to believe all single mothers have the same journey. I do not wish to convey the message that my journey is better or harder than other single mothers. Rather, please focus on my journey as a personal one, a journey I know inside and out; a journey used as a way to educate others; and a journey I feel comfortable disclosing. As this writing continues, I foresee other single mothers sharing their journeys. I understand how for many single mothers it may be a great risk to allow one to focus on their journey while still going through it. Today, after much self-centeredness, I find myself filled with the courage to share my journey.

Hearing the sound of my own voice has been challenging. I have spent years making spaces for other people to hear their own voices. In fact, it has been part of my job, my life's mission, to make sure other people walk this life realizing their own greatness. However, in that journey, I forgot about my own greatness. I have allowed myself to live in silence. SPN allows me to tell my story, in my own words, and in my own voice. This narrative, my narrative, will show other single mothers how they are not alone. I am here for them, and I will continue to write for them. (Erin Baker, "From Welfare Lines to the Ivory Towers: A Single Mother's Journey to Access Higher Education")

• •

My graduate classes opened me up to a new style of writing which embodied constructivism through the process of writing—the Scholarly Personal Narrative (SPN). One of the most powerful tools I gained over the last two years has been the self-assuredness that my own life has meaning I can reference in my scholarship and vocation. I learned to trust and share my voice in my graduate classes through using SPN writing, which is a form of research and scholarship based on the author's own life story and perspective. Indeed, "whether critics of personal writing like it or not, writers are always an integral part of what they observe, study, interpret, and assert." (Nash) To write a true account of the principles and knowledge about educational philosophy and practice I have learned in graduate school, I must be honest and forthcoming about *why* these principles mean something to me and *how* I have seen them demonstrated in my life. Because I am employed in a helping profession, it is essential that I understand my own motivations and background beliefs to build authentic, ethical, and beneficent relationships with the students and colleagues I serve.

The SPN style of writing is gaining momentum nationally in higher education. It does not exclude traditional, objective works of scholarship, but instead, enriches the academy through a different, student-centered approach. SPN presumes an understanding and respect for the way personal experiences are relevant to both our academic research and society. I assert that this is a way to apply the philosophy that "the personal is political" in academic research, and also to allow for the ethic of compassion (the focal point of this paper) to be reflected in the products of our academic pursuits. I am grateful that I had these opportunities to write in SPN. This format has helped me to make greater meaning out of my educational endeavors, and has empowered my perspective and voice. Now, I hope to encourage this empowerment and vocal liberation for future students by contributing this manuscript to the greater body of SPN scholarship.

If this is a new methodology for you, please join along with amicability in the personal stories I will share with you. Understand that this has taken vulnerability and confidence. In these pages are just a few of the moments in my life that sustain my meaning and purpose, and I hope will evoke some of your own self-exploration on my chosen topic. (Annalee Dammann, "The Place for Compassion in Higher Education: My Path Toward Mindful and Meaningful Living")

· ·

James Baldwin observed: "Story is bigger and wilder and more faceted than anyone could have imagined. It's disruptive and raucous, heartbreaking and tender. It offends us and outrages us, enlightens and guides us." Malcolm X once said, "Why am I as I am? To understand that of any person, his whole life, from birth must be reviewed. All of our experiences fuse into our personality. Everything that ever happened to me is an ingredient." This quote means a lot to me and will foretell the scholarly personal journey that I will embark upon. Both scholarly and very personal, this Scholarly Personal Narrative will represent my journey to define who I am really and what I am really capable of, to bring a voice to an "at-risk" African-American male student, who despite what statistics may try to predict, made it from humble beginnings in Jamaica, New York, to receiving a graduate degree from the University of Vermont.

I expect my scholarly personal narrative to provide a counterstory to the dominant narrative of what it means to be a young African American man from a low-income, urban environment in our society today, to shed light on the importance of promoting self-authorship for students in higher education today, to serve as a catalyst for other marginalized identities to use this methodology to give a voice to the voiceless, and to provide a strong rationale on why "affinity spaces" are crucial for identity development for students in higher education. I will also support this methodology with an embedded literature review examining the research in higher education regarding African-American men and their persistence in higher education and defining what it means to be an affinity space. (Devan Carrington, "Men Integrated in Brotherhood: A Scholarly Personal Narrative Understanding of the Importance Affinity Groups Have on College Campuses for the Persistence of African-American Males")

Cancer, Parkinson's disease, Lou Gehrig's disease, schizophrenia, cerebral palsy, multiple sclerosis, Alzheimer's, AIDS—all terrible, painful, debilitating and, yes, some even deadly afflictions of the human body. But as hard as it is to believe, none of these diseases or disorders have stood out to doctors and patients in a way that resulted in the appointment of the moniker "the suicide disease." No, this title is reserved for the most painful condition known to mankind. It is called *Trigeminal Neuralgia*, and I suffer from it. Trigeminal Neuralgia is an extremely rare nerve pain disorder with no known cure and little known research about its causes. It is a progressive disease and while it cannot kill you, it can subject its victim to unrelenting torturous pain that is unparalleled by any other kind of pain experienced by man. More often than not, it is considered to be idiopathic, or from an obscure or known cause, which contributes to relatively little research available for public consumption. My diagnosis is recent and this is my story of coming to terms with my situation for which there is no certainty or visibility—only the fear of what could be.

I chose to tell my story in the writing style of Scholarly Personal Narrative. SPN is a unique way for a writer to include their personal voice in their work and adds a truthfulness and authenticity that the reader would not likely have the opportunity to experience if the work had been written in the more typical qualitative fashion. Scholarly Personal Narrative is the creation of Robert J. Nash, a highly regarded and nationally renowned professor in the College of Education and Social Services at the University of Vermont. Robert's work in promoting SPN has given hundreds of students the opportunity to write from the heart in a truly compelling and surprisingly universalizable manner. The universalizability of themes that appear in peoples' SPN work is what makes this style of writing so powerful. Over the past three months, I have had the privilege of hearing the written work of many of my peers in the SPN course that Robert teaches. People with whom I struggled to find any semblance of a shared experience, other than the fact that we were all in class together, were mere strangers to me at the beginning of the semester. Through the power of SPN I came to realize that despite our differences in culture, upbringing, socio-economic status, religion, political stance, etc. I could identify with at least one truth that each of them shared with our class.

Writing in Scholarly Personal Narrative is not easy despite what some may think. I had made the false assumption that my propensity towards storytelling, my open nature towards self-disclosure, and my undergraduate degree in history (read: many, many scholarly papers) would make me a natural at this style despite it being completely new to me. After countless hours of worrying about how I was going to perfect each section of this writing which resulted in numerous story ideas that never made it off the ground, I decided to just write—free from the constraints of self-imposed perfectionism, and I watched as my story unfolded. Without even realizing it, I found that experiences to date with trigeminal neuralgia closely aligned with what one might expect to experience as they travel through the five stages of grief, as written by Elisabeth Kubler-Ross. I found it only natural to highlight those stages and explore my own journey within each of them throughout this work. It is my hope that none of my readers will ever identify with me in my experiences with trigeminal neuralgia specifically but that universalizability of facing fear and finding strength will reach everyone. (Anonymous [by request], "Walking Towards the Unknown: My Life with a Chronic Pain Disorder and the Implications for Educators")

. . . .

I have always been profoundly fascinated by the power of story telling. From reading a book to conversing with a friend, listening to and sharing stories are passions of mine that I will always hold dear. Most of my fondest memories in college consist of my friends and I staying up all night telling stories to one another. My favorite classes have been the ones that allow me to express myself through my own story and hear the stories of others as much as I can. Whenever possible in my studio classes in college I created pieces that let me share my story in a creative or unique way. Stories have given me the privilege of knowing others intimately and allowing them to know me just as well.

Due to my love of story telling, I have chosen to write my comprehensive exam in the Scholarly Personal Narrative Style (SPN). SPN writing allows for my life and story to inform the subject at hand. I am an atheist. Atheism has informed my life, so I shall give it the same treatment as I write this paper. Sharing my story will give me the ability to give meaning to the theme of my paper. The theme is therefore a direct result of my life and experiences.

However, I do not wish to be selfish and write a paper about myself, for myself. The purpose of SPN writing is not to talk about myself for thirty pages and be done with it. This paper is for the benefit of the reader, as is the true goal of SPN. I hope each section will provide a different insight for the reader to consider and discuss in the future.

Researchers have only very recently begun delving into the societal views on atheism, and in response I will add to this small pool of knowledge to inform and guide the reader into thinking critically about how sterotyped our atheist students are regarded today. I do not expect the reader to set aside their religio-spiritual beliefs when reading this SPN. I would never ask anyone to "set aside what they know" as they read this work; that would be contradictory to my goal. I say this because it is impossible to remove the "self" from the paper when reading it. This paper is fundamentally different when someone else is reading it than how I wrote it *by virtue of its being read*. As you now read this paper you are fundamentally linked to it in this way and cannot "set aside what you know" in order to better understand it. The best way to understand this paper is to bear in mind what you know and let this paper further inform that knowledge. This connection is what truly guides an SPN. (Ray Mattila, "De-Stereotyping the Atheist Student")

. . . .

I am from Senegal, and I have always had a love of languages! During the time I have been a student, writing has become an act of faith. My primary native language is Wolof. My father's native language is Serer, my mother's, Wolof. These two are utterly different! But since Wolof is the National Native Language in Senegal, I grew up primarily speaking Wolof at home. At school we were restricted in the use of our native languages; all learning and conversing had to be in French. However, we managed to find ways to speak our native languages, mostly when we were in the playground, away from teacher supervision. We'd express ourselves instinctively in our own native languages. With time, I ended up picking words from other native languages, and eventually have come to speak fluently three different native languages. French is almost like a native language since the whole educational system is taught in French. So, I express and think in a few different languages, which could be perceived as beneficial at times, and a handicap at others.

When I took your SPN course, Robert and Sydnee, I was thinking in Wolof, Serer, French, and my new language, English. Your course has given me the opportunity to understand that a language is not just a compilation of words; it is a way of thinking and being. Shifting from my native languages to English meant adapting myself to new ways of thinking and being. Nevertheless, this doesn't signify that I had to alienate myself, to let down my native languages, which had configured essentially who I am. It simply means that every time I sit down to write, I can't ignore the clashes of languages inside me. Now is time to think and write in English! The leap I have to make is frightening and enormous! When I sit down in front of a paper, I have all these languages working together and at the same time against each other. In which language should I think and write? I often feel like a bouncing ball going from one language to another. I resolved that to write in English, my primary aim must be clarity. As Boileau stated, 'Everything that is conceived well is expressed clearly, and the words to say it come easily.'

SPN writing has helped me to make sure that my reader understands what I understand or understood, see what I see or saw, feel what I feel or felt. I constantly battle against the fear that my new way of expression could corrupt or alter the meaning I convey. With perseverance and patience, my initial limitations, confusion, and frustration faded in the face of an indescribable need for telling my story. Through the power of the SPN writing methodology, I am able to step out of my original cultural universe to embrace a whole new one. In this process, I found myself journeying to the discovery of others, to the revelation of my soul, of my meanings, of my dreams, my hopes, my uncertainties, my role as an educator, and as an advocate for intercultural and inter-religious dialogue. (Mohamadou Diop Alkhourane Ndione, "Propaedeutic for a Cosmopolite Education: The Philosophical, Spiritual, Professional, and Ethical Growth of a Senagalese Muslim Educator")

· ·

Resources: Example of a "This I Believe..." Statement and Some "Six-Word Memoirs"

· ·

"THIS I BELIEVE..." Robert J. Nash

I believe that *trying to be perfect is an exercise in futility*. It used to be an old, familiar, and agonizing pattern. Everything had to be in impeccable order for my first class of the semester. My syllabi—much too detailed and lengthy because they were calculated to answer all questions beforehand—were piled neatly in a stack. I covered every base in those syllabi, some of which were longer than 20 pages single-spaced. I checked out the classroom many times before the first session.

In those days, as I walked to the seminar room, more ready than any Olympic athlete who's prepared for a single event for years, all the usual "what if?" fears resurfaced. What if there were people in the seminar who were smarter than I? What if I screwed up in some way and looked like a dumbass? What if nobody actually showed up for the first meeting? What if the students hated the course material? What if they laughed at me behind my back, or, worse, to my face? Robert, the first-generation, blue collar/no collar, working class, community college loser, an academic pretender in a "public ivy" university. What if, what if, what if?

Students of mine who are members of Alcoholics Anonymous tell me that it was at the moment they accepted themselves as less than perfect creatures, and resolved to love and forgive themselves despite their imperfections, that they were able to *help* themselves. The hubris that denied all their needs was the same overweening pride that drove them over and over again to drink and fueled their illusions of self-sufficiency.

As for the recovering alcoholic, so too for me, a recovering perfectionist. Humility is the best antidote to perfectionism. I realize that I can be loved even when I make mistakes. My outward displays of grandiosity and pomposity have too often covered up my fear that I'll be found out, if not this week, then most likely next week, and, if not then, the week after. In the old days, when I used to write, teach, or lecture, I did it with a single-minded ferocity for being perfect. It's too bad that I didn't know then what I know now. I was really asking these questions: now that I've proven that I'm perfect, will everyone love me? will I never get sick and die? and will I live happily ever after?

No. I won't live happily ever after, regardless of how perfect I am. And neither will anyone else. Who can guarantee happiness? So, here I am today, trying to overcome my imperious compulsion to be "best enough" and seek, instead, in all humility, to be "good enough." Humility is understanding that the best way to be loved is to love…and, then, in St. Augustine's words… "do as you will." Humility is giving myself permission to leave behind the fear of imperfection that used to torment and diminish me. Humility is the willingness to tell my story to others so that they might learn more about me, and in the process, perhaps learn more about themselves. Humility, in the spirit of the *Tao Te Ching*, is learning how to practice professorial non-interference. No longer will I be the know-it-all scholar who covers all the bases in my teaching. The more I relinquish my need to be the perfect teacher, voila! the more my students are willing to learn for themselves. This I believe…with all my heart. And I'll be working on being kind to my imperfect self for the rest of my life.

• •

Six-Word Memoirs (from R. Fershleiser & L. Smith, Eds., *Not Quite What I Was Planning: Six-Word Memoirs by Writers Famous and Obscure*. HarperCollins, 2008.)

"I asked. They answered. I wrote." —Sebastian Junger

"Dancing in fields of infinite possibilities." —Deepak Chopra

"I live the perfect imperfect life." —Paul Love

"Started small, grew, peaked, shrunk, vanished." —George Saunders

"I inhale battles. I exhale victories." —William Heath

"Fearlessness is the mother of reinvention." —Arianna Huffington

"I read too much…into everything!" —Jessica Reed

"Wounded girl turns life into stories." —Farai Chideya

"Philosophical teen, surrounded, but always lonely." —Nehemiah Blazek

"Loved home. Left to make sure." —Adam Krefman

"Tell your story. That's my story." —Andy Goodman

Dissecting My Own SPN Writing
One Author's Self-Evaluation

ROBERT J. NASH

Writing: proclaiming in front of everyone what one is careful to conceal from one's immediate circle.

—*Jean Rostand*

The paradox [of writing SPNs] is that everything must be written with total commitment, or the work reads falsely and insincerely, and yet all total commitment is to partial knowledge. As writers age and learn, they can't help rethinking and perhaps regretting earlier commitments.

—*Jane Smiley*

Revisiting My Previously Published SPN on Teaching and Learning

I have written three previous books on how to do Scholarly Personal Narrative writing (Nash, 2004, 2012, 2013), but I am going to attempt something here that I've never done before. I intend to reproduce the first piece of SPN writing I, myself, ever did that was published in 2002 by Peter Lang. The piece will remain relatively intact (with some longer sections deleted because of space limitations) except for one very important addition: I will insert a series of comments in **bracketed bold-faced inserts** strategically throughout the writing as to where I think I was successful, *as well as* unsuccessful, in using the basic SPN "tools."

˙ So, think of this chapter as an *ex post facto*, uncensored examination of how I feel I succeeded, and how I failed, to practice what I preached in my first attempt to do SPN writing. I do this not out of a sense of false humility or authorial bravado. Instead, I hope to teach the fundamental SPN tools (not rules) by example. I hope to illustrate in my actual writing the highlights and lowlights of authoring my personal story as a college teacher and learner for over four decades. While it is true that the original version of my "passion to teach and learn" story actually got published, it is also true that, in retrospect, I believe I could have made it stronger.

In fact, I'll go Jean Rostand one better in the above epigraph. Rethinking publicly *what one has already written and published* is the ultimate act of non-concealment. If I had to do it all over again, here is what I would keep, add, subtract, and modify. Here is how I would apply the SPN guidelines today to what I wrote in 2002. At the end of this chapter I will list, and summarize, the main tools for writing an effective SPN manuscript. I will do this inductively by referring back to my own writing in this chapter. I ask each of you as readers to remember that everyone's writing style, thematic foci, and level of personal disclosure are different. This is why I refer to SPN writing techniques as "tools" not "rules."

The Passion to Teach…and to Learn

(Originally appeared as Chapter 1 in Robert J. Nash, *Spirituality, Ethics, Religion, and Teaching: A Professor's Journey.* New York: Peter Lang Publishing, 2002)

Passion is the exhilarating experience of being carried along by a power greater than controlled conscious willing.

—*Rollo May*

My vocation is the spiritual life, the quest for God, which relies on the eye of the heart. My avocation is education, the quest for knowledge, which relies on the eye of the mind . . . . But—unable to blink one eye, shut them both, or live in a blur—I have been forced to find ways for my eyes to work together, to find a common focus for my spirit-seeking heart and my knowledge-seeking mind that embraces reality in all its amazing dimensions.

—*Parker J. Palmer*

[I often use epigraphs to begin my articles, chapters, and books. Epigraphs— introductory inscriptions—are my way of organizing, framing, and focusing the content of my writing. Before I begin, I cull out of many relevant readings those quotations-epigraphs that I think will give the reader some sense

of where I am going in my chapter. As this chapter, and book, are all about the passion I feel toward my teaching, I found the Rollo May quotation to be very apt. The Parker Palmer quotation, however, hit a false note for me. In truth, my "passion" has very little to do with a "quest for God," or a "spirit-seeking heart." Palmer's quotation, in retrospect, is a bit too Quakerish (he's a well-known Quaker) for me, and I would probably replace it, if I were to rewrite it now. By the way, my epigraphs actually serve as outlines for me; these are the only "notes" that I take in preparation for writing. Sometimes I refer back to these epigraphs in the chapter itself; sometimes I don't. It all depends on what works and what doesn't.]

Retirement Is out of the Question…for Now

I have, all of a sudden it seems, reached the age of retirement as a professor. Even so, to paraphrase Dylan Thomas, I refuse "to go gently into this good night." [I have always enjoyed Dylan Thomas's poetry, particularly this line. It seemed to me to be a nice way to set just the right tone for what follows.] I have practiced my craft—teaching—at the high school and college levels for almost four decades [now, it's actually approaching five decades]. Nothing surprises me anymore in the classroom, even though everything continues to delight me. A very insightful graduate student once said to me: "You claim to be a religious agnostic. I think I know why you have the luxury of holding this position. Your work as an educator is actually a religious vocation because it gives you a sense of transcendence. Your church is the university. Your sacrament is teaching. Your community of saints is made up of your students. And your prayer is when you carry on intense, revitalizing, give-and-take conversations in the classroom. Am I right?" [This is almost a verbatim quotation by a graduate student who took a religion, spirituality, and education course with me. It has stuck with me for years, because it is right on the money. So much of my own personal narrative writing draws upon my experiences in the classroom with my students. You might say that I tell stories about my life by using my students as real-life takeoff points. One ethical challenge for me, in my own SPN writing, however, is how to draw flesh-and-blood examples from my teaching without exploiting my students; without using them as fodder for my publications. Another ethical challenge is how to maintain confidentiality in my recounting of their stories without revealing my students' identities, unless, of course, they have given me permission to do so.]

Yes, this student is correct, and I blush at being so transparent. I am not at the point in my life when I am willing to withdraw gracefully to a life of monitoring the stockmarket, sailing, traveling, golfing, gardening, volunteer-ing, or running for the local school board. As worthy as all these activities are, the truth is that I live to teach, to be with students, to read their papers, to advise their theses and dissertations, to write and to learn, and, yes, even to engage in the incessant political maneuvering with my colleagues that tries the patience of so many college professors. I am that strange breed of professional animal who is a proud, lifelong teacher. What is more, I am a happy one, at least most of the time. I was not always this way, however. I have only gradu-ally, at times painfully, grown into my contentment. [**This last, short sentence took me a long time to craft. I wanted to create the impression that my pro-fessional life has not always been smooth-going. In fact, it has been deeply troubled at times (I told my personal story for the first time in Chapter 2 of this book), but always more satisfying than not. Whatever contentment I have experienced has been hardwon and tenuous at best.**]

I first entered the profession of teaching at the high school level, in the year of 1962, in a major suburb of Boston, Massachusetts. While I hated the em-phasis that administrators and teachers in this large, suburban, working-class school (4000 students) put on routine and discipline, or, in their words, "keep-ing resistant students in line by enforcing the rules," I, nevertheless, found much to love in the challenge of teaching a bunch of distracted adolescents the joys of English. I remember glowing for days afterward, for example, when "Liz," a very troubled sophomore, came up to me after class and said: "Wow, this stuff called poetry that we've been studying for the last month is really cool. Would you mind reading a little poem I wrote last night in memory of my little brother who died of leukemia last year?"

Or when "Ken," the president of the school's National Honor Society, ex-claimed that he had just been accepted to Boston College on an academic scholarship and that, thanks to my course, he was declaring himself to be an English major. Ken eventually went on to earn a doctorate in English, and he is today the chairman of his department at a very prestigious university. What is more, Ken's books on postmodern literary theory are well known in the academy. I beam with pride whenever I announce to my students that I knew the author when he was a high school English whiz. I also point out that he was a very competitive basketball player. To this day, I enjoy telling my students the tale of suffering a broken nose during a pick-up basketball game when I foolishly attempted to challenge Ken during one of his signature, hard-driving layups to the basket. To compound my physical pain, I was the one who was charged with the personal foul! [**Ken was really a pain-in-the-ass when he took my English class because he was a know-it-all. He still is, in fact, but** so am I in some ways. Actually, omniscience is the quality most prized by the professoriate, especially in their respective disciplines. This is the way we are socialized throughout graduate school, at department meetings, and at our professional conferences. I debated as to whether I should have expressed my true feelings about Ken in my SPN. I opted, instead, to be kind, for fear of seeming snide, or of offending Ken should he ever read the book. The cat's out of the bag now, though. Strangely, I feel relieved. An important SPN question still remains however: How honest should you be whenever you describe real people in your writing? The answer is simple: Be as honest as you need to be to make your point. But remember, too, that you don't need to leave a trail of dead bodies in your wake.]

Of course, I vividly recall my terrible disappointments in that school as well. Noteworthy among them was a junior, "Paul," who sat for days at a time in the back of the classroom, glaring sullenly at me, and never opening his mouth. Throughout the term, I continually asked him to stop by after school to talk with me, but he never appeared. I later learned that he dropped out of high school. When he returned his textbooks to the assistant principal, the words scribbled in large boldface on the cover of his English text were these: "Mr. Nash is a fucker! [Not a single reader so far has complained about my using this obscenity. I debated as to whether I would retain it in reading the galleys, but decided to keep it. This is the word that I remember most vividly on that bookcover.] I hate him, and I hate English." When Paul did make a connection with me a year later, it was in an angry letter. The words were meant to taunt and hurt me, and they did: "High school was bullshit! So were you. I'll bet I'm making more money driving a truck cross-country than you are teaching your crap. You know what? I don't need poetry or grammar to make it in the world. When are you going to get an honest job, make some real money, and do something useful for a change?" [Paul taught me more than he will ever know. If I had to make a choice of a class full of Pauls or Kens, I would choose the Pauls. Paul had strong convictions; he was willing to express them; and, for me, hate is not the opposite of love, indifference is. Paul "hated" me because he actually had a strong emotional connection with me; I stirred up some intense passion in him. Maybe, if Freud's theory of projection is corrcet, he hated in me what he hated in himself. As a teacher, I can work with hate and passion, but not with apathy. I would love to break bread with Paul, now, some fifty years later. I wonder if he ever returned to school. Is he still driving that truck? Is he still so sure that my English class was a waste of time for him? On the other hand, in the past, I have actually gone out of my way to avoid smug and arrogant Ken at conferences.]

Then there was "Millie," a trailer-park child old beyond her years, a senior, already a divorced, teenage mother, and the daughter of two severely depressed, alcoholic parents. Millie was also brilliant, the possessor of a near-photographic memory and a fertile, creative mind. I took it as my solemn mission to raise her educational aspirations. I cajoled her throughout her senior year to take the SAT exam, and to apply to colleges. She managed to gain admission to Northeastern University, a cooperative education college that would have been a wonderful fit for her. There, she could have worked for her tuition and studied at the same time. She was also accepted to Smith, an exclusive women's college in Massachusetts, which came up with enough financial aid for her to get through at least the first two years.

Millie was killed in an automobile accident shortly after her high school graduation. Her blood-alcohol level was almost three times the legal limit, and she was also six months pregnant. Her older sister later told me that she had no intention of ever going to college, despite what she was telling me and her friends. According to the sister:

"Millie liked and respected you very much, Mr. Nash, but she felt tremendous pressure to gain your approval. She told you what she thought you wanted to hear when all along she really wanted you to be her friend. She was so deeply lonely and needy to have an adult confidante she could trust. All you ever talked about with her was how important it was to have a college education. She could never understand why you weren't interested in her personal problems. These problems, I think, are what turned her to booze and eventually killed her."

[To this day, I can't think of Millie without tearing up. I dramatized her situation here, but only in order to conceal her identity. Her memory will remain with me forever. I think that I did a good job in telling her story, and its impact on me, in such a very short space. I only wish that I had told some more personal teaching stories in this chapter, though. I think that some of my self-revelations that follow in this chapter would have been more powerful if I could have told at least a few more concrete stories. I've got hundreds of them. Not all my experiences in high school teaching were so dramatic, however. I could have related some of the more typical tales, I think, without undermining the central themes that I wanted to present in this chapter and throughout the book. Finding that delicate balance between *theme* and *story* is something that is a real challenge for me. I tell stories in conversation more easily than I write them. I am good with concepts and thematic foci in my writing, but less sure-handed with stories. I still have a lot to

unlearn from my earlier academic training—where abstractions and name-droppings were, and are still, prized—in order to be a good SPN writer.]

I left high school teaching forever, knowing that I had failed with too many Pauls and Millies. I left mostly to lick my wounds, and to figure out why teaching had been such a bitter-sweet experience for me. I hated the public school bureaucracy. I could not understand the sarcasm in administrators' voices whenever they talked about teachers and parents, or the cynicism in teachers' words whenever they referred to administrators or, sadly, to their students. More personally, why did it seem that for every soaring success I experienced in the public school classroom I also suffered an offsetting and dismal disappointment? Why was it that on some days I could not wait to get to school in the morning, while on others I yearned to call in sick? Why was it that so many of my colleagues deep-down intensely disliked teaching, yet still chose to stick it out year after year—complaining, conniving, and gossiping, and, in the process, casting a pall of gloom and discontent over all the rest of us? I wondered: Were my ambivalence and my doubts about my work and my colleagues normal? Was all of this professional misery somehow inevitable? [**This is a pivotal "hook" paragraph, the one that sets up the reader for my decision to leave the public schools forever. I think that it works. I worry, though, about my tendency to write tediously long sentences, replete with seemingly endless series.**]

I decided, after much soul-searching, to return as a fulltime student to the university, to find refuge in the books, papers, and solitude that I had always loved. I began my doctoral studies at Boston University in philosophy and educational theory with high hopes. Experiencing a crisis of religious faith, I wanted to deepen my formal understanding of existentialism, a very popular 1950s and 1960s philosophy which I taught my high school honors classes. I had enjoyed assigning my honors students a number of readings by such authors as Albert Camus and Jean Paul Sartre. These writers rarely failed to touch something vital in the hearts of my bright, questioning adolescents, and, not coincidently, in my own heart as well. At the time I was struggling with the age-old philosophical problems of making meaning, finding purpose, good and evil, freedom and determinism, creation and chance, theism and atheism, the individual and the community, and with the starker realities of coming to grips with my own human finitude. I vaguely sensed that existentialism might be able to provide some answers, or, at least, some ways of asking the right questions about such difficult philosophical puzzles. I hope to describe some of my learnings on these topics in the chapters to follow. [**Here's another "hook" paragraph with a central theme: My teaching, at least in part, reflects my**

own spiritual and philosophical struggles. This is a theme that has continued throughout my personal and professional life.]

I also wanted the systematic opportunity to examine the ins and outs of
educational theory. I needed to look objectively at what I could have done
as a high school teacher to be more effective and to gain a greater peace of
mind. Teaching was still my obsession. In fact, it was behind everything that
I thought about during the three wonderfully reflective years that I spent at
Boston University. The combination of philosophy and educational theory
hooked me from the start. I knew almost immediately that I would become a
philosopher of education. I also knew that I would someday return to teaching—not in the public schools but in the university. Moreover, I knew that I
would make my academic home in a professional school, a college of education, rather than in a philosophy department. [**I wanted the reader to know in
this paragraph that I am an applied philosopher. This was important to me
because, throughout the book, I make the thematic case that nothing can be
more "practical" for a teacher than having a sound philosophy and spirituality of education.**]

This academic home is where I have resided for over three-and-a-half decades, and I have never once regretted my choice. It is here in the university
that I have gained a deep sense of vocational satisfaction, along with a modi-
cum of spiritual peace. As will be apparent in subsequent chapters, though, I
am still restless when it comes to matters of the spirit. Most of all, however,
I have found in teaching something that I can do every day of my life with a
special gusto, with what some of my students today love to call "passion." Sadly,
this term is so often used in the helping professions that it is fast becoming a
cliché. It is a word that, in my opinion, cries out for thoughtful deconstruction
and reconstruction. This will be one of my aims in the pages that follow.

[**Finally, I get around to discussing passion. The challenge for me here
is to talk about passion in such a way that it doesn't sound trite. I don't like
the use of the words "deconstruction" and "reconstruction," though. They
are the jargon of an in-house academic group in the academy—the literary theorists—whose choice of language I have always found theoretically
overwrought. I wouldn't use these words again.**]

Passion, Eros, and the Classroom

I cannot think of another human undertaking that is as painful or as joyful, as
mundane or as spiritual, as the profession of teaching, unless it is being a parent
or a lover. Ironically, the root of the word passion (L., *passio*) conveys these two
antithetical meanings: a powerful fondness or enthusiasm for something; and

suffering, endurance, and pain, as expressed in the Christian Gospel narrative of Christ's passion and crucifixion. It will be one of my hypotheses in the chapters to come that effective teaching, similar to effective parenting and loving, requires considerable passion. This reality, though, sometimes turns out to be a mixed blessing, because passionate educators always run the risk of oscillating between the extremes of a soaring exhilaration and a grinding depression as a result of what happens in their classrooms.

I remember an educator once remarking somewhat irreverently to me that teaching is a lot like dying and then being reborn: When things go badly in our instruction, we die a little bit, but when things go well, and inevitably they always get better, we experience a resurrection better than Jesus Christ's. I also recall another teacher, less eschatological, saying that "when my teaching is successful it's better than sex and chocolate; but when it's a disaster it's worse than unexpected airplane turbulence and root canal surgery." [**These are my two main thematic paragraphs. They are also my favorite paragraphs in the entire book. I got many of my intellectual interests in here: philosophy, religion, and word origins. It is one of my beliefs that *passion* is a word that has been bandied about by therapists, educationists, and self-help, life-coaches for too long to be taken seriously anymore. My goal in the book, in part, was to reclaim this word for educators. I do worry, though, about my continuing inclination to show off the fruits of my Latin and Ancient Greek training. I often overdo this.**]

I, for one, do not know how anything truly worthwhile can happen in a classroom unless teachers experience a powerful fondness, indeed even something akin to a lustful enthusiasm, for teaching, learning, and subject matter. In this sense, teaching is an erotic activity. I am not talking about being sexually attracted to some students, although this is more of a reality in teaching than most of us would care to admit publicly. We are, after all, naturally libidinal creatures for whom sexual energy can, and ought to, be transformed into something wholesome and creative in our teaching. Rather, I am referring to eros in the way that the Greek writer, Hesiod, did: Eros was the god who emerged from Chaos, a being who drew all things together into an order. In this sense, eros is the supreme creative and binding force in the universe, and, in my estimation, in the classroom as well. [**As a lover of the classics, I decided to throw in this reference to Hesiod. In retrospect, the reference was too gratuitous to be effective, though. I wouldn't use it again. This is one of those times where I tend to display my background knowledge in such a way that it distracts the reader. One intrepid student, after reading this paragraph, told me that the ending was too obscure, and he had trouble understanding it.**

"Who the hell is Hesiod? Who cares? What's your point?" he asked. "You start off talking about something interesting—sex—and you end up with Hesiod. What's that about?"]

Eros is the unapologetic love of beauty, relationship, and truth that I believe ought to underlie everything that we do with students. It is the major source of inspiration for our continual search in life for meaning and purpose. It is the primordial human energy that attracts us to each other and binds us together in affection and generosity. It is the moral and aesthetic force that enables us to live the good and beautiful life. Eros fuels the passion for knowledge, relationships, and practice, and it has the potential of turning a dull classroom into something dynamic and memorable. Eros is clearly a synonym for the way that I understand spirituality. [**Notwithstanding my** *ex post facto* **bracketed comments above, I still went on about eros. I should have been asking myself: What is my point? Could I have explained the relationship of eros and spirituality in language that even a bright high school student would understand? If not, why not? Could I have made my point more effectively without the eros allusion? This is a case of being infatuated with the sounds of my own cleverness, and writing, not to clarify and exemplify, but to strut my stuff.**]

bell hooks [*sic.*], the *transgressive* (her term) Black educator, believes that it is only our passions that make us whole, that "expand rather than diminish the promise of our lives." hooks does not think it possible for us to bridge the "world outside and the world inside the academy" unless we are willing to display an erotic passion both for ideas on their own terms and for students on theirs. She says: "To restore passion to the classroom or to excite it in classrooms where it has never been, we teachers must find again the place of eros within ourselves and together allow the mind and body to feel and know desire." How else, I wonder, is it possible to get beyond those awful, desiccated times when the classroom venture gets hyperstressful or hypertedious? In my estimation, many supporters of the back-to-basics and standardized-testing movements in the schools, especially in the upper grades, including the colleges and universities, attach very little value to passion. For them, this is a dangerous emotion teachers must keep securely in check. After all, or so these critics reason, if physicians and lawyers must struggle to keep their feelings under strict control in order to make the tough professional decisions their work requires, why should teachers be any exception? [**Usually, bell hooks tends to turn me off with her use of the dense language of critical theory and oppression ideology. What she says in this quotation, though, is striking. I wish that I had developed the role of "desire" and "sexual attraction" in teaching**

Greek God of carnal love
Latin = Amor
He made people fall in love by shooting an arrow in their heart.

much more than I did here, particularly its sublimated benefits. Frankly, I was afraid to go there. And yet I feel that I left a lot unsaid that is pivotal to my central theme: the need for passion in teaching. I admire hooks for her willingness to go there in her book *Teaching to Transgress*. Someday, someone will write an honest book about teaching that deals upfront with the presence of desire and sexual attraction in classrooms and how to handle these natural human tendencies in very constructive ways.]

I have even heard a well-known teacher educator, who is a devotee of a no-nonsense approach to teaching what E. D. Hirsch, Jr., calls " basic background knowledge," announce to a large conference gathering one day that, whereas empathy, enthusiasm, and warmth are certainly desirable in working, say, with younger students, they are "contra-indicated" with older students. According to her, the best high school and college teachers must strive to become "more authoritative and objective and less affective." They must do this in order to make the unbiased, professional judgments necessary to control unruly behavior, as well as to transmit and to measure the acquisition of core subject matter more efficiently. Sadly, to me, this perception stereotypes teachers and students at all levels. It limits the expression of feelings to teachers of elementary and middle-school children and relegates critical thinking to teachers of high school and college students. It bifurcates the heart and head by making passionate professionals appear unaccountable, anti-intellectual, manipulated by their feelings, uncool in the literal sense, that is, interested only in pandering to the hot emotions of their undisciplined charges. [**This whole paragraph bothers me no end. It sounds too abstract given the point I am trying to make about eros, emotion, and "cool-hot" teaching. It's the one paragraph in this opening chapter that causes me to wince whenever I reread it. Who, nowadays, references E. D. Hirsch, Jr.? In the crude words of Clint Eastwood's Harry Callahan, who "gives a rat's ass" about going back to the basics? Whose "basic background knowledge" is Hirsch talking about? What counts as "basic background knowledge" to some scholars might not count for others. Who in the world of education today would set up such a rigid dichotomy between the intellect and the emotions? I set up a straw man here that deserves to be demolished.]**

It is revealing to note that the ancient philosophers thought of passion as a type of madness that people must assiduously avoid. The ancients would never have agreed with Rollo May's assertion in the epigraph that introduces this chapter that often "controlled conscious willing" can actually be a hindrance to experiencing the deepest forms of love, freedom, and power. For May, to be completely caught up in love for a person or an idea can oftentimes be incredibly liberating and empowering. It can also be profoundly inspiring.

In contrast, the Stoics considered passion to be a fatal misunderstanding and an enemy to reason because passion leads too frequently to loss of control, frustration, weakness, and unhappiness. Who in their right (rational) mind would want to be out of control, frustrated, or unhappy? Later, Christian theologians, following Plato and Aristotle, taught that what makes humans most divine is their reason, whereas it is their passions that threaten to engulf them and sweep them away. Immanuel Kant disdained the passions as bothersome "illnesses," diseases to be cured rather than gifts to be celebrated. When the Enlightenment thinker, David Hume, made the outrageous declaration that reason is, and ought to be, "the slave of the passions," philosophers at the time were shocked. [I admittedly had fun drawing on my knowledge of the history of philosophy here. Since its publication, I have had a mixed reception to what one critic called the "occasional sidebars of erudition" throughout my book, though. Some readers like them; some don't. I guess that at this point in the manuscript I was having some problems in identifying my best voice and point of view in my book. Who am I as I write? A philosopher? A teacher? A student? A seeker? A cynic? All of these? None of these? Some of these? What is my authority? Do I need to show off some academic pedigree in order to gain legitimacy? Who am I writing to? What ground am I standing on here? What story am I trying to tell?]

Passion as Artful Madness

What Hume meant, of course, was precisely what I believe is a prerequisite for passionate teaching: While reason is obviously necessary for stimulating a student's intellect and even for touching a student's heart, it is rarely sufficient. Reason without strong feeling is unlikely to motivate either teachers or students to reach beyond their more narrow self-interests. Hume's "natural human sentiments" must always accompany rational calculation, if teaching is ever to hit the mark of inspiring students to reach beyond themselves in a strictly non-utilitarian way. I prefer to think of passion as a kind of artful madness, whereby teachers skillfully direct their own intense excitement for learning to the furtherance of one primary goal. This is the goal of generating an intense excitement in students for the intellectual and emotional work that both sides must undertake together if anything truly breathtaking is to happen in a classroom.

In fact, as both Blaise Pascal, a seventeenth-century philosopher, and Friedrich Nietzsche, a nineteenth-century thinker, knew so well: Every passion contains its own quantum of reason. To paraphrase Pascal's more ironic language: The heart has reasons which reason knows nothing about. The passionate teacher, then, is someone who vividly understands that heart and head are intricately linked in the teaching-learning venture; that agony and ecstasy, insight and ignorance, feeling and thinking, are ubiquitous and always precarious bedfellows. When I speak of the passion of teaching, then, I describe a paradoxical awareness that, for teachers and learners, what is ultimately at stake in teaching is staggering, even though what happens day-to-day in the classroom might appear to outsiders (and to some insiders) to be merely humdrum and customary.

When I speak of passionate teachers, I think especially of those teachers who are unavoidably, helplessly, in love with their work. I think of teachers who feel intimately, indeed amorously, about their subject matter, their students, and the whole magical experience that sometimes transpires whenever learners and teachers come together in the confined, artificial space called a classroom or a seminar room. I think of teachers who are so deeply in love with ideas that they cannot wait to share an exciting insight garnered on their own time—perhaps something learned from a conversation with friends, or from reading a particularly challenging book, magazine, newspaper, or journal article, or from attending an engrossing lecture, film, or play. Nel Noddings's words to describe this exuberant, personal giving are poignant: "There ought to be gifts freely given in education."

Aristotle once said that teaching does whatever it does "as to a friend." In the discussion of religious, metaphysical, and existential questions, teachers and students are both seekers. Teachers tell stories, guide the logic of discussion, point to further readings, model both critical thinking and kindness, and show by their openness what it means to seek intelligent belief or unbelief. Students long for gifts of this sort from their teachers.

Passionate teachers are those who have thought long and hard about the nature of knowledge, about what makes students of all ages want to learn even when they are most surly and resistant, and about what young people really need to know, and do, in order to be good and decent human beings—of no imminent danger either to themselves or to others.

I think, also, of teachers who experience the same kind of breathless excitement that Aristotle did when he reached the startling conclusion that ultimate knowledge resides, not in some distant Platonic World of Ideas, but in the fresh, uncensored questions of eager and curious children and young adults. How then, Aristotle asked, can a teacher ever dismiss out of hand any student's wonder, no matter how seemingly impertinent, naive, off-track, stupid, irreverent, or subversive? Finally, I think of teachers who, by virtue of the incredible intellectual, emotional, and physical energy they expend while working at their profession, eagerly await vacation breaks as a time for necessary spiritual rejuvenation. However, these are the same teachers who soon grow bored with the time off and begin furtively to look at the calendar with the anticipatory excitement of starting yet another school term or school year. Away from their classrooms, they know that they are fish out of water. [**Although, I am a philosopher first, and an SPN writer second; and although I am proud of my ability to write philosophically in such a way as to make it at least vaguely interesting to practitioners, I wish that I had peppered these last several paragraphs with more personal stories, more particulars. For example, I might have told a story or two from my own experiences in the classroom in order to illustrate Nel Noddings's wonderful insight regarding teaching as a "gift freely given." My paragraphs, as they now stand, are strong on concepts and theories but weak on stories, an all-too-familiar writing malady of mine. Whenever theory-overload happens in SPNs that I read, it makes the writing appear to be untethered to anything tangible. The tone of voice then sounds pontifical to me. The reader of a theory-loaded SPN is likely to experience the author as surveying the world from above rather than from below. Even though I am well aware that no author ever has anything more than a worm's-eye view of the world, I wrote these paragraphs as if I had a bird's-eye view of the world. I needed to be more like the worm and less like the bird. This is something for me to keep in mind as I do further SPN writing. In fact, this is a good way to live an ordinary life.**]

Teaching with Cool Passion

I think of myself as a passionate teacher, albeit, on occasion, I can be a strategically cool one. As I enter the 33rd year of my career as a university professor, I find that I am growing more passionate about my vocation almost by the hour. I know regretfully that the end of my work is in sight, but I also know that teaching continues to be the core of my life. As most teachers know, a vocation, in the religious sense of the term, is a calling, a summons by God, or by some superior power, to perform a particular, sacred function. I must confess that I have never been moved by this definition. It implies to me that the decision to teach comes from a force outside rather than from inside the person. Instead, I like the notion of teaching as a profession—this, also, understood in the religious sense. Professionals, like religious leaders, are obligated to profess, to make an open declaration that they believe in the worth of something with all their hearts and minds.

In fact, the comparative religions scholar, Diana L. Eck, goes so far as to say that "the word 'credo,' so important in the Christian tradition, does not mean 'I believe' in the sense of intellectual assent to this or that proposition. It means 'I give my heart to this.'" By implication, for me, teaching is always more than an "intellectual assent" to some external administrative or practical imperative. Rather, it is an open avowal of the heart's commitment that nothing else matters quite as much as professing a special kind of love for students and subject matter. This is a love that is committed to helping students grow in the kind of self-knowledge which, in some cases, might ultimately lead to major personal and social transformation. This is the kind of love that says: I give my whole heart and soul to this undertaking. I can do no less.

Despite the high-sounding words in the preceding paragraphs, however, I am also a cool realist. I realize that I have failed, as often as I have succeeded, to profess, and to exemplify in my practice, my love for students and for learning. I must admit that nothing has the power to exhilarate or dispirit me as much as the act of teaching. The highs in my day-to-day, year-to-year work with students know no equal in any other area of my life, but, truth to tell, neither do the lows. I have walked away from some classes and courses thoroughly elated, and from others totally drained and dejected. More often than not, my students inspire me, but they can also depress me. There are occasions when I love my students, especially when they respond well to my intellectual entreaties, and when they treat each other, and me, with kindness, respect, and forbearance. Sadly, though, there are times when I dislike them, particularly when they are ungenerous toward each other and me, or when they are lazy, self-centered, and manipulative.

There are occasions when I would rather spend my free time with students, more so than with friends or colleagues, or, in some instances, even with loved ones. There are other times, though, when I desperately need relief from students (and, I am sure, they from me) because I am exhausted and empty. I cannot honestly give a single one of them another minute of my riveted attention. Their demands overwhelm me. During a recent year-long writing sabbatical spent at my home, I purposely scheduled several leisurely breakfasts with my students at a nearby cafe, mostly at their initiation. I did this because I genuinely missed my classroom contact with them.

I was honored and touched that so many of them chose to linger a bit with me during their zealously guarded free time. Listening to them share their out-of-classroom joys and sorrows, their hopes and fears, with me over a bowl of granola, a blueberry scone, or a western omelet, I realized that I felt closer to them as real people than I ever had in a seminar or in an office. (I will speak of this experience at greater length in the last chapter.) However, in all honesty, I would not have chosen to do this nearly as often during a typical semester of teaching, advising, and university service. I know from years of experience that revivifying periods of time away from students are absolutely necessary if the time spent with them is to be mutually productive and satisfying. **[Now I'm 46 years into my teaching career. I am most proud of these last three paragraphs because they are honest, and because I still believe them with all my heart. Although I love my students, there are times when my feelings toward them are just the opposite. "When they are good, they are very, very good; but when they are bad they are horrid." Having said this, however, I need to acknowledge quickly that some of the closest, and dearest, people in my life are my former students. I would do anything for them. Maybe one of the main reasons they are so dear to me is that they still like me even when I, myself, am "horrid."]**

As a teacher, although I am passionate, I suspect that my passion is a bit cooler and more tempered than Rollo May's, whom I quote in this chapter's epigraph. On the one hand, I am not as willing as he, at least not yet, to subordinate my critical, rational faculties to a "power greater than conscious, controlled willing." I am, after all, trained as an analytic philosopher. On the other hand, however, I find it impossible at this stage of my career to teach in an impersonal or dispassionate manner about what have been the scholarly loves of my professional life—moral philosophy, ethics, educational theory, and religious studies. I am struggling to this day to achieve some kind of a balance between hot passion and cold dispassion. I have learned the hard way that a teacher's unrestrained cool passion can sometimes intimidate and overwhelm students; ironically, so too can an uncontrolled hot passion. Either way, students are silenced.

According to the seventeenth-century philosopher, Thomas Hobbes, "hot passions unguided are for the most part mere madness." While I do not agree a whit with Hobbes's attempts to justify the existence of an authoritarian state by urging people to relinquish their personal freedom in order to gain civil security, I do respect his warning about the dangers of unguided hot passions. Thus, I believe that something tantamount to a cool passion is the best compromise. It is what good teaching is all about, because, at least for me, this paradoxical combination best balances the forces of heart and mind, affect and cognition, personal investment and critical detachment, as well as private disclosure and professional formality.

I believe that I have been at my best both as a teacher and scholar whenever I remain calm yet cordial, controlled yet responsive, independent yet relational.

I have been at my worst when my teaching and writing have been so frenzied and ideologically driven that they border on the frantic and politically self-serving, or so imperturbable as to appear chilly and distant. I am striving in these, my later years to be a teacher and a scholar whose cool passion speaks to both impassive and impassioned students. While I want to be cool, I also want to be perceived as warm and responsive. In the sixth decade of my life, I crave connection. As a professorial elder, I have become, in Erik Erikson's word, "generative." I pursue affiliations with students that are mutually caring, supportive, and affectionate. I believe that deep down these are the essential conditions for intellectual and spiritual growth, both theirs and mine. I will talk in greater detail about these types of connections, and their potential to enhance pedagogy at all educational levels, in the chapters to come.

For now, however, it is important for me to acknowledge that what has kept me passionate about my teaching, in addition to my insatiable love of knowledge and my wish to infect others with it, have been the wonderful relationships that I have formed with students for lo these many, many years. I continue to correspond with hundreds of them. I have attended their weddings and, sadly, their funerals. I have met their parents, partners, and children. I have seen some of them become college professors in my own disciplines. Others have gone on to become teachers and administrators in fine schools and colleges throughout the country. Also, I am in the rare and enviable position of having observed several generations of students come and go in my classes, a few even from the same family. Some of my older students from the 1960s are now grandparents whose grandchildren have already made an appearance in my classroom. I have observed up close the human chain that links what colleagues call the "community of scholars," and what the Quakers call the "society of friends." I am delighted to be a living link in this unbroken chain.

Always I am reminded of Parker Palmer's important observation that the literal meaning of the word *truth* has little to do with correspondence, revelational, or coherence theories of knowledge. It has everything to do with faith and trust, encounter and engagement, and dialogue and connection with others. The Germanic root of the word truth is actually *troth* as in betrothal, an entering into a faithful and lasting relationship with persons. Thus, etymologically, truth, like teaching, is first and always relational: It aims mainly to secure trust and initiate a relationship with others. My single most significant objective as a teacher through the years has been to help my students get to the point in private and public conversations where they, and I, are ready to relinquish the dogmatic dimensions of ourselves. We endeavor to do this in order to grow into some kind of binding connection with each other. The actual

Latin derivation of the word religion (religio) means to bind people together in community, to fasten human ties. This communal pursuit of truth requires an uncommon humility, a luminous generosity, and, above all, a limitless capacity for self-transcendence. [**This entire section, "Teaching with Cool Passion," feels like it hit most of the right notes. I was able to combine concept, theme, and story in a very salient way. I was also able to be genuine here, acknowledging what I enjoy and what I don't about my students; how they can be the source of both exhilaration and frustration to me. I also found a way to refer to two thinkers who have had a huge intellectual influence on my life—Diana Eck and Rollo May. Eck's work as a comparative religions scholar intitially got me interested in enlarging my understanding of cultural pluralism to include religious difference. May's work decades ago drew me into the philosophical and psychological dimensions of existentialism. Both scholars have left such an indelible intellectual imprint on so much of my writing and teaching during the last decade that I finally found a way in these paragraphs to acknowledge their contributions to my philosophy and pedagogy of education. I also love the concept, "cool passion." I think the original phrase might be Nietzsche's, but I'm not sure. What I do know for sure, though, is that the concept succinctly captures the best and worst aspects of my personality, insofar as I experience myself as myself. I wanted to develop the meaning of the phrase further here, at least initially, because the rest of my book can be read as an extended commentary on these two words. I first worked with the concept in my *"Real World" Ethics*, published in 1996 and revised in 2002, but only in a truncated way.**]

My Spirituality of Teaching

At this point in my life, spirituality is the name I give to the never-ending struggle that for each one of us is inescapable: the need to provide satisfying answers to life's most insistent questions about meaning. For Parker Palmer, quoted earlier, spirituality is the "quest for God." For me, God is only one, tentative answer that some of us give to such questions as: What am I?

- Why am I?
- Where am I going?
- How should I act?
- What is worth knowing?
- What do I stand for?

- What should I believe?

- What should I hope for?

- Why should I believe?

- What is worth dying for?

- Whom should I love?

- Whom should I help?

- Who is my neighbor?

- To whom or what should I belong?

- What is the source of my joy?

- Why do I and others suffer?

- Is social justice truly possible?

Why should I be moral? Also, for me, God is better understood as an aesthetic concept rather than a theological one; as a poetic expression rather than a philosophical proposition; or as a story to be narrated rather than a doctrine to be believed. [**Finally, I say it straight. I separate myself from Parker Palmer's Quaker-Christian spirituality. I come up with a definition of God and spirituality that I can believe in: one that is humanistic, secular, and existential. The Latin root of the word spiritual is spiritus—breath. Breathing in and out, something we do unconsciously, is what keeps each of us alive. The attraction of meditative, mindful breathing to so many of my students today is that it slows down their breathing, relaxes them, quiets the "chattering monkeys" in their minds, and, therefore, adds another dimension to their lives. For me, personally, spirituality is all about cherishing those moments in my life that actually take my breath away. I want more, not less, breathlessness. My students' stories often leave me breathless. I want to live my life always open to surprise, novelty, vulnerability, adventure, and, most of all, to being able to discover the extraordinary in the ordinary moments of my life. I am less interested in controlling my breathing (although this can be a focusing activity) as I am in becoming breathless—in both the physical and emotional senses.**]

I will attempt to make the case in upcoming chapters that constructing a spirituality of teaching is a prerequisite for fostering a genuine and lasting passion for teaching. What I mean by this is that I do not believe an invigorating passion for the demanding work that we do as teachers is possible without a spirituality of education to ground us and to deepen our commitment to the profession of teaching. A spirituality of teaching attempts to help students formulate their own soul-satisfying answers to the questions I ask above. Walter Kaufmann, the existential philosopher, comes at spirituality in a similar way when he talks about ontological privation. He chooses to use the term "ontology" rather than spirituality. For him, ontology is the technical branch of philosophy that deals most adequately with the questions I raise in the previous section regarding being, existence, ultimate meaning, mystery, and human finitude. He says: "We all experience ontological privation, whether we are aware of it or not: we need to rise above that whole level of being which is defined only by our psychological and physiological needs and their satisfaction; we need to love and create." **[In my opinion, the Kaufmann quotation is one quote too many in this first chapter. "Ontological privation" is a jawbreaker. It ends my chapter on a pretentious note. Even philosophers don't use the term "ontological" anymore. One of the problem areas in my writing through the years has been my tendency to throw in polysyllabic (this is one!) words whenever I'm not clear in my own mind about what I want to say. I love putting a rich vocabulary on public display, but I am still learning how, after almost five decades in the academy, to keep it in check; not to overdo it. I recall a wise colleague, who was collaborating with me on an article, once confronting me over this: "When are you going to learn to prune the clutter from your pompous language? You're already a tenured full-professor with lots of honors and awards. Who the hell is left to impress?" Ouch! but exactly right!]**

The chief implication for educators of what Kaufmann is saying is this: Teachers and students have a fundamental human need to create meaning by loving and creating, and by pursuing higher levels of aspiration. The person who is content only to spend inordinate amounts of time trying to gratify psychological and physical desires is also someone who is frequently restless, unsatisfied, and bored. To deny or to ignore one's ontological privation—to be oblivious to the spiritual questions that I ask above—is to settle for a life lived only in the present, hedonistic moment. The consequences of ontological privation, both for teachers and students, can be disastrous. According to Kaufmann, an inability, or refusal, to rise above the physical and material routines of our everyday personal and professional lives means that our fundamental need for love and creativity goes unfulfilled. Whenever this happens, we burn out or we dry up. Worse, some of us become aggressive, hostile, and alienated. We get paranoid, or we grow numb. **[Well, yes, but except for the last three sentences, what am I really saying?]**

This book, therefore, is one educator's humble **[Did I really mean to use this adjective? Is it honest? Does the reader see through it? Can I be trusted? I don't really see myself as "humble" or even modest. Who am I trying to deceive? Why?]** attempt to speak to teachers at all levels, teachers-to-be, and students everywhere, who want desperately to experience a deeper and richer meaning in the important, day-to-day work that they do. I want especially to reach the minds and hearts of those teachers who might be restless, unsatisfied, even bored. I hope to say something worthwhile to those educators who refuse to settle for a life superficially lived. **[How pompous and presumptuous this last sentence sounds.]** I want to speak to teachers in schools and colleges who are concerned more with the search for a lasting meaning and less with the pursuit of a frenetic careerism. I wish for my words to reassure the hopeless, and to revitalize those who have grown numb and lifeless. I have been there many times during the "dark nights of my soul." **[This last figure of speech is a spiritual cliché. I should have come up with something fresher. It's also dishonest: I don't believe in a soul, except as a form of music or food.]** My aspiration is that my own passion for teaching, and particularly for my subject matter, might become infectious, might somehow prevent at least a few other teachers from drying up or burning out. It is my firm conviction that a spiritual approach to teaching is the only way to keep from dying to ourselves and to one another. **[I like this final clincher sentence, although it's a bit over the top for drama. I do believe, though, that I was candid in expressing my sentiments about teaching in this very last paragraph that ends the chapter.]**

. . . .

So, What Did I Learn in Writing My First SPN in 2002? A Summary of My Use of SPN Tools and a Self-Evaluation

Jane Smiley, in the epigraph that introduces this chapter, remarks that the writer's commitment is always to a partial knowledge. Hence, the writer is always rethinking and, at times, regretting, earlier commitments. This is the nature of the writing beast. For my own part in writing this chapter, I am proud that I was able to take another look, a critical look, at an SPN I wrote several years earlier. I was able to rethink and regret. Again, in Jane Smiley's words, I will "never stop working over the largest questions that life has to offer." So, in retrospect, and in summary, what did I learn? Here's a brief self-evaluation report card.

- **Establishing Clear Themes**. This was my strong suit. I identified clearly who I was, what was important to me, and what message I wanted to convey to my readers. In my opinion, I focused and hooked (captured the reader's attention) very effectively. I also asked provocative questions, both of myself and of my readers. Grade: A.

- **Combining the particular and the general, the personal and the formal, the facts and the values**. This was my weakest suit. Too often, my philosophical generalizations tended to crowd out the grittier, and more interesting, personal details of my teaching life. I forgot E. B. White's advice: "Don't write about humanity; write about one human being." I must learn to write more locally, and more subjectively, in order to balance my natural intellectual tendency to think globally. Grade: B-.

- **Drawing larger, more universal implications**. This was another very strong suit of mine. I have a knack for seeing the large in the small; for extracting from my story universal ramifications for my readers' stories. I just have to learn how to think, and write, more often in the small. Grade: A.

- **Drawing from background knowledge**. This was yet another strong writing suit of mine. I know well how to mine the many and diverse fields of knowledge that interest and excite me. I know how to cross disciplinary boundaries. But I have not yet found the happy medium that exists between overwhelming and underwhelming the reader with what I know. This is still a work in progress. Grade: A-.

- **Telling a good story**. This was my most sought after, yet most elusive, goal in writing SPNs. I want to be able to *write* a story as well as I can *talk* a story. My SPN did tell an intriguing story (at least at the beginning of the chapter), but, at times, I lost the story amidst the lessons I wished to impart. I became didactic, an occupational hazard for philosophers and professors, but especially for story-tellers. I lost my feel for narrative tension in my writing, and in my teaching, in my zeal to teach something. Consequently, I ended up telling when I could have been narrating. I need to learn how to let the story itself convey the meanings I think important. I need to learn better how to teach by narrative indirection in my writing. Grade B-.

- **Showing passion**. I am not a stoical, distant, or "objective" writer or human being. I can be skeptical, though. There was much passion in my SPN. In Annie Dillard's words: I "spend it all, shoot it, play it, lose it…" The key for me, though, was to be able to express my passion in passionate language. This meant taking more writing risks than I might have been comfortable with. My instinct when I wrote my SPN was to go with the language of a thinker. I needed to develop an instinct to go with the language of the feeler as well. Grade: B+.

- **Writing in an open-ended way**. My postmodern philosophy of life has well prepared me to be open-ended, qualified, even tentative in all my assertions. I was not out to convert, proselytize, or sell anything to my readers in my SPN. I honestly tried to write softly and elliptically. If anything, though, I might have held back too much. I could have been more forthright in declaring my truths without attaching all the caveats and qualifications. I tried to be more assertive in the last two chapters of my book. Not so coincidentally, these are the chapters that my students like most of all. Grade: A-.

 Being editorially meticulous. I am proud of my self-discipline in being able to sit still for long periods of time to complete a writing task—day after day, week after week, month after month. I wrote the entire book in three months, six to eight hours a day. I am also pleased with the meticulu- ous care I take with all of my manuscripts, but especially this one. I think that I was a good craftsman in my SPN. I did tend at times, however, to tweak something to death, so much so that it didn't sound spontaneous. I bled the life out of it. I needed to learn how to let go and let stay. But, in the end, I still worked very hard to be true to Stephen King's ruthless editing and cutting formula: 2nd draft=1st draft–10%. Grade: A.

- **Using "non-show-off" citations and references**. I believe one of the strengths of my SPN was my ability to cite very relevant authors and to produce apt quotations that illustrated rather than obfuscated, at least most of the time. I had a good eye for the catchy quotation. I could entice my readers to go to the primary sources, not always, of course, but many times. In my SPN, most of my references and epigraphs were good ones. Occasionally, though, I was tempted to show off, and so I padded my text with flashy quotes. In Annie Dillard's words, I "aim for the wood" instead of the "chopping block." As a result, I often ended up only with with something ephemeral after the first intellectual tickle. Grade: A-.

- **Loving and respecting language**. I write because I love to play with language. I write because I appreciate the sound and sight of words. I strive for clarity, but, more than I would like, it escapes me. I work constantly to rid myself of my irritating writing tics. My SPN reflected my love of language, I believe, although, at times, I overwrote—words too complex; sentences too long; too many series (like this one); an endless array of adverbs. Also, there were times when I let the glitter of my language overshadow my content. I was a very willing accomplice in allowing all of this to happen. In spite of it all, however, I am working hard to produce Richard Rorty's "tingles" (my favorite postmodern philosopher) in my writing, even though I know that I am a very poor metaphorist. I see the world in words rather than in visual images; I hear before I can see. Grade: A-.

Postscript: A Series of Thematic Maxims about Teaching and Learning

As I was reviewing this chapter, I decided to put into a series of thematic maxims (no more than a paragraph or so) what I believe is my spirituality of teaching and learning. (The word *maxim* comes from the Latin *maxima proposito*, meaning "greatest premise.") I was only slightly surprised by the influence of Zen Buddhism and Taoism on my philosophy of education, because Eastern philosophy and spirituality are among my favorite topics to teach. I couldn't have compiled these maxims without first writing this chapter and then drawing out the implications for my philosophy of education. I love writing pithy (succinct, full of substance and meaning) propositions. Nietzsche thought of maxims as "shorthand bursts of kinetic intellectual energy…like a tub of cool water…quick in and quick out." I have found that when delivered either inside a classroom or a publication, a maxim results in an insight that stays with learners…long after the "water in the college tub" gets cold.

Not all scholars are as infatuated with maxims as I am, however. One of my colleagues said this to me: "Some of your maxims remind me of fortune-cookie sayings." I decided to respond with yet another maxim, which I'm sure confirmed for him the truth of his fortune-cookie charge: "To each his own wisdom, and my own wisdom is pithiness with a small 'm' for 'maxim.'" For me this is what I believe: whether or not someone likes my writing, or whether I like someone's writing, is pretty much a matter of personal taste. I have never been convinced otherwise. What I am convinced of, however, is that I, personally, tend to remember (even take the time to memorize) maxims, proverbs, aphorisms, and, okay, even a few fortune cookie sayings in order to share these with my students. I tend to remember these trenchant words of wisdom far longer than I do all the constantly changing, hyper-technical, tenure-track terminology and convoluted, theoretical explanations I've endured (and, yes, perpetuated) through the decades as a university professor.

For me, a maxim is where I can best express my *thematic artistry* as a writer. As a thematizer, I need to be bold, brief, dramatic, clever, and evocative. I also need to be personal. Not only are themes the *sine qua non* core of SPN writing; they also become the central takeaways for my students whenever I teach and write because they hold such subjective significance for me. My students remember my thematic maxims long after they leave the classroom and graduate. Why? I believe it is because a succinct thematic statement actually crystallizes a short story in a creative way and, in the process, teaches a lesson that stays with learners. While a thematic maxim serves as the climax, and even the denouement, of a narrative, it is also the true north on the SPN writer's compass. It signifies personal meaning. It is the "scholarly" guide that always brings the writer ("the-me") back to the major points of personal narrative writing.

Below is a bulleted list of my thematic maxims about teaching and learning. Please note that these maxims also represent the meaning that teaching and learning have for my life. They represent what makes me whole. I return to them whenever I need to heal from the trials and tribulations of my work as a university professor. They put me back on track, because they remind me of what gives my life the most meaning. Before I move on, however, I want to describe two core thematic truths that underlie my pedgaogical maxims.

Core Thematic Truth I: Ask yourself these two related questions whenever you go into a classroom, lecture hall, or office and are tempted to over-exaggerate the professorial impact you must make on your students: "How many of my students do I think will remember in one year, five years, ten years, and more, even a single one of my brilliant, intellectual insights, or references to "important" scholarly readings, or the titles of even one of their assigned academic texts? In fact, how much do I honestly remember from those long-ago days when I was a student?" (Truth in Packaging I: I, Robert, a former English major, do not remember even one of the numerous critical-theory book titles assigned during my undergraduate years. More telling, however, I remember only the names of two of my professors, and not a single paragraph (or even sentence, to be honest) of content in any of the lengthy papers I wrote for their courses. Granted, all of this happened a long time ago, but still…I mean, really? Why aren't we able to keep it all in perspective and focus on what is truly important and worthy of remembering?)

Core Thematic Truth II: Except for a precious few (perhaps a couple of those rapidly disappearing souls who might go on for a graduate degree in your field), what your students will remember, if anything, are the candid life stories you tell in those rare, unguarded moments in a classroom or office that touch their hearts and souls. The truth is that we do the most good as teachers whenever we have less to tell and sell as scholars and more to expose and share with our students as fellow collaborators in the universal search for meaning. (Truth in Packaging II: I, Robert, am able to recall almost word for word many of the impromptu, unguarded, out-of-classroom conversations that I had throughout my undergraduate and graduate years with faculty mentors who took a personal interest in me beyond the "trials and tortures of tests and term papers."

These were the rare, hence memorable, teachers who tried to personify in their everyday lives the lessons they taught in their disciplines.)

The Thematic Maxims

- Perhaps the one pedagogical principle that all of us might be able to agree upon someday is that, in the end, our educational work is not all about us; it's really all about them—our students.

- Selfless teaching, like selfless love, is at the heart of real learning and caring. But the degree of selflessness is the teacher's choice; and this is contingent on each teacher's particular temperament, taste, timing, training, and talent (what I call my "Five Contingent Ts").

- The teacher who teaches less, who experiences little or no need to be the god-like figure in the classroom, laboratory, or lecture hall, is also the teacher who teaches most. This might be called a "pedagogy of minimalism." And, in keeping with Taoism and Zen Buddhism, it is the most effective way for us to be with our students and with our subject matter.

- Learning begins and ends in love. Every single one of our students is a miracle waiting to happen. So, too, each of us is a miracle waiting to be born…every single moment we, and they, spend in the classroom is a potential birth experience.

- As an educator, dare to experience the world as a child does. Or, better, as you once did when you were a college student grappling with the complexities and mysteries of the academic disciplines for the first time.

- Look for the miracle of joy in your educational work-settings first, before looking for the joylessness. Often this miracle can be found in the most unexpected places—in unconventional, sometimes zany, questions; in candid and impromptu classroom reactions to something said or read; and in the generosity and support that educators and students are more than willing to give to one another, if it is the norm to do so (and, in some cases, even if it isn't).

- Be generous with everyone you know in your teaching in the name of saving, not condemning, their cherished propositions. And look always for the personal story that lies behind each student's persona. Find that story and, eureka, you've found the student (and colleague) as a real live, flesh-and-blood human being.

- Stay in the present in the classroom. It is here where genuine innocence, vulnerability, passion, and compassion live. It is the location for healing, becoming whole, and creating meaning. In contrast, it is being stuck in the past and agonizing over the future where the opposites of these qualities sometimes reside: guilt, insensitivity, apathy, and aggression.

- Don't give in to the periodic brokenness and burnout that sometimes come out of teaching and learning—boredom, self-criticism, uncertainty, physical and mental fatigue, unrealistic expectations, restlessness, and self-doubt. Ironically, it is in this brokenness where true joy and freedom are waiting to be born.

- As teachers, we tell our stories to prove that we've lived, that we're still alive, and that we intend to live into some unknown future. Without our stories, our lives are missing form and content. So too with subject matter. When all the technical trappings are removed, subject matter is really one group's storied view of the world, and the story changes often. Find the story of your favorite subject matter, and you've located the hard (and soft) core of your academic discipline. You've also brought it to life...for yourself and for your students. Even better, tell your students when, where, why and how you yourself fell in love with the story of your discipline.

- Amidst those periods of our worst anguish, only faith and hope remain. Teach with hope (optimism). Live with faith (trust). Help students to create stories of meaning that will sustain them through all their own anguish, faithlessness, and hopelessness.

- Hold students close but only with arms wide open. Prepare them well for the flight into the rest of their lives by encouraging them to make the leap from the cliff on their own. And as at their dying, they are condemned to make the leap into an unknown future alone, almost in spite of the comfort they will receive from others. Only they, as only you, will know how to "go into that dark night."

- At times each of us will need to "let go" of our teaching-learning projects as our exclusive, "big-fat-ego" possessions. We will need to "let be" in our interactions with students and colleagues in order to realize our best hopes as teachers. When we give away whatever knowledge we possess, sometimes we get it back wrapped in a wiser package. And, when this happens, many of our students will do the same for us...and for one another.

- Whenever we can give up exclusive ownership of our teaching, and be content simply to plant the seeds of learning and understanding in others—

when we are willing to evoke, more than revoke, provoke, or invoke—then, miraculously, our students will learn to do all these things themselves. Not always, of course, but more often than we might think. What this "miracle" will take from us is the courage to "let go" and "let others."

- We must learn how to match our inner and outer lives, at least some of the time. We must struggle always to find that perfect symmetry between our feminine and masculine powers. We need to learn how to be true to both our heads and hearts without always compromising one or the other. We need to learn how to blend our *yins* and *yangs* as best we can in order for us to be whole people using our whole hearts and heads in our work.

How "Deep" Writing Heals
When It Comes to Love,
"We Are All in the Same Boat"

ROBERT J. NASH

Deep writing is engaged writing. What is engaged is your whole human being. You bring everything that you are to your writing. The wind stops whistling. The clock stops ticking. The universe stops for the sake of your deep writing. Deep writing is work meant to mean and not just entertain, garner applause, or demonstrate one's skills…Each deep writer has a dream, a problem to solve, a truth to tell, a moral imperative, a holy quest, all mixed up together.

—Eric Maisel

We are all in the same boat. We are full of secret shames and desires, real loyalties and real idiosyncracies, keen self-understanding and spectacular self-idiocy. We are all capable of making every human mistake possible, and we all go ahead and make tons and tons of them. We also all aspire to becoming meaning-makers…A meaning-maker is a person who takes her humanity and experiences and attempts to put them together coherently, artfully, beautifully…for her own sake and for the sake of others. That product may or may not change the world or even reach the world. But a meaning-maker can do nothing less than struggle to make meaning, because meaning-making is a moral imperative.

—Eric Maisel

 ### "We Are All in the Same Boat"

For almost half a century, I've been teaching in one college classroom or another, seeing students in some college office here or there, and meeting students in a number of off-campus sites to talk about their studies and their jobs, their dreams of success and their nightmares of failure, and, even, at times, their loves lost and loves gained. Each student looks different in physical appearance, to be sure. Each one comes from a unique family background. Each one has shaped a personal history that is special. The details in all the stories I hear are what separate my students (at least superficially) from one another. And so I listen carefully. I affirm when necessary. I ask questions when I need more information. I avoid giving advice unless asked. But I'm always working hard to identify the *background* nuances of each student's story so that I can *foreground* the deeper issues that demand my professorial attention. I am also looking for the narrative overlaps in all their individual stories, because I am convinced that this is where the common core of the human condition resides.

None of this is easy, of course, but all of it is what gives me the satisfaction, and the drive, to continue to do what I do, and have done, for a very, very long time throughout my career. Yet, no matter how many times I hear the candid, no-holds-barred stories of my students of all ages, majors, stages, and wages—once they relax and let go—Eric Maisel's (a Ph.D. creativity psychotherapist) insight in the second epigraph of this chapter remains constant for me: "we are all in the same boat." We are all contradictory containers of meanings. Sometimes we shine, sometimes we whine, and sometimes we're just fine. At all times, however, and each in our own way, we are just trying to make sense of what William James (the creator of American pragmatism) once called the "blooming, buzzing confusion of our lives."

In one student's writing (Jarett) that I will share below, some of the issues that touch all our lives will be evident, once we get beyond the details of the writer's particular story. Maisel is spot on. Even I, a later-lifer, am amazed at what I have in common with quarterlife students decades younger than I. At the very least, they and I tend to make the same human mistakes over and over again. They and I are capable of wonderful achievements, but, so too, are we capable of "spectacular self-idiocy." In the thousands of SPN essays, theses, and dissertations I have supervised through the years, I am one with each writer's quest for meaning. My struggle is their struggle...and vice versa.

Like them, I want others to hear my story. I want to understand what common humanity I might share with these others, despite my irritating idiosyncrasies and insecurities. I want to know how to create a life-story that is coherent, purposeful, and cogent and that might make some sense even to complete strangers. And I want more than anything for my story to make a difference—even if it might be for only one other human being besides myself. As for Maisel, so, too, for me: this is a "moral imperative." In the language we are using throughout our book, I feel morally obligated to have my story make a contribution (even if does not make a dramatic difference) to the healing, meaning-making, and wholeness of others. In the end, this is why I teach, write, advise, mentor, consult, and counsel. Why else, pray tell, would I continue doing what I have been doing professionally when every single one of those colleagues who arrived at the university the same time I did have long since retired and/or died?

"Deep Writing Is Meant to Mean…"

During the time I was thinking about the overall theme for this chapter, and looking for a piece of writing that, even though very particular, would also be universalizable (demonstrating that all of us are, indeed, in the "same boat"), coincidentally, one of my students sent me a very personal letter. His name is Jarett Chizick (not the "Jared" of the 1st chapter), and he has taken two graduate-level courses with me. I read the letter very carefully, because Jarett has worked hard to learn how to write in a personal way. He's actually a much deeper, inspirational writer than he thinks he is. He is the graduate of an Ivy League university, and his academic training there was very traditional. He had little practice, if any, in doing personal narrative, non-fiction writing. I was touched by his willingness to be so open and vulnerable in his letter. He made it a point to talk transparently about the power of love in his life. When I finished reading the letter, I realized that as different as he and I might be, we share something very important in common. We both believe strongly in the truth of what Shantideva, the 8th-century Indian Buddhist scholar, once said: "To free myself from harm, and others from their sufferings, let me give myself away, and cherish others as I love myself." For Jarett (who volunteers his time at our college health and wellness center), and for me as well, love is the single greatest healing force in the world.

As you read Jarett's letter below, remember the words of Eric Maisel in the epigraphs that introduce this chapter: Deep writing is "meant to mean." A la Maisel in his epigraph, Jarett's intention is not to show off a superior intellect or to elicit sympathy. Neither is it to engage in confession for its own sake in order to win redemption. And, most certainly, the intention is not to seek retribution for wrongs committed in some near or distant past. Instead, Jarett's "deep writing" is meant to highlight candor, to share a dream, to solve a problem, to tell a truth, to ask questions, and, above all, to identify at least a few universal human themes that unite, rather than separate, us from one another. And, even though his thoughts about love are written in the form of a non-academic, personal letter that he wrote to me, his instructor, in a time of need, they will serve as the background theme for an extended thesis he intends to write in the next year.

And so, dear reader, no matter how different from Jarett your family circumstance, community of friends, temperament, physical health, education, and background beliefs might be, ask yourself these "deep-meaning" questions (indirectly inspired by Eric Maisel) as you read Jarett's letter to me about love:

- In what ways am I in the "same boat" as the writer? Or are we all on different boats floating off in different directions?

- What is there in the writer's story that could be "healing" for me?

- What are some examples of authorial courage in what I am reading? Is it possible for me to be courageous in my own writing, particularly if self-disclosure and vulnerability have been a challenge for me in the past?

- Are there at last a few resonant themes in the writing that I can apply to my own life as I go about the task of making meaning?

- What have I learned from the writing about putting together a "coherent," "artful," and "engaging" manuscript of my own?

- How has the writer framed the manuscript in such a way as to tell a story that has a narrative arc containing a beginning, middle, and end? How much is left up in the air, and how much, if anything, has been resolved?

- What are my own "moral imperatives" that I would like to write about? How do I go about identifying these? And how do I do this without moralizing?

- What is my particular "problem to solve" in my writing? What "truth" do I have to tell? Am I on a "holy quest," or am I on a quest that is more secular than sacred?

· ·

Jarett Chizick's Personal Letter

Love does not give up. Love is kind. Love is not jealous. Love does not put itself up as being important. Love has no pride. Love does not do the wrong thing. Love never thinks of itself. Love does not get angry. Love does not remember the suffering that comes from being hurt by someone.

—I Corinthians 13:4–5 (The Bible, New Life Version)

Dear Robert:

Having the opportunity to write about my stories and share them with others in your classes has been an ongoing healing experience. Chronic pain has been an ever-present protagonist in my life. The chance to speak about my chronic pain issues, the undiagnosed illness during my undergraduate years and the places in life I allowed them both to take me, was not available earlier in life. Writing about my stories has been nothing short of transformative. I can only hope the meaning I have found through this process will continue to help myself and others.

I come from a small rural town in Western New York outside Niagara Falls. While working on an Ivy League degree, I suffered from a chronic, degenerative, arthritic condition that went undiagnosed for three years. At the time, the doctors told me I would have to learn to live with my illness. There was no assistance to discover how to manage my chronic pain, just a bunch of pills. And, so, I manifested poor coping skills in order to tolerate the suffering in my life. After many years of struggling, and simply coping, I made a choice to manage my life situation. I no longer wanted to live a life filled with sorrow, broken relationships, or regret. Choosing a path to wellness and expressing myself through writing has helped me to find the meaning behind my circumstances and choices.

I recently had an event that changed my life path. My relationship with my son's mother had become estranged. How do you respond when someone you love asks how they should proceed with their life? How do you find meaning when they believe hospitalization is necessary in order to heal and find wholeness again? I did the only thing I could do—I loved. I dropped everything I was doing in order to just be there for whatever she needed.

Over the next several weeks I comforted, supported, and assisted her on her meaning-making journey. But, no matter how hard you strive, some things are just out of your control. Life unfolded. Circumstances and situations arose I was not expecting, nor prepared for. Choices needed to be made, and my character was tested. We make our own choices and decisions, but our emotions don't always immediately follow. It doesn't matter how many right or correct decisions we make in a row, because just one incorrect thought that becomes an action can change the course of the rest of our lives. External factors began to multiply for me and turned my frustration into fear and anxiety. At all times I tried to remember St. Paul's words. I wanted my love to be "kind." I didn't want my love to be "angry." I refused to live in the memory of a "hurt" love. I did not want to "give up" on my love for my son's mother.

I managed to survive all of this, and, in the process, even do some good for my son's mother, but I was long overdue for a holiday after the drama and tumult. I needed to go for one of my long "drives," but I knew that running away was not the solution to my problems. Jon Kabat-Zinn puts it frankly, "Wherever You Go, There You Are." My Sufi friend's grandfather used to tell him "Don't make the same mistakes; learn from new ones." We learn from our experiences in life, from the joys and the sorrows. Trying to balance joy in the midst of sorrow is difficult because time is fleeting. We have only this present moment to choose from. We are human and find it difficult to manage joy and sorrow at the same time.

Acceptance of this human imperfection has taught me to let go of past suffering, whether it was self-inflicted, caused by others, or by uncontrollable factors in my life. When I look at my present juncture, this helps bring about joyful living and love to my actions. By viewing our vantage point of thought in such a way should bring joy to our reality each and every day.

I believe in the "goodness" of humanity, that we are all kind, caring, and good-natured at heart. Christopher Phillips views these as "Socratic virtues," and he defined them as temperance, wisdom, and courage. In class, Robert, we talked a lot about the etymology of "courage" meaning "core" or "heart," or even "love." I know I am imperfect, but I have always tried my best to make it possible for others in my life to embrace their own path. I may or may not be courageous, but I do want to be loving.

The unconditional love of my wonderful family, friends, and community echoes these "virtues" and has seen me through some of the most trying times in life. When all else seems hopeless, this *agape* love" is there to shine a light on my circumstance. For the Greeks, *agape* love is unconditional. For the Christians, "greater love than this no man hath but to lay down his life for his fellow humans." Love, according to the Buddhist, Thich Nhat Hanh, is patient, has no limits, is understanding, endures, and is healing. At a time in human history when we have mapped human DNA to reveal we are 99.9% identical, I have found that true peace can only come from acceptance of myself before moving forward with others. I need to experience a kind of *agape* love toward myself first as a precondition for expressing this type of love toward others. My family and community provide this type of environment for me to do this.

I have wanted to return home for the fourth of July for years. This celebration has always been special to my home town, and this year I needed that catharsis. Being home was both a joyful and poignant experience. I don't think I have ever cried so much in my entire life. Many reasons contributed to this. It had been three years since my "traditional" nuclear family was all together. Previously it was for my grandmother's funeral. This was different. It was planned, scheduled, and a time for jubilation as my sister was expected to be married. My older brother brought his three daughters and wife from California, my sister was coming from Philadelphia, and my younger brother had his daughter with him from Florida. This was an opportunity to commune with family, friends, and meet nieces I had not met before.

It seemed unfair that I had allowed life to get in the way of these gatherings. Time had quietly passed us by. Everyone seemed to have something personal going on. My sister was dealing with feelings around her relationship. I understood her hesitation in marriage; my own relationships have never seemed "to go as planned." How can you truly love someone when you don't have open communication with them? How can you be honest with yourself and another human being if one of you perceives the other to hold on to bitterness, resentment, or pain from the past? What if there is a child involved—biological, non-biological, or given up for adoption, as mine was? Robert, is it possible when abuse, trauma, or loss are concerned for others to let go and let love heal?

Though my sister had canceled her wedding plans, our family turned the time into an opportunity for reconnecting. My younger brother and I had the chance to catch up playing mini-golf with his daughter. He was managing a personal life situation of his own. Being there with him and his daughter quickly quieted my mind. The power of love to heal became evident as the week unfolded.

The next day my brother and I had plans for the evening, and we met our sister as she came into town. Being there face-to-face allowed us the opportunity to share in person what could not be done over e-mail or the phone. No technology could duplicate that level of communing. Love was there. The beginning of our family reunion, deepening our ties and healing, had begun. Watching the Fourth of July Parade in our hometown at our friend's house hadn't happened for almost ten years. It was simply wonderful to experience this again with everyone. Moreover, open and honest communication brought about a sense of wholeness while we enjoyed each other's company. My nieces loved the interaction with our family, friends, and community. Experiencing the traditions of a small town fireworks show can bring out *agape* love with the people you hold most dear.

Robert, there is no time like the present. I couldn't let the opportunity to spend time with my family pass me by. I made sure I was available for everyone. My older brother had a flight out of Buffalo the same day my younger brother had a flight out of Rochester. I drove them both to the airport. An unscheduled delay in Rochester allowed us to visit my aunt and uncle before my brother's flight. My sister and I then spent the early evening reading and writing at Hamlin Beach. Sitting there I pondered the book I was reading, *Einstein's Dreams*. While she sat and read, I put the book down and wrote: "Imagine a world where time stands still. All you can hear is the crashing waves on the shore, the gulls cawing on the beach. A fish jumps in the water. You feel the sun on your face and the wind in your hair. Peace has been achieved. Time stands still…"

Joyful living starts with forgiveness of self and others. I've found this to be a matter of attitude, desire, and altruism. When we do loving acts for others it helps free us from our selfishness and in some cases pity (for self and others). Having a strong sense of belonging fosters this learning. The support of family, friends, and community helps this growth. I've heard it said that time heals all wounds. In the present moment, time does not exist; therefore it is love that heals. Now is the only choice I can affect. I have an obligation to make the "now" meaningful. Love is born out of this understanding.

Recognizing the effort I put forth, not only for my own personal healing, but to try to help our family grow, my sister reached out to me and signed a little note before leaving. It was inside a brochure where she was the guest speaker. It says, "I love you Jarett!! Never underestimate the power of Love!! ☺" Jenée

I firmly believe that doing is love in action and action is love by doing. Freeing yourself through the experience of agape love helps heal and build stronger relationships. Thich Nhat Hanh puts it another way, "…our life is not for ourselves alone, but for our ancestors, future generations, and our society also." Here he is talking about love, respect and understanding, knowing your trueself. If 80% of life is showing up (Woody Allen), then the other 20% is perspective and attitude (Rubin). Love, Robert… I believe in the power of Love.

I laid awake in my old bedroom looking at a picture I took of a sunset on Lake Ontario. Reflecting back on haunting and healing memories, I felt compelled to write a maxim atop the picture. A few days earlier my sister gave me "Life's Little Instruction Book." She received it as a high school graduation gift. "Never Waste the Opportunity to Tell Someone You Love Them." I inscribed it on my picture of the sun shining through a wooden heart-shaped chair with the lake and sunset as a backdrop (H. Jackson Brown Jr. #347). Both the picture and quote have special meaning for me and will continue to help me heal.

The night before returning to Vermont I visited a close personal friend's mother. Conversations with her and her husband are always enlightening given my life's circumstances. She tells me every time I see her, "Jarett, I used to tell my kids, it doesn't matter what you do with your life. As long as you wake up with a smile on your face and are joyful, that is what you get to do that day. Go do it! If not, change it." She writes this on graduation cards, and she shared it with me before I left.

"For J.—With Love: From Mama Campbell

Laugh, Cry, Listen;
Sing, Love, Make Messes;
Dream, Let Go, Dare;
Become all you can be…
And always remember, the truest test of success
Is liking the person you become…
Enjoy the Journey!"

As I return to Burlington, this love experience continues. My life with all its ups and downs has molded me for the "greater good." It took each and every situation I have encountered to bring me to the current moment. And every moment of my life, including this one right now, is a fresh start. I have learned that healing, meaning-making, and wholeness are an ongoing process no matter what. Everything affects everything else, and change happens whether we like it or not. It shapes us and molds us into what we are and who we will become. I only need to have the courage to admit when I am scared and have the ability to laugh even as I cry. I need to have the nerve to speak up even if my voice is shaking. I must muster the confidence to ask for help when I need it and have the wisdom to take it when it's offered. If I have successfully gathered these tools, then I have everything I need to get to a better "place" in my meaning-making journey. In essence, I have become comfortable with my discomfort, and I am learning to let go of pain as my antagonist. This is the true power of writing my way to meaning and wholeness, Robert—telling part of my story and living a life of Love.

Always Your Friend With Joy and Peace,
Jarett Chizick

. . . .

The Need to Love Puts Me in the "Same Boat" with Jarett

. . . .

One of the great satisfactions I get from my vocation as a professor is that, through the years, several of my students have asked me to be the officiant at their weddings, civil unions, and renewal ceremonies. Almost always, I begin my wedding remarks with a quotation from J. Krishnamurti, the Indian mystic and philosopher:

If you have no love—do what you will, go after all the gods on earth, do all the social activities, try to reform the poor, enter politics and education, write books, write poems, accumulate wealth, enhance your power and influence, become famous—but you are a dead human being. Without love, you will be lonely, your problems will increase, and multiply endlessly, you will be isolated. But with love, you have everything. With love, you stand on sacred ground.

—J. Krishnamurti, *On Love and Loneliness* (1993)

I choose this passage because it sums up everything I believe about the power of love. It is an eloquent reminder to me, and to my students, that fame, fortune, and fun can never be substitutes for genuine love. Krishnamurti keeps all of us honest. His words serve as a dramatic reminder that, in the end, love is all we have to deal with the most vexing existential life-issues that face all of us. No matter our passing successes and/or our failures, our triumphs and tragedies, there is one constant alone that makes life worth living and keeps us whole—love.

When it comes to my need to receive, and give, love, I am in the same boat as Jarett, even though in many other ways our individual lives are floating off in very different directions. Jarett's long overdue get-together with his family in upstate New York came at a time when he needed it the most. He was reeling from a traumatic experience with the mother of his child in trying to help her heal. As a result, he needed a kind of unconditional love from his family in order to heal, and rejuvenate, himself—what the Greeks call *agape* love. He found it in the joyful reunion with his family in upstate New York. I, too, find this kind of love with my wife, children, grandchildren, and a small group of former graduate students whom I have embraced as my "family" and, also, as my close friends.

Just to know that these people are there for me—regardless of how many books I've published or fail to publish (or that receive good or bad reviews), or of how many positive or negative teaching evaluations I receive at the end of a semester, or of how many mistakes I might have made in my professional or personal relationships—confirms for me the truth of Krishnamurti's take on love. Neither Jarett nor I appreciate being "lonely" or "isolated." During our most trying times, we need the love of others to revitalize. We do not want to become Krishnamurti's "dead human beings." Jarett came back to life in upstate New York on a July 4th vacation in the company of people who loved him. I experience my own resurrections in the company of people I trust, who are my confidantes, and who see the strengths in me especially when my weaknesses seem ever so conspicuous.

And, so, whether the message of the healing power of love arrives in a student's surprise email, or appears in the classical work of an acclaimed philosopher, or shows up unexpectedly in a give-and-take conversation with a student or colleague over a relaxed breakfast accompanied by a cup of steaming hot coffee or tea, the universal truth of the message is unmistakeable. Whether it's

Jarett's new-found, quarterlife awareness that "joy is love and love is joy," or my later-life observation that the best teacher is always a lover, both of wisdom *and of* students, the larger truth is clear that he and I are, actually, in the "same boat." In his letter to me, he and I have managed to reach across the chasm of differences that separate us from one another, and yet we still manage to come together in a mutual display of love and support. He trusted our relationship enough to write me such a personal letter, and I reciprocated by reading it and responding in a very personal way.

Discerning the Love—Wisdom in William James and Bernard of Clairvaux

I close this chapter on how "deep writing heals" with two of my all-time favorite quotations on love. These maxims sum up my philosophy of education and my philosophy of living my life to its fullest. It has taken me many decades to arrive at a place where I can even discern the wisdom in these insights, let alone put the lessons into practice. But I am trying…each and every day of my life, I am trying. Like Jarett, my intention is to continue to grow as a loving human being until I am unable to grow anymore. When I reach this point I shall retire as an educator. But I promise all those who love me that I will strive to love them back with everything I have—until I pass once and for all.

First, here is William James:

> I am done with great things and big plans, great institutions and big successes. I am for those tiny, invisible loving human forces that work from individual to individual, creeping through the crannies of the world like so many rootlets, or like the capillary oozing of water, yet which, if given time, will rend the hardest monuments of human pride.

Jarett has reached a time in his life when he realizes that, while an Ivy League degree is a wonderful achievement, there is something even more wonderful. His personal tragedies and disappointments have taught him to cherish the comforting, non-judgmental love of other human beings. He knows now that this kind of love is the greatest success of all. He is learning how to give, and to receive, this kind of love. There is no substitute.

I, too, during this later period in my life cycle as a professor (and as a parent, grandparent, friend, and husband), am far less centered on the "big life-plans," changing the "great insititutions," and living through the "big successes." These worldly goals are the dreams of the everyday quarterlifer, and, unarguably, they are important motivators in the developmental process. These dreams meant everything in the world to me decades ago, but at this late stage in my life, they are mere ephemera. I am proud of my worldly achievements, to be sure, but I am far more grateful for those "tiny, invisible, loving human forces" that fill my life each and every day. I want these forces to "creep through the crannies of my life" wherever I am and whenever I am doing what I do. I sometimes say this to my students: "On my deathbed, I will not be screaming for someone to hand me a copy of my just-published book or read me a glowing book review. Neither will I be demanding from my financial advisor my current bank statement or TIAA-CREF retirement update. No. Instead, I will be asking for the special people I love to be at my side to comfort and inspire me like no book or bank account ever could.

And, now, Bernard of Clairvaux:

> There are many who seek knowledge for the sake of knowledge: that is curiosity. There are others who desire to know in order that they may themselves be known: that is vanity. Others seek knowledge in order to sell it: that is dishonorable. But there are some who seek knowledge in order to edify and love: that is teaching.

Here in four, packed, aphoristic (colon-separated) sentences is a lifetime summary of where I've been, where I am now, and where I would still like to go as an educator. In response to Bernard of Clairvaux, I have always been a curious seeker of knowledge. This is why I have gone on to earn multiple degrees in the course of my lifetime. And, for a large part of my professorial career, it was the need to be known by others that was far more important to my vanity than the need to seek wisdom for its own sake. I regret this pursuit of fame for its own sake, because not only is fame fleeting, it is also fickle.

Finally, while I was never outwardly a seeker of knowledge in order to accumulate wealth, I did use the knowledge I sought to publish and to travel the country as a highly sought-after, well-remunerated national spearker. I sometimes wonder at this present time in my life, however, where all the money went. Was it truly worth it? What Bernard of Clairvaux says about knowledge in general has its wonderful upsides and its disappointing downsides, to be sure. But it has only been during the last couple of decades as a teacher that I have found the fullest satisfaction in my vocation. It has been during this time that I have consciously tried "to edify and to love." Is the mark of a true teacher anything other than this? Is anything more lasting or fulfilling? I, for one, will remember the personal letter from Jarett, as well as similar inspiring letters from scores of other students, far longer than I will remember all the academic honors, generous yearly salary increments, and the highly sought-after invitations to speak throughout the country. Of this, I am sure.

Chapter 7

Some Pungent Reflections on How to Do Personal Narrative Writing
Inspired by Maya Angelou

ROBERT J. NASH

The following will serve as my closing thoughts about the art and craft of Scholarly Personal Narrative Writing as a methodology. All the remaining chapters in the book will talk less about *how* to do the writing and more about how the stories themselves can *heal, create meaning, and make us whole human beings.* The chapters following this essay will be living examples of how some authors (including my co-author, Sydnee Viray) have used this kind of writing to work their way through the darkness into the light. These chapters demonstrate the validity of Maya Angelou's observation about the need that each of us has to write our way to a truth that will set us free: "Personal narrative writing is telling the truth about being human through our own stories—what we are capable of, what makes us lose, laugh, weep, fall down, and gnash our teeth, and wring our hands, and kill each other, and love each other."

Maya Angelou (b. 1928) is the master of personal, non-fiction writing, having authored six of these types of books. Her breakthrough personal narrative was *I Know Why the Caged Bird Sings* (1970). Her first book of poetry in 1971, *Just Give Me a Cool Drink of Water 'Fore I Die,* was nominated for a Pulizer Prize. She was honored with the National Medal of Arts in 2000. For me, Maya Angelou's sagacious observations about writing skillfully capture both the complexity and simplicity, the challenge and the satisfaction, of putting together the stories of our personal lives.

Angelou's fundamental truth about writing is that it is impossible to separate how we write from who we are and what we have to say about who we are. Effective story-telling is, therefore, a triple-threat: It relies on creativity, self-understanding, and candid self-disclosure. None of this is easy, of course, but the goal is within the reach of all of us, if we are willing to work hard, take risks, believe in the value of what we are doing, and stay the course until the project is done. For most of us, the triple-threat will become a triple-treat once our stories have been told. Nobody, in my mind, has done all of this better than Maya Angelou. So, I begin each of my closing reflections on SPN writing with quotations taken from Angelou's extensive interview in the *Paris Review Interviews*, Vol. 4, 2009, pp. 236–258.

"Easy reading means damn hard writing."—Maya Angelou

Who is it who said: "Writing is easy; all you have to do is sit down, open a vein, and bleed." Or "death is easy; writing is hard." Or, my favorite: "I have to rewrite something dozens of times to make it look as if it came easy to me the first time and didn't need any revisions." My students will sometimes say that many of the assigned readings for their courses are hard to get through because they're so "technical and boring." I think what they mean is that so much formal, academic writing sounds like first-draft writing because the writer is aiming for inaccessiblity as a badge of expertise. Why? This is the mark of the scholar for so many of us—make yourself tough to read because this means you are an expert who is the only one capable of understanding yourself.

The best (most pleasurable to read) writing I do is the writing that I tweak constantly. I aim for clarity and readability, not complexity for its own sake. I have to be careful here, though, because too much tweaking threatens to remove all the spontaneity and risk-taking from my writing. Sometimes I achieve my aim; sometimes I don't. The rigid training of the academy is tough for me to overcome. I remember working on an article for a prestigious religious studies journal that took months to write. The required 8,000 words dragged on for what seemed like forever. Now I've written entire books in three months (some good, some bad, some better off unwritten)…but one, short article consumed months and months of work? What was that about?

Much later, when I received national recognition for this article, someone asked me if it took long to write it. After some thought, I said, it took me months, but it was actually in the works for years. I had poured out my heart, head, and soul into that article, and, as a result, the writing was the hardest I've ever done. I was trying to say in a minimum amount of words what I had been reading, thinking about, talking about, and teaching for decades. And I had to distill it all into 8,000 words. This distillation process added up to my doing 10 drafts of this article. Yes, this was "damn hard writing" for me, but the effort was worth it. Many of the responses from readers included a comment like this:

"Even though your article on 9/11 was easy to read, I know that I'll never forget it. 9/11 changed my life forever." (See Robert J. Nash, "How September 11, 2001 Transformed My Course on Religious Pluralism, Spirituality, and Education." *The Journal of Religion & Education.* Vol. 29, No. 1. Spring, 2002, pp. 1–22)

It takes me forever to get my words to sing. I work mainly with the language…even more than the plot and the characters. I really love language; it allows us to explain the pain and the glory, the nuances and the delicacies, of our existence. —Maya Angelou

Ah, the magnificence of language! I am a wordophile, always was and always will be, like my father, probably, but, sadly, not like most of the teachers I've ever had. I do remember a college professor, though, who would often say: "The more words you know, the more power you have in the world. The person with the most words has the most clout, especially in the professions." What this professor of mine was missing, however, is Angelou's artistic insight that we need to get our language to "sing." It's not the number of words we know; it's whether the words sing. I must say that I tend to remember the lyrics to my favorite ballads even more than the prose of my favorite writers or the verse of my favorite poets.

I want my own words to sing for my readers. Some words do and some don't. I think before I die I am going to try to write a song. Perhaps this will teach me to use language lyrically. My co-author, Sydnee Viray, does this well. Here's a confession: I've never written a poem. Maybe I'll also try to compose a short verse sometime soon. Meanwhile, thanks to Angelou, I've set up a project for myself to complete over the next few weeks: Can I make a list of the most vivid, memorable words in all the musical ballads that I love that I can use to describe the "pain and the glory, the nuances and the delicacies," in my own life? My reminder to myself will be to avoid "in-house academic argot." Hey, I like the phrase I just made up—"in-house academic argot." "Argot" has only five letters, but it comes from the French word meaning "to get one's claws into." Isn't this, after all, what we esteemed professors are trying to do with our students in order to dazzle them with our specialized vocabularies? Why am I always so easily tempted to "argotize" what I don't know so that it looks as if I really know it?

Never let the facts alone obscure the truth of your narrative. The truth is what your life felt like…Personal narrative writing is telling the truth about being human through our own stories—what we are capable of,

*what makes us lose, laugh, weep, fall down, and gnash our teeth and wring
our hands and kill each other and love each other.* —Maya **Angelou**

A fact is a *datum*—Latin for that which is given. I believe that Angelou recognizes a basic truth of the human condition: Nothing is ever given to us as if it can be immaculately perceived, beyond the influence of the stories we inhabit at any given time in our lives. We do not see pure "facts," because purity exists only in our imaginations. What some of us might consider to be a scientific, well-researched "fact," others might see as a preconceived tendency to call something a "fact" because it fits our "privileged" story of truth. If I am trained to be a quantitative researcher, then my, and your, truth must be expressed in numbers. If I am an ethnographer, my, and your, truth must emerge from structured, "objective" interviews. If I am a lawyer, my, and your, truth must meet the standards of the law as recorded in court-upheld, legal precedents. And so on…

Angelou, in contrast, believes that, for the writer, the truth of a narrative lies in the emotional power of the story we construct that gives meaning to what we perceive. For some of us, like Angelou, our feelings determine the truth of what we experience. For Angelou, there is no prior purity when it comes to truth. Truth, etymologically *(troth)*, means "trust." Angelou wants us to trust our own, and others', authorial feelings above all else. Angelou is convinced that the "true" narrative is the one that evokes, and invokes, the author's, and reader's, strongest passions. Everything else is beside the point—interesting and important to be sure, but never the final word.

Underneath my wish to become a skilled, non-fiction, creative story-teller, is an ambivalent Robert J. Nash. I love to read my students' stories that are rooted in anger, joy, grief, sadness, exhilaration, success, loss, tears, hate, and love. I want to write this way, myself, because I know that nothing rivets the attention of a reader the way that expressions of honest human emotion do. But, the academic Robert needs to ask Angelou this question: Why can't facts and feelings co-exist? Isn't there anything that the writer and the reader might be able to agree on that lies outside of us…outside of our unique meaning-making minds?

When is the story I am telling in my writing a lie? Or is it all dependent on the authenticity of the emotions I am recalling while I'm constructing it? For example, in the past I've made angry accusations to loved ones that I've long since regretted, because they have not been "true." I mean "true" in the sense that they objectively described a situation that neutral bystanders would agree on. Instead, in retrospect, I realized that my accusations were the imagined by-products of my unrestrained fury, my soaring ego, my too-easy tendency to jump to conclusions prematurely. While I agree with Angelou that my feelings have the potential to produce writing that is most honest in the sense of being unvarnished, what else does it produce? What do I want it to produce? And is it "true" that anything can ever be completely "unvarnished"?

And yet...and yet. The most effective SPN writing really stems from what my life feels like to me right here, right now, right away. I'm writing these words on the hottest, most humid day so far of a Vermont summer, and there is no air-conditioning in my study. My six-year-old granddaughter from North Carolina, Kailee, who is staying with us for a month, is clamoring for my attention because her grandmother went to do an errand, and I'm the only caretaker in the house. She claims to be "bored." Moreover, I just received a very troubled email from one of my students asking for my immediate help to register for a summer course or she won't be able to graduate in the early fall. It seems that I forgot to notify the continuing education office that she is an official graduate student in my program. And, oh yes, I have to pick up another granddaughter in less than an hour from her soccer practice or she will be stuck without a ride home. This will necessitate a long drive on my part that will take me away from my computer. My allergies are also out of control due to the stifling humidity and the deadly pollen floating about in the air outside, and even inside, my study.

Doesn't all of this buzzing, swirling, totally distracting activity have an impact on what I'm writing right now? Maya Angelou, you make me feel schizophrenic because, at the moment, the right and left sides of my brain are at war with one another. Perhaps writing this book will help me to heal my ambivalences. But perhaps not.

There is one main theme in all my writing: we may encounter many defeats, but we must not be defeated. A second theme is that human beings are more alike than unalike. Every human being wants a nice place to live, a good place for the children to go to school, healthy children, somebody to love, the courage—the unmitigated gall—to accept love in return, some place to relax on Saturday or Sunday night, and some place to experience their God. —**Maya Angelou**

One of the natural gifts that I admire so much in Angelou's writing is her ability to move effortlessly from the "1st-person singular" to the "1st-person plural," from the "I" to the "we." She knows that, as a writer, she is both unique *and* connected. What she narrates about her own life has implications for other lives. She understands that what binds us all together as human beings are the common themes that we all share by virtue of being human. We are all "more alike than unalike."

I often say to my students—"It's the resonant human themes in your writing that will speak to the heads, hearts, and souls of your readers. So, it's okay to *personalize* and *thematize* whenever and wherever you think appropriate. And don't be afraid to both show *and* tell. Maya Angelou does, and so do many other great writers like her. Personal narrative writers understand that the word *theme* actually includes two words—"the me"—and, for them, this is more than a coincidence. They know full well that "the me" is an inseparable part of "the we," and vice versa. Thus, universalizability is inevitable. The complementarity of the "me" and the "we" makes up for what is lacking in either the singular or plural pronouns when they stand alone.

Angelou sums up my own philosophy of being, believing, and becoming so beautifully in the above quotation. Her two universal themes are the ones that come up time and time again in my students' writings. Living a life of victorious resilience, and understanding what, at the core, binds all of us together, despite our differences, are what so many of my students strive for. They talk about this. They write about this. They deep down believe it, even when their personal lives are in chaos and even when the external "enemy" seems so obvious. All of us want to love and be loved. All of us want something to live for, something to die for, and, yes, something to leave to others. The best SPNs are stories of being lost and then found; of being defeated and emerging victorious; of losing love and gaining love; of being helped by others and helping others in return; and of turning nightmares into transcendent, yet realizable, dreams.

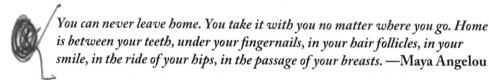

You can never leave home. You take it with you no matter where you go. Home is between your teeth, under your fingernails, in your hair follicles, in your smile, in the ride of your hips, in the passage of your breasts. —**Maya Angelou**

This is an extraordinary example of the writer as artist. Maya Angelou sums up in three incredibly visual, image-filled sentences the impact that our past is destined to have on our present and future. Her words do, indeed, "sing." Her use of language is earthy. It is inspiring. It conveys the kind of gritty "truth" that she writes about in the two preceding quotations. While it is true that, as adults, we may never be "able to go home again," it is also true that we will never be able completely to leave our home behind us…once and for all. Our pasts—good, bad, and indifferent—are with us until the day we die. Our past is indelibly embedded into the core of our psychological and physical beings.

I sometimes say to my students: Tell me what you think the difference is between a "house" and a "home." Some will recall the Gladys Knight lyrics from her hit song, "A House Is Not a Home." Some will say they have no idea of the difference, because their "homes" were never anything more than "houses."

And some will say just the opposite. I will remember forever when I asked a tearful 5th-grade student this same question, during my visit as a guest speaker to her elementary school class, and she said the following: "A house is when I go to live with my father during the summers; a home is when I live with my mom for the rest of the year. I hate houses." For me, this comment captured the gravity of her personal story so poignantly. I hope, someday, that she is given permission, even encouragement, in school to write this story.

Does this mean, therefore, that we are nothing more than our pasts? Is the self really a motley collection of unavoidable family memories (some good, some bad) of how each of us was raised? Can we ever cast off the more lethal aspects of our pasts, or are we doomed to relive them forever? Will I, Robert J. Nash, always be the unconscious product of the orphaned parents who raised me and the siblings whom I never really knew well enough to love or to hate? After writing Chapters 1 and 2 for this book, I'm not really sure I can walk away so easily from the deeply-ingrained influences of my "home," or maybe it was only my "house." I thought I could. Either way, my past has left its mark. Maybe, when all is said and done, I *am* the sum total of my background. Maybe all my learned talk of reconstructing life narratives and creating new and improved background "fictions" is nothing more than my attempt to escape Angelou's "down and dirty" truths about the lasting impact of our upbringing. Maybe. Maybe.

Part 2

The Emotional Impact of Scholarly Personal Narrative
Writing from the Gut

What does it mean to *write from the gut*? This type of SPN writing ignites an author's motivation to undertake a personal journey starting from the "inside" and traveling to the "outside." But how deep inside does the scholar have to go in order to begin the journey? What will be the overall emotional impact, and the take-aways, both for the scholar *and* the reader? This type of soul-stirring, inside-outside writing is *gutsy*, because the writer must be both candid and courageous. At times, the writing will be raw. The gut-based writer must risk narrating what can sometimes be the most painful, heart-breaking self-disclosures. These disclosures are not meant to evoke pity from readers. Instead, their purpose is to show how it is possible for all of us to make meaning out of our own suffering. All of us have the capacity to live our lives as victors not victims, no matter how dire our pasts. As the SPN writer narrates the personal journey from the inside to the outside, it is possible for a radical self-transformation to occur. In the words of Viktor Frankl (2006), "…everything can be taken from a person but one thing: the last of the human freedoms—to choose one's attitude in any given set of circumstances, to choose one's own way" (p. 66). In the chapters that follow in Part II, Sydnee demonstrates the transformative power of "writing from the gut."

Chapter 8

Connecting My Isolated Self to My Communities

SYDNEE VIRAY

Reclaiming My Language

My first language spoken is Tagalog. My second is American English. My third is Parisian French. My current language, as a university administrator, is coded in policy and procedures, rules and regulations, strategies and goal setting. How far away I have drifted from my native tongue! Now, I use the tongues of others to enforce, control, and convince. I use the tongues of others to impress, persuade, and allure. But my native tongue is still the tongue I use—especially when I love, when I care, when I affect. My body holds the vibrations and cadence of my native language. My lips point, my hands wave, eyebrows lift—all to communicate an intimate message of "over there," "over here," and "I see you." However, in this society and in my office dwelling, my body is misunderstood. I am "heard" or "seen" as weak and silent—passive. I am heard incorrectly; when I say "open the light" my colleagues remind me that lights can only be turned on or off. While they correct me, I think to myself that only people can be turned on or off, but they should not worry as my eyes and heart can be open and closed like their light.

My mind and heart anchor my native tongue in the river of my soul. And as my mind and heart speak its foreign dialogue, they adapt in the name of survival, freedom, and truth. This is how I connect and maintain my authenticity in a country where I am swaying to the rhythm of my own heart, even if I have a coded accent.

Writing teaches a positive self-discipline. The exercise empowers the student-writers to push themselves by placing painful and exhausting obstacles between the student-writers and their objective of a completed, though never finished, manuscript. I believe we cannot help others for long unless our own needs are met. We are agents for ourselves, first. We need to be self-sufficient, not co-dependent, whether in short-term or long-term relatioships. I suppose the ideal progression would seem like this: help ourselves first, then our families, then our communities. What does this have to do with writing toward healing and wholeness in the 21st-century academy?

Before we can write about our stories and the stories of those who grace our lives, we first must understand the power of our attitude toward ourselves. I am not sure there is much different in how I perceive myself, from how I talk about myself, and how I represent myself to the world. I believe that eventually how I think about myself will be, at the very least, how I portray myself in my writing. One lesson I have learned is that Scholarly Personal Narrative is not for the faint of heart. For us, SPN is vigorous writing. It has the ability to touch the fringes of our soul as we unravel the meaning in the hidden crevices of our truths. Yet, we should not feel that this writing is an opportunity to self-efface. SPN writing is not about pleasing our readers and making them comfortable with our stories. Rather than self-indulge, we are forced to take some scholarly risks and write daringly.

As the Buddhist scholar, Geshe Kelsang Gyatso, states, "Normally we divide the external world into that which we consider to be good or valuable, bad or worthless, or neither." I had to learn to discriminate that my stories were very valuable and worth every moment I put into them. I had to discriminate toward my choice to tell certain stories over others. And by using SPN, I had to discriminate which scholars would serve my narratives best. Throughout this chapter and the ones that follow, you will see how I engineer my scholarship, economically, toward supporting every limb of my narratives. You will also witness my attempt to connect with what SPN scholars refer to as "universals," or "universalizable truths." All of these elements are critical as I describe my journey from student to author, story-listener to storyteller, and assimilated community member to community engager.

This type of writing process develops from soleful to soulful. Here is what Anne Lamott (1994) says, "Writing and reading decrease our sense of isolation. They deepen and widen and expand our sense of life: they feed the soul. When writers make us shake our heads with the exactness of their prose and their truths, and even make us laugh about ourselves or life, our buoyancy is restored. We are given a shot at dancing with, or at least clapping along with, the absurdity of life, instead of being squashed by it over and over again. It's like singing on a boat during a terrible storm at sea. You can't stop the raging storm, but singing can change the hearts and spirits of the people who are together on that ship" (p. 237).

Wherever I Go, There I Am

Dear *Where am I?*

"Hey, daddy, where are we?" I asked my dad when I was five years old. We were traveling from a sprawling Midwest city to a quaint Northeastern town in the United States. "Where am I" is a lyric that has played on repeat since my earliest memory. At such a young age, I moved thousands of miles from the Philippines to the United States. I moved so many times that the novelty of the actual geographic location of *where I was* faded to become merely the scenery of my life. For me to feel connected to where I was geographically, and to feel grounded in that landscape, my external question quickly created a portal to my inner world: where am I in my *self*?

Jon Kabat-Zinn, the founder of the Stress Reduction Clinic and Center for Mindfulness in Medicine, Health Care, and Society at the University of Massachusetts reminds me "Wherever you go, there you are." Similarly, Heraclitus, a sixth-century Greek philosopher simply states, "I sought myself." Both of these philosophers' statements emerge when I am seeking to understand my place in my own meaning-making. I like Kabat-Zinn's gentle truth that wherever I go, there I am. It's grounding, affirming, and validating. I have interpreted this statement through fearful memories of my past.

When I was in high school I was a practicing Catholic who went to church every Saturday afternoon at 4 pm and on all the holy days. I looked forward to returning to the church as the house where I was able to return to my solitude. Alone, I would go to church on Saturdays. Within my solitude I explored my emotions, my values, my desires, and dreams of my future.

My solitude was profoundly interrupted one Saturday evening during the winter, when the air was brisk and frigid; I walked alone on the main street to the church only a few blocks from my house. A black pick-up truck pulled over across the street. I recognized the men who stepped out of the truck from my high school. They were white American men; one wore beige cargo pants and the other wore blue jeans with his steel-toe boots. I looked over at them, acknowledged their presence, and returned to my solitude. I was very cold, and my scarf was keeping the frigid air from freezing my lips and face. My head was down as I contemplated the degree conversion of the evening air—then all of the sudden, I was grabbed and picked up. I gasped and with great fury, I was lost. I did not know where I was going. I made the split-second assumption that it was the two men who were my kidnappers. I fought as hard and with as much strength as I could. I kicked and tried to wiggle myself from their grasp. They threw me into the truck. The one captor with the cargo pants beat me and beat me hard. This is when I truly faced my loneliness. He yelled racist remarks, "China dolls are not supposed to talk. Shut up!" I retreated so quickly into my inner world. I did not know where I was, but *there*. That is where I went to seek myself. Each slanderous utterance became my voice questioning myself, "Why is this happening? What did I do to arrive here, in their truck, with them?" You see, these were the beginning threads of my sexual assault experience. I was kidnapped and beaten. I was brought to a residential wooded area to be ravaged by two high school-aged men who fantasized this experience into our reality.

But my saving question was "where am I?" The wooded area, where I was raped, was an area that I knew very well. It was my landscape—cold, harsh, and snow-brushed. It was where the old train tracks were laid. I remember visualizing the train traveling over and through my body. But just as a train's whistle evokes alarm, so did the silence that surrounded our predicament. These men were so frenzied about what they were doing that I took their abuse and planned an escape. I was not inside my pain. I was in my strength. I was in my survival. I was in my mind logically planning my journey back home. One of the men became so paranoid about someone hearing me scream and yell that he ran away. He just left. I clung to my strength and survival by doing the only thing I could do. I returned to my inner world. In short time, the man who was on me stopped and ran after his accomplice. I was left, there, in my solitude.

Brown (2011) reflects in her meaning-making thesis, "To this day I still struggle with the weight of blame for what happened to me." I was left by my assailants in my solitude, but my solitude was now mired with fear of death, anxiety, and physical pain. In fact, my solitude faded into loneliness and despair. I felt the weight of my reality. I was to blame. I was their "China Doll" that did not shut up. I was so driven toward my solitude in the church that I wanted to walk by myself to commune in my inner world. This experience did happen to me. It forced me to seek myself in ways that I did not dare imagine I could. The aftermath of my survival revealed that these men were misogynistic Asianophiles who kept each other company by detailing their fetishized thoughts of me while in school. They were obsessive, sick loners who spent hours learning about Asian culture and objectifying Asian women. They even journaled about their desires in a handwritten manual on "How to Get a China Doll Girlfriend." But I still bore the weight of blame because I was the only

Asian woman in my school. I was the one tangible object that converted their fantasy to an attainable goal.

This weight of blame hangs on my heart whenever I find myself in my despair and loneliness. It appears before me in negative and demeaning soundtracks that are repetitive. And as the teenage girl states in *Socrates Café* (2001), "So shit happens, and sometimes because of the shit that happens, you kill yourself. And in other times you make big changes in your life that make it worthwhile enough to go on living." And so I chose to make my life worthwhile—living, despite the terrifying experience on that cold winter day. I could have died, yet somehow I did not kill myself.

> *The heave is the root of the light.*
> *The unmoved is the source of all movement.*
> *Thus the Master travels all day*
> *Without leaving home.*
> *However splendid the views,*
> *She stays serenely in herself.*
> *Why should the lord of the country*
> *flit about like a fool?*
> *If you let yourself be blown to and fro, you lose touch with your root.*
> *If you let restlessness move you,*
> *you lose touch with who you are.*
>
> —Lao-Tzu, *Tao-te-Ching*

This poem by Lao-Tzu reminds me of my answer to the question posed in Christopher Phillips' *Socrates Café*, "How can I get from here to there?" I remained loyal to myself after my assault by not allowing the external restless energy to control my very being. I did not lose touch with who I was because I had literally been taken from my journey, but only temporarily. I held firmly to my root. I moved from my external assault (here) to my internal solitude (there) by holding firmly to my root. This is where I am—looking within to find safety in my solitude. Wherever I go, this is where I am.

In solitude,
Sydnee

My Survival in the Aftermath

The vehemence of emotion, stirred by grief and love within me, was claiming mastery, and struggling for full sway; and asserting a right to predominate: to overcome, to live, rise, and reign at last; yes,—and to speak.

—Charlotte Brontë, *Jane Eyre*

One of the outcomes of this tragedy is that I later became a rape crisis counselor. I sought an occupation to help those who had experienced the trauma of sexual and domestic assault. During my night shifts, I would sit on the phone with an anonymous voice speaking her truth of survival. She would recount her story of anguish and her fears of not being able to make it to see the next sunrise. I would gently listen and remind her that her voice alone was demonstrating her love for herself. The irony here is that, during my time as a counselor, I was petrified to retell the details of surviving my own sexual assault. I remember telling close friends and partners that it was hard for me to talk about. It was hard for me speak about it. I remember one such person who said to me, "Sydnee, because of you, I am able to now speak out about my own experience."

I still struggled to recount this tragedy. It wasn't until I sat down to write an SPN essay that my own survival story materialized. I learned that through our stories we can achieve mastery in our lives and we can reframe our tragedies to rise above our fears to believe in ourselves and in our own stories. This is the greatest healing of all, in my opinion: to allow our stories to heal us no matter what others may think or believe to be true.

●

Chapter 9

Creating Wholeness Amidst the Brokenness of My Everyday Life

SYDNEE VIRAY

Truth 1. The fear will never go away as long as I continue to grow.
Truth 2. The only way to get rid of the fear of doing something is to go out and do it.
Truth 3. The only way to feel better about myself is to go out… and do it.
Truth 4. Not only am I going to experience fear whenever I'm on unfamiliar territory,
but so is everyone else.
Truth 5. Pushing through fear is less frightening than living with the underlying fear
that comes from a feeling of helplessness.

—*Susan Jeffers*

How do we write our way into wholeness and healing especially when our inner and outer worlds can feel so broken, shattered, and overwhelming? This is the challenge with any writing; and this apparent conflict is often the obstacle to doing the writing that needs to be done. One of the pieces of advice that we share with the students in our writing course is to *lean into* the writing that seems impossible to do. "Feel the fear and do it anyway" attitude helps to force the scary to the surface; if nothing other than to get it out and to let it go so that you can continue on with your writing intentions. It can liberate the narrative voice from an internal world of uncertainty, pain, and anguish. In this chapter, I hope to unpack a couple of what I call my *break through-to-break free* writing pieces, where I, rather than feel helpless in my own suffering or within my own insecurity about writing, just wrote. I wrote one word at a time and wrote, and wrote until I arrived at my wholeness.

Drawing on My Breath: A Letter to All Souls That Have Felt Broken

If you let yourself be blown to and fro, you lose touch with your root.
If you let restlessness move you, you lose touch with who you are.

—Lao-Tzu

Whenever anger comes up, take out a mirror and look at yourself. When you are angry, you are not very beautiful.

—Thich Nhat Hanh

To All Souls Who Have Ever Felt Broken:

She stands body erect yet bruised and battered, scraped and scarred. She has a cigarette that hangs slightly from her lips, lips that frown slightly when relaxed and lightly covered in lipstick smeared from the battle. Her physique is slim with a strong and steady posture. Her gaze is also strong filled with intent, clarity, and wit, yet her irises are starkly black. Her arms rest folded and crossed in front of her. A close look at her knuckles and you will see they are swollen and red. She dons faded and tattered skinny jeans, a bomber jacket, with a scarf that covers her neck. She has a boneless tongue strong enough to break someone's heart. She wears boots for a firm and steady stance with heels high enough to give her the appearance that she is floating off the ground. She has a thick belt with a buckle ornate with a blue heron. She looks at you. She says nothing.

But you know, she is a veteran; she has been through battles. She has fallen on to the concreteness of her self-hate. She has slept with and clutched a broken heart and lived inside her loneliness. She has lived in the shadows of her past. She has walked in the rain's storm. She has run with the wild horses of her life most of the time bareback all the while aware of her fence that keeps her contained—the fence she calls fear. She reveres acts of reckless love.

This describes my broken inner self. But don't let the description fool you; she is serene, yet jaded. She is a representation of love, my inner love. That is what I call her. She has softness when I am honest with her. She sees my shame and immediately understands all that I have done wrong—especially the harm I have caused to others. She embraces me when I have fallen down, and then puts me on my feet. She has never abandoned me nor has she rejected me. She is there inside watching, observing. She is the knower behind the thinker I have become. She is the knower behind the feeler I have become. She is the inner wisdom that gives me the conviction that I need to protect myself. She lives in the space that is *never not broken, she is Akhilandeshvari.* "Ishvari" in Sanskrit means "goddess" or "female power," and the "Akhilanda" means "never not broken"; in other words, *The Always Broken Goddess*. She is the kindness within me that I have come to know.

In his book *El Poder de la Bondad* or *Survival of the Kindest* (2005), author Piero Ferrucci discusses what people who suffer need. He writes:

> People who are suffering don't need advice, diagnoses interpretations and interventions. They need sincere and complete empathy—attention. Once they have the feeling that the other person is putting themselves in their shoes, they are able to let go of their suffering and head down the path of healing.

When I read this passage, I discovered the reason why I am broken and jaded... I have been ignored, not seen, and not heard. Moreover, I was hiding from my inner wisdom, ignoring my inner voice. I did not empathize with how I got the first bruise on my face, why I needed the cigarette to hang from my mouth, and how my wit was necessary for survival. My heart was an inner glacier with soul serving its apocolyptic landscape. However, it was only through forced self-retreat could I hear kindness, gentleness, and happiness; through meditation, writing, and easing up on my own brittle and stale beliefs, I found a fertile place to nest the seeds of my own self-compassion. I have removed myself from my life routines to find sanctuaries—refuges. These retreats forced me to pay pure attention to my inner wisdom; a wisdom trapped and whose desperate screams were echoing in the chambers of my hardened heart.

In my refuge, I had to be kind to myself. I had to learn *what is my kind of kindness*, how did it differ from kindness towards others and kindness of others? I had to learn to pay attention to my needs and myself first; and if my needs were not easily identifiable, I had to exercise extreme patience with myself until I was clear. From my humble place, this is where I started to feel alive again.

The Deeply Disturbing Episode

The best people possess a feeling for beauty, the courage to take risks, the discipline to tell the truth, the capacity for sacrifice. Ironically, their virtues make them vulnerable; they are often wounded, sometimes destroyed.

—*Ernest Hemingway*

A rupture of my very being occurred a couple of weeks ago. I lost my connection with myself. I lost my vision—I could not see who I really was. The eruption was like this: the heat that rose boiled the liquid in my body to the point of intense perspiration. My eyebrows furrowed into an almost permanent stance at my forehead which forced my eyes to cross its visions of fire and light.

I screamed while I was falling into the abyss. I punched the couch. I screamed. My face was red with fury, rage, anger. I left the room… to breathe out the fire blazing, roaring inside. I couldn't stand the fury. My hands turned into stone-like fists and my arms became their catapults—and crack!

Connection!

I punched myself… in the face on my jawline and again at my eye socket and began to bleed.

In the middle of our life journey, I found myself in a dark wood. I had wandered from the straight path. It isn't easy to talk about it: it was such a thick, wild, and rough forest that when I think of it my fear returns.…I can't offer any good explanation for how I entered it. I was so sleepy at that point that I strayed from the right path.

—Dante

Wake up!

Wake up.

I had fallen…I was desperate. My ears rang of the hateful messages from the years of torment that preceded all of me. I lashed out rabidly trying to escape these projections. I believed so deeply in the notions offered by my abusive father, my rapists, and others who had racially bullied me.

When a man gives way to anger, he harms himself.

—M. Gandhi

Was this what it meant to lose my faith? In that moment, it was. I defined myself as having lost all faith in myself. I cannot even justify my hurtful and harmful actions. There is no explanation when your soul hides under the torment of internalizing abuse. Yes, I am a good person perhaps because I do have a soul, but my deed was the furthest thing from good. It was unruly rage coming from the depths of all that had happened before that moment. After this experience, the rage left only ashes of regret, remorse, sorrow and deep wounds that pang to this day. For the nights that followed, I had the most haunting nightmares of being burned alive at the stake, and this death witnessed by those whom I have hurt. I woke up emotionally ravaged with despair. How could I have been so cruel, so hostile, so…dangerous?

I had written the following verses just prior to my out-of-control detour into violence:

I remember the injustice:
I gave away my most vital organ—my Heart.

I try not to think about her. I have discovered that my mind is the traitor that
sold my Heart in payment for its egocentric treat.
So I lay here sobbing, looking up. I cry, "How it hurts so."
I have been drowning in the tears that have filled my Heart.
This has been the barter between my Mind and Heart.
It's the detachment of the loss of her that is painful.
If gold wants to be purified it pasess through fire first.
My Soul is passing through its fire during the darkest of nights
Each time it reaches for the beautiful sunrise.
My Heart has the fragrance of a silent, peaceful, meditative Lotus.
I have tried my best to capture its scent, but the mystery remains a mystery.
My Heart is the Lotus, and confused-lust is the mud that smears its facade.
I ask her to stay with me. Stay with me. Do not be bartered away.
Though the only currency I can offer are my tears.

My rage is a dangerous demon, an evil fountain that gushes inside of me. It is completely untamed and immature. It rises out of my inner shadows. *Why? Why now?* Can my faith in myself really save me now? These were all questions I had to answer—alone, where I am often saved—in my solitude.

So I left. I fled my dwelling to spend time in my shadows—alone. And to heal, I lit a candle, a candle that flickered on the wick of forgiveness toward myself and others. The deep gutteral and primal cries and screams I whelped while alone taught me that my suffering has such painful origins. These were the screams I needed when I was raped, but I couldn't scream, or when my mother left me and my sisters, or when my father dominated and controlled my life. These were the tears that ran; tears that had been locked up; and finally, the detachment allowed my internal spirit to fall. I licked my wounds as I attempted to defile my shadows. There were times in the past where I was close to this edge, but now I had jumped off completely and as one would expect, I hit rock-jagged bottom. Here is another poem I wrote from this place of fertile solitude:

In Darkness, Detachment and Descent Are Witnessed

In Night's darkness, the Tree shivers in the frost-thick air.
The Tree detaches of an autumn Leaf requiring the Tree to let go and witness the Leaf's great descent:

The Leaf falls gliding, twirling, determined to make this last dance to the Earth notable.

The Dragonfly observes the Leaf's dignity, and dances with the Leaf, accompanying her descent.

Leaving the ballroom of the sky the Dragonfly departs as the descent continues.

Like changing partners, the Western Wind supports the Leaf's flight, stabilizing her glide.

With a warm whisper of support the Wind waves a goodbye and blows a good luck wish as the Leaf continues to fall.

The weight of Gravity weighs on the Leaf's chest.

Pressing, pounding, penetrating at the very heart of the Leaf.

Then before folding under Gravity's pressure, the Leaf unfurls, parachuting its determination to survive under Gravity's power.

Before long, Rain surrounds the Leaf: some droplets change the Leaf's composition, and some express the sadness that the Leaf has held since the beginning of this dropping descent.

Where is the Sun now? Did the Tree pursue or reach for the Leaf? Will the Leaf ever be caught and held?

The Leaf realizes that the Rain is actually the Leaf's own tears; the Leaf begins to drown in these tears.

Scared, afraid, decidedly alone as the Leaf feels the space in the solitude.

The Earth appears just below. The Leaf grounds and anchors as it reaches for the Earth.

The Leaf's fantasy of finitude brings forward the one single savior.

Herself.

Her brilliant colors, her comraderie with other leaves, all are faded now.

Her heart, her self-love, are what remain.

She reaches for the Earth and gently lands on the strength of her extended stem...so effortless, so brave.

She sits, settles, and bows to her new host, the Earth.

With gratitude she draws out her final breath.

This breath connects her heart, the Earth's groundedness, the Tree's love and nourishment, and she lets go of her only desire—being closer to the sun.

The Dragonfly, Wind, Gravity, Rain join her in her final exhale; they honor her boldness.

The Tree who demonstrated this art of letting go shares this atonement:
I never meant to leave you in the darkness of the night.

—Sydnee Viray

Deserving Detachment

You yourself, as much as anybody in the entire universe, deserve your love and affection.
—*Buddha*

In this, the dark night of my soul, I discovered what I finally had to let go of and what I had to learn to embrace. I had to let go of all of my previous suffering (perhaps all of my suffering from lifetimes ago that I am not even conscious of) and finally embrace the only person present—me. I still fear things like narcissism and selfishness as an unintended outcome of this dark night journey of my soul, but I have learned to trust that I will find humility. My humility is what has gotten me through this darkness. My physical and emotional stillness has shed light upon the spaces that I need to grow and evolve. My humility is the hidden flame that will light up this darkness. So I tread lightly and carefully in my humility and accept the deeds I cannot change of my past or the deeds others have done against me.

> *Rather than allow ourselves to be burdened by regret for our past misdeeds, we must strive to develop the inherent goodness which lies hidden in our souls, beneath layers of tarnish left by our sins.*
> —*Rabbi Joseph Stern*

In the Jewish tradition *teshuvah* is practiced during the high holy day of Yom Kippur (A Day of Atonement) and is understood as *getting rid of the bad*. Many rabbis and teachers have suggested that to seek getting rid of the bad one might search for the good. I swirled with restless questions in the aftermath of my storm: *What was the goodness that could be discovered in bad actions? What is the good lesson that can come out of a bad decision? Where and how can te-*shuvah *turn bad relationships into friendships, or at least grudges into forgiveness? Rather than banishing the evil, could I simply crowd it out with the goodness found within me?*

> *When the mind is disturbed by improper thoughts constant pondering over the opposites is the remedy.*
> —*Pantanjali*

In my refuge, I set forth to reconcile my ailings with the idea that for every sin or bad habit I engaged in I would create or install a new, positive practice to replace it. This opened a new way of being and living; it's not that I denied the bad, the tarnished, the damaging experiences. I just chose to unhook my focus from the destructive. This freed me to finally be on a journey to find my core self while I anticipated a result of wholeness and deeper meaning. I had reached my turning point.

The questions of *why did all of this happen?* and *why am I engaged in such cruel acts of violence?* are still before me. And I am discovering that no matter what, my greater purpose is self-control through self-love. This self-love can show up in acts of non-violence, expecting nothing, radically accepting, and generously allowing my love to brighten my world with no attempt to hide it. As Helen Schucman and William Thetford (2009) state: "Your task is not to seek for Love, but merely to seek and find all the barriers within yourself that you have built against it."

The Cycle Transforms

The Precious Moment of Transformation, My Inner Goddess Manifesto: Invitation to Become a Person of Soul, Heart, and Mind (in that order)

Dear Self,
Her hands are clean
She washed her hands.
She had done the deed.
She washed her hands.
She was not her skin.
She washed her hands and only she knew that she was washing with her own tears.
—Sydnee Viray

So after I have wailed my heart and soul's cry, what have I left? Well, all I have left is to love. To love myself first and to take baby steps away from my clear attention and fixation on my soul/heart's needs.

We have to decide—every day, every minute—which is it going to be? Cruelty has evolutionary value. Kindness does too. But we can't have both at the same time.

—*Greg M. Epstein*

My heart needs to be protected as my mind sorts through the betrayal that I feel so deeply. I, now, spend at least ten hours meditating each week. I also spend time writing, and I consider myself lucky if I can get ten hours or more of uninterrupted writing. I began this "practice" as a way to distract myself from my most feared emotions. Then I realized that while I would be trying to distract myself from the internal wounds, I was actually writing my way toward meaning and discovering my purpose. This practice brings me closer to the pain, and as I leaned in and listened to its messages, I began befriending the hurt and the suffering in a new way.

From a strong inner base, I dealt with the pain. According to Ferrucci, each of us has a core where we are not hurt, where we are healthy, receptive and strong. "I am convinced that even people who have suffered greatly, carry this healthy core inside. Finding this core may well be the most beautiful quest of our lives. If we return to this middle point—even for a moment—arguments and revenge are unmasked as an absurd waste of time." When I find in myself the place where I am happy and whole, I achieve a level of forgiveness. I find myself in alignment with Lewis Smedes (2007), who wrote, "...forgiveness is a positive quality. It contains joy and faith in others, generosity of spirit. Illogical and surprising, sometimes sublime, it frees us from the ancient chains of resentment. Whoever forgives, feels uplifted....To forgive is to set a prisoner free and discover that the prisoner was you."

I am still hurting; don't get me wrong. Now, I have a practice to help me pace myself as I begin to heal. The challenge lately has been to stay way from re-wounding. I feel sometimes like an addict who can't seem to stay on the wagon of recovery. Now I ask myself, Are you really addicted to your negative feelings like guilt, regret, remorse, helplessness, etc? What I have come to learn is that for me to live with tremendous guilt and negative feelings, I had to become habitually connected to the hurting. I had to create some drama in my life—for example, I did not apply to go to medical school despite being a great candidate. Why did I not go to medical school? Well, I couldn't afford it for one, and instead of dealing with the pain, ironically, I bought a costly BMW. Now, that is dramatic. Why couldn't I just deal with my feelings and grieve the loss of such a dream. Oh, no, no. Sydnee had to buy the BMW to prove something to herself. I had to prove to myself I was worth part of my dream, even if it was materially grounded.

So as I sit here, right now, I am looking at getting a new car, again; but I am doing it slowly and with more attention to my breath. This is in an effort to remain in alignment with the truth I seek and to break my inner struggle to maintain peace. I may not buy a new car, but I have achieved a newfound consciousness. I do not pedestalize me as having reached a guru-level enlightenment…I am far from it. However, I am more clear that the anxieties I experience are here to tell me something.

It's not about reaching some higher plane; it's about discovering that as I write my way into healing and wholeness, I am coming to accept, and adapt, my life's stories. I used to be someone who was driven by what others thought of my life and circumstances. I allowed myself to attach to other people's inner projections much like if water tried to stop and attach itself to each rock in a riverbed—each rock would become water. Instead, now I try to imitate the nonattachment that water has shown me. Most days I try to emulate the stillness I have observed from a placid lake. I try not to be afraid of my own beauty, of my light—as Nelson Mandela warned from his prison cell. I believe that my experience is really not that unique. I have met many people who struggle to be kind toward themselves.

So I have committed to just showing up, to listening and being present. This is perhaps the first real conscious commitment I have made toward myself. Before I would judge my faith. I would question what I preferenced. And now, I am clearer than ever. In fact, I am so clear, I can see myself loving myself in a different way. A slippery slope albeit, but I am content with the pendulum swinging this way for a bit as I get used to this break on my path. I am conscious that I choose how I want to live life. But this choice is not a static one… it's very dynamic and reliant on the relationships that I build.

A year ago I told a friend that our greatness is equivalent to the average of the top five people we spend the most time with. This equation (by the way, I love equations; they help to sum up complex ideas in a short-hand way) is really a formula to measure how our "average" choices impact whom we spend time with of those that are around us. This is a sacred selection process. When I told her that this process was selective, she immediately declared that she had vacancies in her top five. I liked her notion of having vacancies. For me, my top five represent people who are able to see who I really am and be able to put my behaviors and attitudes into a perspective related to my narratives. My qualifications for the people in my top five are transparency, consistency (behaviors and words line up), openness to new ideas and thoughts and ways of being, patience, and humor. I believe in making a choice toward interdependence as a step toward being good to our selves.

> … *goodness is a choice. It is the most important choice we can ever make. And we have to make it again and again, throughout our lives and in every aspect of our lives.*
> —*Greg M. Epstein*

I have been asked what my religion is and I really can't say. All I can say is what I try to practice. I think I fear stating an affiliation and then not being able, at some future time, to commit to it fully. I just want to *be* (mistakes and all), because I really am open with others. But you know, at the end of the day, we will die. And can we really take our dramas into the grave? I am not so sure. But I can say, for me, to remain on this journey in misery is just not what I have signed up for. So I will attempt to live each difficult moment in another way or at the least to minimize the impact of the difficulty on my future moments.

My manifesto of a healed, whole, meaning-full life is really a declaration to align my words with my actions, and with my inner spirit. I will make mistakes, but hopefully the practice will show itself to be evolutionary, revolutionary, or perhaps, counterrevolutionary.

I believe that if we stop to think, it is clear that our very survival, even today, depends upon the acts and kindness of so many people. Right from the moment of our birth, we are under the care and kindness of our parents; later in life, when facing the sufferings of disease and old age, we are again dependent on the kindness of others.

—Dalai Lama

So I will end my letter here. Be Kind (to yourself and others). Rewind (to the present moment). Breathe (your only life support). Smile (more often). Repeat (as many times as is necessary).

That's all for now.

Sydnee, your fellow journey maker

A Final Reflection on How I Found Wholeness in SPN Writing

In my above SPN to those who are broken, I dive deep into my darkest moments. The climax is my description of being harmful to myself. This unmasking is risky. There is risk that the reader will be judgmental, concerned and not able to connect to my suffering. I also expect readers to be skeptical about my healing journey. But the honest, raw truth is, I am not attached to the reader's judgments or thoughts. I am so clear that I make mistakes as a human being. I also show up in my writing as devastatingly imperfect. I reference the writings of others as signals that others have written about the journey toward healing. My narrative strives to show that even in our darkest moments, we can, do, must survive. One of the points I really want to be clear about is that I do not love myself for causing harm—either to me or others. I do not feel like a better person for even telling this narrative. But what I can clearly say is that I am finding my wholeness in the brokenness of the existence I live. I am my own hero and anti-hero. Isn't that the ultimate wholeness—to have both heads and tails in the coins that we flip in our life? Each day I choose to live according to the narratives of my heroes and anti-heroes. And in this narrative I am choosing a path of non-violence through knowing that violence is an act that is so easy to choose.

Chapter 10

Revealing the Healing Ironies
of My Everyday Life

SYDNEE VIRAY

The Webster's dictionary definition of irony—a combination of circumstances or a result that is the opposite of what is expected; an attitude of mind characterized by recognition of the incongruities, contradictions, and complexities of human experience.

The definition of irony in SPN Writing—on the one hand, writing (one word at a time) is easy; on the other hand, writing (your personal narrative) is hard as hell.
—Sydnee Viray

I have always been a disciplined self-starter. So I wonder, did SPN writing give me self-discipline, or was I already a self-disciplined person, and didn't the other people lack it who discontinued their writing despite wanting to master their SPN writing? From this perspective, self-discipline was not something I learned. It was an inherent part of my makeup. The relative success of my writing experience resulted from my self-discipline. This seems ironical that I would receive as a benefit from this kind of writing a quality that I already possessed. I do believe, however, that my self-discipline was enhanced by the practice of writing. While I might have dropped out of my early SPN classes, the many sufferings I endured strengthened me and rewarded me. I learned that the self-discipline to sustain my writing no matter how raw, how emotional, or how gutsy it got, I still wrote to the end, to the finish.

My co-author, Robert, often says, "You know you are a writer when the pain of not writing is greater than the pain of writing." I agree. Many of us enter the world of writing because we are passionate or we are seeking passion in our life's work. Remember the word *passion* means "ecstasy" and "agony." Writing can be equally pleasurable and painful. Moreover, many who have written using SPN methodologies have been known to *bleed on the page*. Nevertheless, some of us are drawn to the tension of the love/hate relationship to writing. Writing is hard work requiring many psychological tricks to get the words on the page. Yet, the only advice I can give is that writing begets writing. As the co-teacher for the SPN writing course, the only directive I give is just write one word, and when you are done writing that one word at least attempt another one.

Irony: Cutting My Complex Life Down to Size

I am an ironist. One of the writing techniques that I employ is the use of *irony*. To me, irony cuts my complex, drama-filled life stories down to size. Through discovering the ironies in my everyday lived experience, I discover the whole of me. I manage to enjoy the life I have led through my ironic discoveries, because I can never be the worst or best at living my own life. Ironies create a kind of zero-sum gain which dissuades me from thinking myself better than anyone or pitying my own existence. I think of my writing process as having a cool, detached attitude of mind and heart, characterized by the inevitable incongruities and complexities of my experiences. Yes, I am an ironist.

There are many ironies that reveal themselves in our everyday situations. For example, I use ironies to carry at least two seemingly opposing themes in my narratives. The contradictions of our lives are hard to avoid, and, for me, being able to write from one theme to another helps me to see the meaning of my life come around "full circle." The following is an example of writing my way toward meaning and wholeness, as I size up my work experience in the academy.

To the Bullying Manager:

It is with ironic enthusiasm that I write this letter of resignation. That's right, enthusiasm. I am enthusiastic to leave behind being shackled to your desk; being wedged between your biasly crafted bamboo ceiling position title and your sticky floor compensation package. (Asian women have historically experienced the *bamboo ceiling* in their achievement and the *sticky floor* of their earnings). I reject your judgments of me as being a timid, meek, and mild leader. I am leaving behind a six-foot grave, shovel and all, in exchange for the limitless horizon of opportunity by letting go of you and your style of leadership and accountability.

Ask me how ecstatic I am and I will tell you—I could just about jump from the highest mountain peak shouting "See you close to NEVER!" and then I would wait around to hear my word NEVER echo as it bounces back at me. I just cannot bear the brokenness of your short-sighted leadership. *Why are you so happy to deliver this news?* you ask. Let me take up a bit of space and describe my experience as I see it:

When I was brought on board you promised me the sky's limit of "running my own show." But I should have known the seats to my own show would be empty since you did not offer me any more compensation for the passion, energy, and grit I delivered day in and day out on the job. I racked up months of work that spilled into laboring 60- to 70-hour weeks. You took advantage of the fact that I was *exempt* from the labor laws that stated that you should pay me my hourly rate. You painted abundance in the pictures of professional growth, and yet after testing the waters I discovered your painted canvas only displayed a mirage that disappeared when I requested various opportunities. You were quick to distract me with more work to allow me to utilize my strengths by ghostwriting your memos, emails, announcements, and other communications. In a sense, you would say "Jump, Sydnee, prove yourself to me!" and I would so eagerly reply, "Ok, boss, now how high? Is this good enough?" All the while I was jumping, you were ignoring my exhaustion.

I dedicated myself to working by your side—you, another woman in a man's world of numbers, business affairs, deadlines, and competition. I remember, after I had received an award for my outstanding leadership as a woman and then again, separately as a person of color, you told me, "I have never thought about being a woman in leadership in all of my 20 years of working here. Do you think it's really that important?" Shortly afterward, you would disclose to me how you were not sure you were up to the task to be a leader, and then you would ask me, "Sydnee, would you ever want my job?" I never really knew if you were joking or not.

I proudly hung my awards in my office and thought to myself, "I guess I am really doing it...climbing this ladder of success." And, yet, all the while I was actually digging myself a six-foot grave. My awards?...Each one of them became a flat note when you would mention your disappointment in my work. I would demonstrate with my statistics that I had processed 1,000–2,000 records nearly single-handedly, and you would invalidate the work I had accomplished. "Sydnee, I must say I am extremely disappointed and frustrated that once again your work submission is past my deadline." You scarred me with your words. My pride, my dignity, and my ego all went down. I missed YOUR deadline...but you seemed to forget that I was busy with YOUR other demands to serve. Your verbal warnings would leave me gasping for air as each warning felt like a sucker punch to the integrity and dignity that I brought to my work. You would flex your occupational brawn, and I would cower and not make eye contact with you, for fear that I would receive another negative judgment that would shatter me.

And one day, I left my office; I unchained my legs from your desk and met with a high-level administrator who described my work with the most healing words, "Sydnee, you are so eloquent and dignified. Let your commanding voice be heard." It was like a lightning bolt that healed my wounded ego and heart. I am not one to believe entirely in miracles, but I did feel a dramatic shift. I felt a radically liberating shift away from my co-dependent participation in your assault against my dignity.

Here is my ironic shift:

I would like to offer a Eucharist, which literally means "thanksgiving."

I offer this moment of gratitude for the lessons you have shared with me: You have taught me how to sacrifice, to surrender, and sit in my silence and stillness. Your surveillance of my movements as a professional has taught me that all of our actions and spoken words are on record to be misinterpreted and screened for flaws. You have asked me to paraphrase what I understand to be written down in your policy manual and rulebooks that govern the operations of your department. You have made an example of me to those who are new to your order. You have cloaked me in your judgments. And you have shunned me.

Why am I grateful to have learned these lessons? I am grateful, because I have learned that I no longer want to be steam-rolled by your insecurities, your perceptions, and your labels. I am grateful, because I know that others value me as a professional. I know my worth. I am unique, I am eloquent, I have dignity. You do not possess me. I am not here to serve you as your ghost, writing the official communiques that represent this department. Rather, I am here to learn, listen, and grow. I am here to add an innovative thought, a question not yet thought of, and I am here to serve, not you, but the values that embody our university community. You will not single me out on my being the only person of color in the department. No! Never again! Never. Again.

At a university, students and faculty are seekers. They are seeking inspiration and as administrators, we are here to facilitate that process. I know your business perspective has you counting the heads and the dollars, but my educator's perspective has me measuring the quality of their educational journey. I am here to turn the anxious perspiration that comes with dealing with our department into an inspiration that they can carry with them every day of their lives. I coach, mentor, sponsor, and advocate for the students who struggle to be heard. I listen, guide, and support the faculty who are frustrated by the bureaucratic rules and regulations that crack the very foundation of why they are here—to teach, publish, and innovate. You have taught me the ironic lesson that by being chained to a desk I now know the full meaning of connection. I am not referring to a connection to my emails or phone; rather, I am talking about the most important connection that any of us can make in higher educa-tion—validating the self-worth that comes with the privilege of serving others.

I am sorry for the ways you have been taught leadership. I am sorry for the ways you have learned to control your environment. I am sorry for how tightly others have micro-managed you. Ironically, you have taught me to look within myself for my own strengths, courage, and voice. You have taught me how to drown out your voice while you judge me and silence me. And while you rant about how I could be doing a better job, I am listening, quietly, to the beats of my own song. I have learned the how, the why, and the when of Maya Ange-lou's "caged bird that sings." I have learned that to be a caged bird is not victim-ization but rather an opportunity to expose the victor hidden within all of us.

These truths I hold: you are a leader, and you are responsible for the welfare of all your employees. I support you in continuing to find your inner strength and act on your inner courage. Just be careful. Because in order to do this you need to be perceptive to the gifts of imperfections that we all bring to our work. Be grateful that an employee like me is here traveling this journey with you at least for now. Because one day, you will be calling me from your own cage, asking me to set you free, and I will only have one response to give you: Keep singing while you work. One day you will realize it is not I who can set you free. You and only you can set yourself free. This letter is my own declaration of freedom. Here is to Maya Angelou's cage, the bird's song, and the freedom that lies within each of us; may our journey be heroic, and may we surround ourselves with people who believe we are worth living and working for.

How a Resignation Letter Can Be a "Song of Freedom"

...his tune is heard on the distant hill
for the caged bird sings of freedom.

—*Maya Angelou*

In this chapter, I use Angelou's epigraph as my inspirational backdrop to thematically weave a universalizable notion of freedom into my narrative. The haunting nature of the visual metaphors I construct— like "being chained to a desk," "ghost," "six-foot grave," and "Eucharist"—are all used to juxtapose my ultimate purpose in writing this piece: to ironically describe what freedom is not. This SPN is in one part a resignation letter and in another part a Eucharist, or a gratitude letter. This paradox transforms the letter of indignation into a letter of declaration of freedom from anxiety and fear. When I wrote this letter, I opened myself to the possibility that perhaps there was something to be thankful for in my occupational despair. To use an ironic metaphor, the only way for me to see the good in my situation is first to see through the bad in order to discover the good. It was through my SPN writing that I am able to find the wholeness and meaning in my challenges. These challenges are recognizable to many employees across the globe. They echo a song that is familiar to all those workers who might feel like "caged birds," but who must still depend on their work to provide them sustenance for daily survival. While I could remain battered and bruised being a "caged bird," I find solace in my narrative that, in the end, I can set myself free. Free to do what? Here is the most supreme irony of all: possibly I might be able to find in the resignation a path to healing my relationship with my oppressive boss.

Chapter 11

"Walking My SPN Talk"
Writing My Healing Is the First Step Toward Helping Others Write to Heal

SYDNEE VIRAY

Self-Validation Precedes Universalizability

In the previous chapters, I have narrated my journeys from my weak and vulnerable solitude to my insecure and dangerous attitude that make up my unique story. Without fabrication or exaggeration, I have detailed how difficult it has been to reflect on a life of highs and lows. Throughout, I use scholarship to highlight the notion that, while I have my own perspective and experience, others might be able to take my story and find hope and healing in their own story. This is what SPN writers refer to as "universalizability." In the letter that follows, my "declaration of independence" is my way of reconstructing my life narrative so that others may do the same. As an administrator who works directly with students, I hear their day-to-day struggles at my university. One thing I know for sure is that each of them has a unique voice—a story to tell. I am a firm believer that first-person storytelling allows us to show up, with humility and forgiveness, in our narratives.

My Declaration of Independence May Help You to Declare Yours

Below is a personal "Declaration of Independence" letter to myself which serves as a manifesto of how I will strive to push beyond the oppressive bounds that have blocked my thinking of the past. Sometimes during the writing process, the isolation that I feel while rewriting, reliving, recounting my past experiences can leave me fixated and dwelling on painful, hurtful thoughts. Like all humans, I am drawn to the negative, to know what to stay away from, or to problem solve, in an attempt to fix the situation. And sometimes, I can get short-sighted in my thoughts, forgetting to ever acknowledge the healing that may occur. As Dr. Stacey Miller, a respected Residential Life director, once said to me, "Sydnee, it's like you are driving in the dark sometimes and the low-beams of your car just won't let you see but 800 feet in front of you, when what you want to see is the whole terrain."

I respected what Dr. Miller was saying to me, and yet I didn't want the blindspot of not being able to see far enough determine how I might experience my own path. So I wrote this letter. I hope that this serves as a demonstration of how SPN does allow me to feel liberated from the confines of what is possible, once I let go of the impossible. Someday, I will forget about the hurts, the reasons I cried and who caused me the pain. I will finally understand that the secret to being free is not revenge, but letting things unfold in their own way and own time. After all, what matters most is not the *first*, but the *last* chapter of our lives, which will show how well we ran the race.

· ·

Dear Sydnee and your shit luck:

This is a declaration of independence for your soul to be freed from your oppressive notion of your shame, wounds and scars. Sydnee, I want you to break free from holding back your power. I no longer want you to live with only your low-beams on. I want you to shine so unequivocally that others abandon their own shadows. I want you to break away from the undermining thinking of the *dependent* world—and choose some *independent* thinking, some firecracker, celebrating, birth-giving thoughts. As of this very second, allow yourself to be blessed. Allow yourself to be uncorked, unabashed, and showered with delicious good in every facet of your life. Why don't you take the road toward your greatness and head toward your goodness?

You don't need to fit in anymore in the world of struggling, suffering, complaining, belittling, judging, blaming, shaming. Be willing to have things be easeful and brimming with sheer wonder and curiosity, and be willing to deserve this. None of us deserve the other. That's why it's grace. It's not about deserving.

Sydnee, you are ready. Your work here doesn't have to be oppressive. No need to plod uphill anymore, dimming your song, or accepting crumbs and crusts, and bowing your head. Just keep your heart wide open and parade through wide-open doors in a welcoming world. I believe you want every golden circumstance. I believe you want to experience more fun, jubilance, connection, generosity, nurturance, prosperity, and synchronicity than ever before. I believe you want to know your nature—and your nature is not one of limitation or punishment or lack of any kind. I believe there are doorways to your kindness that haven't been opened yet, so be willing now to let go of the familiar and invite your unlimited love to heal. Be willing to let go of what you think is possible or right or worldly or to be expected—and allow yourself to rampage through this new declaration of your own independence, dance through it, breathe through it, dream through it.

Lastly, allow yourself to be treasured, cherished, and nourished wherever you go and in whatever you do. Don't you dare think it's asking too much, because there are so many dimensions of goodness and promise that you have yet to experience. The more you allow yourself to receive—the more you will experience true love.

Wipe away the shit-luck and revel in your deserved-luck. You have earned it.

May you be free,

Sydnee

. . . .

Filling the Blank Pages: SPN as Mindful Writing

In Asian languages, the word for "mind" and the word for "heart" are the same. So if you're not hearing mindfulness in some deep way as heartfulness, you're not really understanding it…You could think of mindfulness as wise and affectionate attention.
—Jon Kabat-Zinn

Inspired by Zen Buddhists, we lead each SPN writing class with a mindfulness activity. When I facilitated my first mindfulness session, I quickly realized that it was a moment for me to "walk my talk." If I was asking my students to be present and mindful during class, I had better help them get there by being mindful myself. Basic mindful exercises like meditation, muscle relaxation, and creative visualization help calm the frantic mind, heart, and body. These simple exercises enable me to witness my own groundedness and centeredness where insecurities, woundedness, and brokenness can lie just below the surface. By modeling the use of these techniques, my hope is that students can take away mindful tools that will aid them in their writing process. Mindfulness activities free our new SPN writers to create the space to let go of their distractions, to listen to their inner voices, and to engage in some of the toughest writing they will ever do.

You have always written before and you will write now. All you have to do is write one true sentence. Write the truest sentence that you know.
—Ernest Hemingway

Just like Hemingway and thousands of other writers, when I write my narratives sometimes I struggle to fill a blank page. When I do, I just start with a metaphor or an epigraph that sparks an emotional response. This allows me to write toward that feeling. I anchor the feeling to a concrete experience. Then I think to myself—why tell this story, right now? I think about the people who I would like to connect with: the students I run into, the faculty members I know (but am pretty sure they don't know me), and the strangers who ride the bus, or who stand dazed in the check-out lines at the supermarket with me. *How can I write to them?*

Like Hemingway, sometimes my first *one true sentence* is a question I am personally exploring. These questions are existential in nature; they resemble a type of—what counselors might call—"self-appreciative inquiry." This self-inquiry beckons or evokes my authentic self narrative; it gives me an opportunity to write my way toward meaning. During my time as an insecure undergraduate student, I was asked to keep these questions out of the mix as I conducted focus groups and wrote my summaries of the "data" that I would review. I would find that I would intellectually tell myself that my story was not enough and I was determined to leave the *me* and the *I* out of my writing. Brene Brown has put it so efficiently: "Maybe stories are just data with a soul." Maybe she is right? Maybe, while I was leaving *me* and *I* out of the data mix, I was leaving out intentions and realities that really needed to be present and forthright. Maybe, just maybe, this idea of narrativizing our lives is the best way to document the data that only our lives can represent. After all, just because a survey asks us questions, we never really know how the survey's results will serve our best interests. The investigator is the only one who has control over that story. So with this lesson, I began to trust that, in order to help others write their way toward meaning and wholeness, I had to learn how to write my own way there, too.

This does not mean I execute SPN with the agility of an expert. This does not mean I can perfectly identify with the S-P-and the N of my writing. This definitely does not mean that I know all the ways that SPN writing can heal. But, I do know one thing—it's worth giving it a try. Writing my way to meaning and wholeness does not mean I seek out others' stories, but rather that I get to the healing that my own story enables. And when I do that, I let go of some of my insecurities, injustices, and infractions that may have influenced my personal choices. When I am asked to share these stories, someone on the other side of the universe may find connection, and therefore, community. And perhaps, just perhaps, my stories may help others heal.

Part 3

The Transformative Power of
Scholarly Personal Narrative
Writing about Change from the Field

The three SPN authors in this section are highly respected professionals in their fields. Wind Paz-Amor is the Associate Director of the Living-Learning Complex on the University of Vermont Campus. Madelyn A. Nash is a recently retired elementary school guidance counselor who has worked in Vermont public schools for several decades. And Jennifer Prue is a University of Vermont professor who has been trained as a clinical psychologist, and who is currently a faculty member in the teacher-preparation program in the College of Education and Social Services. What all three SPN writers have in common is their steadfast belief in the proposition that change must start from *within* the person before change can happen *outside* the person—whether in the workspace, the playspace, the homespace, or the schoolspace. Each author tells a unique story of personal and professional transformation. Each author writes from the heart as well as from the head. Each has made a profound difference in their respective professions.

Chapter 12

See Me, See You
Finding and Accepting Your Authentic Self

WIND PAZ-AMOR

In writing this chapter about authenticity and autonomy, I was forced to really think about what it is that makes up my own authentic and autonomous self. I came up with a list of keywords that I have used as subtitles throughout this chapter, concepts that I later turned into shorter Scholarly Personal Narratives (SPN). The SPNs are broken up into three overarching sections; see me, see you, and finding and accepting your authentic self. I chose these as sections because I realized that I found my deepest understandings around authenticity and autonomy by learning to see myself in every person I meet. Among the top keywords I used were: beauty and body, love and loss, family, courage and resilience, reciprocity, honesty, and integrity—or as I learned it—"do what you say," "walk your talk," and always be able to "hold your head up high." These and many more are the values and beliefs that I hold dear to myself and my philosophy of life.

To gain further understanding of my own authenticity and autonomy, I developed and posed several questions to myself along the way and offer that you, the reader, do the same. What do you risk when you are being your most authentic self? How would you describe authenticity for yourself? What rules in your life have you lived by? How did you come to those rules? Who helped you? How do you continue to hold your truth? How do you grow and make meaning from those truths? Finally, each section will have my own poetry threaded throughout, as poetry helped me to make sense of my experiences while further bridging me to the truths I hold.

My hope is that this chapter helps you, the reader, to understand that like most things, authenticity and autonomy don't come with clean or neat recipes. WARNING: It will get messy. It takes risk, time, effort and most of all it takes love, courage, and reciprocity. "We never know how our stories might change someone's life—our children's, our friends, our parent's, our partner's, or maybe that of a stranger who hears the story down the line or reads it in a book"(Chodron, 1994, p. 3). I hope that you can see from this chapter that the stories in our lives serve to give us opportunities to learn who we are and heal from what or how we have learned it. The most important thing I would like you, the reader, to take with you is to be gentle with yourself, appreciate your stories, and never stop growing.

I. see me

I begin with the section, "see me," because in my own life, I had to first learn to love and see my full self, inside and out. If I could honor and accept myself, I learned I was also more able to honor and see the authenticity that others bring. "See me" is about the ability to see, own, and love who you are first; in doing so we begin to find our seamless rhythm into discovering, accepting and nurturing our most authentic and autonomous self.

The SPN below is what I think of as a live streaming moment in my life that visits me at times with relentless vigor. It reminds me of the long struggle I have had with my weight and my own notions of beauty. As loving oneself unconditionally takes long and hard work, so too does the process of unlearning and learning anew. What self-talk no longer serves you? Through learning to love my own body and seeing my own beauty I am able to feel more natural and grounded in myself. When this fills me, my approach to myself and others is both rooted and genuine.

Beauty and Body

It's 7:40 AM and as I look in the mirror one last time, the question hits me again. Does this make me look too fat? A deep sigh and a quick blinking of the eyes that ends with silence and my hands gently over my heart. I regain my breath and open my eyes to stare at a sticker stuck on my bathroom mirror that reads, "CAUTION: reflections may be distorted by socially constructed images of beauty." I smile, take a deep breath and remember that I possess every ounce of beauty right now, in this very moment.

"We already have everything we need....All these trips that we lay on ourselves—the heavy-duty fearing that we're bad and hoping that we're good, the identities that we so dearly cling to, the rage, the jealousy and the addictions of all kinds—never touch our basic wealth. They are like clouds that temporarily block the sun. But all the time our warmth and brilliance are right here. This is who we really are. We are one blink of an eye away from being fully awake" (Chodron, 1994, p. 3).

Am I too fat? Is my hair too kinky? Is my skin too light or dark? Is my voice too loud? Do I speak well? Am I beautiful? Am I worthy? Am I courageous? Do I stand for something…anything? Who am I? Who do I want to become? And how do I get there? In my own life, I have learned that the questions never end, and with every question I look forward or backward. In doing so, I miss out on the valuable moments of, "*my-me*" in the now, or as Pema Chodron says, "being fully awake," accepting *your* full truth of who you are in this very present moment. "The truth is inseparable from who you are. Yes, you are the truth. If you look elsewhere, you will be deceived every time. The very being you are is truth" (Chodron, 1994, p. 3).

All of these questions and many more didn't really ever help me. They just led me to doubt myself more. In fact, it wasn't until later in my life when I realized that the questions were not helpful because they were not the right questions. They focused primarily on the judgments and responses of others—and little to nothing to do with my own understandings and thoughts of myself. If you wait for others to tell you who you are, you will never find the right answer. Authenticity is about knowing your truest, realest, juiciest self and honoring it. Knowing what you value, what you believe in and honoring it with courage. For me in particular, this included my body and working to shift my own feelings towards it. As far back as I can remember, the one thing that has felt most complicated for me was my body. I had to learn to interrupt the chatter that puts down my body and replace it with gentleness and compassion that in turn creates healing that resonates and echoes my true genuine self. Early in my life, I learned that through writing poetry I could express the "unexplainables" in a way that I could then digest and further understand. I found healing that I could offer myself and in doing so learned more about *who* I was at my core.

Oshune to Moon

Woman to Woman
Sistah' to Sistah'
I have something to share with you
Gather close
While I whisper to you my truth
I am beginning to understand that everything I have ever hoped for, longed for—

Is
And always has been
Within me
Two shades of brown
Shimmering from the moon's light
To all the women who ever thought beautiful was too strong of a word to use for self
My love flows out for you, for me, for we.

—Wind Paz-Amor, 2010

We have those moments of awakening and truth throughout our lives, and it's within those moments, those deep pockets of "shift" and transition within our lives, where we begin to see all of the pieces that create our truest selves. It is in those moments where we begin to build compassion and love towards seeking and accepting our authentic selves—and that authentic self is always growing. Did you know there is an inner rhythm that will tell you when those moments are happening? Take a moment and think about a time when you loved deeply, when you suffered loss, when you found great joy or great pain. In those moments of deep feeling, were your senses heightened? If asked, could you remember a smell, a vivid color, what someone was wearing? Could you remember moments of how it felt? Was your stomach clenching? Were your palms sweating? Was your jaw tight? Was your face hurting from smiling? In those moments and many more we are forced, not asked, to deal with ourselves, to feel fully and authentically in the present moment. Those moments, those pieces of our journeys whether good or bad, whether win or fail, shape us, and the meaning we make from it becomes the wisdom we take into the next day. Through it we learn to make "rules" or lists for ourselves around how we walk through the world. Living those learned rules or lists helps us to reach our truest, realest, and most authentic self.

Come and Gone

i am moon.
daughter of rain.
sister of dark.

i travel like ancestors in the night
hiding beneath skin, searching for inside.
within shadows of pensive and quiet I lie.
i reveal truth only to those who can hear me.
and disappear among the sun's light.

—Wind Paz-Amor, 2010

Beauty and Body have been major mountains in my life. "Looking back I can see how I have caused much of my own suffering. For reasons of pride, ego, and insecurity, what is left unsaid. Pain and ache are felt in the unexpressed parts of my life—when I didn't' speak up, spill open, and be truly who I am" (Ward-Harrison, 1999). My body often betrays me. It has since I was a child. In addition to falling prey to illness, it holds on to weight in a way that is sometimes challenging for me to understand. It has taken a great deal of love and compassion for myself to begin to understand that in many ways I DO love my body, and in many other ways I feel my body has put me through many feelings of loss. I am always healing when it comes to my body both figuratively and literally; it has given my life great meaning. Mostly, it has given me the deep understanding that life is to be cherished and our experiences are our greatest clues to discovering who we really are.

The following section is an SPN on the first time I experienced falling in love and the shame, epiphanies, genuineness and acceptance that came from it.

Love and Loss

I certainly do not hope to alter the world. Perhaps I can put it best by saying I hope to alter my own vision of the world. I want to be more and more myself. As ridiculous as that may sound. And suddenly it became so light and clear to the inside. The heaviness of all this lifted and I could breathe into me as I am

—Wind Paz-Amor

Love and Loss have been staples in my own life. I use them to hold together the chapters of myself. Love is how I strive to walk in the world. Loss, although painful, has offered me some of my greatest life lessons that lend towards creating my understanding of why I walk the world the way I do. Below is a small Scholarly Personal Narrative (SPN), followed by one of the initial lists or "rules" to help steer my life, that I made after my first heartbreak. The biggest lesson I learned…love is a risk, but what better to risk for.

My thoughts were lavished with lavender hues and the thick, layered undertaking of love. Although a long time ago, I do remember that being seventeen is not as easy as it looks. I would compare myself during that time in my life to a baby giraffe taking its first steps into the wild. I felt shaky, wobbly, constantly on the brink of fumbling, and unapologetically top heavy. What I remember most about being seventeen: the first time I ever fell in love which also happened to be my first year as a college student and the first time I ever "came out" as a lesbian. I'll set the stage for you…It all starts with the very conversant "shame of down there."

In my own upbringing, I was never taught to really speak about "down there." It was an anomaly to me. Growing up in Catholic School run by nuns wasn't exactly the best place to get answers—not for the "real" questions I needed to ask, that is. High School wasn't that much help either. Aside from health classes that focused more on reproduction or safe sex, nothing was really spoken about in regards to women and loving our…"downstairs." So, like most women, I walked around at that time not really knowing much about…myself. Until that is, I came to the understanding and acceptance that I was attracted to women—and like most great stories it starts with falling in love for the very first time.

I grew up hearing stories on TV about how love, "makes colors brighter," or love, "opens your world." From cartoons to most movies, love is displayed as adventurous, mysterious, sweet, tender, worth fighting the world for, an epic journey, bells and all. The romanticized love that most people long for involves pieces of that "magic," and why shouldn't it? There is no greater truth than love. What they don't tell you is that love is work. It's hard, endless, incredibly rewarding—and at times taxing work. Authentic love or, "real love," adds a flare of stinky, whole, persevering, compassionate, belly laughter, tree roots, eye stare-down kind of love. It even comes along with a dash of everlasting, if you nurture it.

This was not that kind of love. It was more of a "young, misguided love." It was a love that brought about tremendous revelation about me—and how I walk the many melodies of love—but had little to do with the other person, and who we were together in love. However, it was the love that freed me from the looming shame of "down there." It was in that time, that I discovered how misguided I was about the myths! Most women will understand what I mean. "Shame is organized by gender. The expectations that fuel shame for women are based on our culture's perception of what is acceptable for women." The "whys," the "how comes," and my personal favorite, the "holy shit, that's what that does!" With those discoveries came a release of the shame around it. A veil, so to speak, was lifted, and underneath was love and wonder. "Shame is universal—no one is exempt. If we can't talk about shame and examine the impact it has in our own lives, we certainly can't be helpful to others" (Brown, 2007, p. 18). This was the first time in my life that I can remember where I felt like I discovered my own truth, and I vowed to myself to live it. To own and honor my body and my identity and live who I knew I was, out loud and with authenticity and autonomy. Although that love did end in what felt like heartbreak and betrayal by a seventeen-year-old me, I came out of it that much stronger.

Here is what I learned that later became rules for me to live by:

- Love is a risk, but does a better risk exist?
- Don't give your heart to a fool, and don't be a fool with your heart.
- Don't forget to ask yourself, "Is it fit? Or fear?"
- Let go of the word "downstairs"—downstairs reminds you of basements, and basements feel creepy and dreary. How about "over and yonder"? That feels like you're approaching a meadow and might run into a mystical creature along the way.
- Be true to your heart and make sure that what you think and what you feel align.
- When your toes twinkle, you know you're on to something good!
- Don't worry about what others will think of you; focus on loving yourself.
- Last but not least, there are going to be times when you are afraid to live your truth; when that happens remember rule number 1 and that loving yourself is the greatest love of all.

Learning to "see me" or to see your self is only the first step in discovering, owning and loving your authentic self and how you walk the world. It's a great place to start and in my own life served as the only place to start for me that felt real and right. How do you know when something is right for you? Is is it a feeling? A thought or memory? Do your toes twinkle? The following section will look at what and who has shaped you; how do you make and honor your connections? What experiences and stories do you have to share about what has made you who you are today?

II. see you

What has shaped you? What do you hold dear? How have family and friends helped you to further discover who you are? Family, courage and resilience are pillars in my understanding of myself. The Section "see you" looks at the critical times in my life that have guided me in developing rules, lessons learned, and guides that I later translated into the laws that govern my own life. The section then connects how the rules that guide me allow me to live my most authentic self. The section names the importance of learning to see others and yourself in them.

The SPN in this section echos an experience in my life that contextualizes why I value family as a central core; it further dictates why family, courage and resilience are such important facets of my being. Through this experience and many others like them I was able to develop one of the most important rules that I live by: love with courage and resilience and love your family.

Family, Courage & Resilience

We lived in connected houses on East 51st and Kings Highway in Brooklyn, NY. It was a street lined with trees on both sides. If you stood at the front of the street you could see how the tree tops seemed to be kissing when they reached their peaks. They were untouched by the reality of gunshot, and crack dealing in the area. They seemed to dance in the wind regardless of what the night brought ahead. Although I could not name it as a child, resilience is a dominant theme throughout my authentic makeup. Much like the swaying trees, I too had to sway and dance with and against the changing winds along the journeys of my own life.

Pow, Pow, Pow, Pow, "Mi hijas, bájense!" (My daughters, get down!), my mother's voice echoed in the night in between the bullets that ricocheted amongst the walls. She and my father crept on the floor until they got sight of my sister and me crouched on the floor with our hands over our heads and our faces towards the ground. They quickly covered our bodies with their own until the loud, crashing BANGS dissipated into the darkness.

The house seemed to go from shaking to completely still within minutes. My mother and father, as they always did, first made certain that my sister Jeannie and I were unharmed and okay, then themselves. Before I knew it sirens filled the air, neighbors filled the streets and police filled my home. It seems the neighbor next door, the same one my mother was convinced was running some kind of escort service out of her home, had made some enemies. Enemies who came to our tree-lined block with connected houses and un-loaded several rounds of bullets aimlessly at her house, rounds of bullets that missed and hit our house instead. With windows inches apart, our house be-came an easy target. Our sense of safety shattered like the windows themselves.

My sister and I were quivering, but not my parents; they were focused and steady. My mother leaped towards a detective and began screaming in his face, "I have been calling and calling about this neighbor and you have done noth-ing, and now this. If anything happens to my daughters, I will kill her." She continued by saying, "Write it down. If you won't protect my family, know that I will." "The spirit of fire spurs her to fight for her own skin and a piece of ground to stand on, a ground from which to view the world" (Anzaldua, 1987, p. 3). She didn't blink an eye, my mother; there she stood barely 5 feet tall, fair skin with an olive undertone, fiery red hair that always matched her chestnut eyes, and she didn't blink an eye. The next day my parents put up our house for sale and before I knew it we were packing up our lives in boxes and loading them onto a moving truck. I was 14 years old. We moved to Paramus, New Jersey, and as my father says, we never looked back.

Bullet Lullabies

Resting to the sound of bullets firing at night
Like a symphony of fireworks to a five-year-old me.
Sweet-sweet dreams
Every night
While sounds of exploding guns carried me away into a peaceful rest
I remember always being able to sleep when I was a child growing up in Brooklyn.
Because after a while sounds that mean violence can come to take a rhythm that
causes a schism between what we hear and how it makes us feel. And when you're a
young baby you make things that make you feel crazy go away by hoping, wishing,
praying, humming......

—Wind Paz-Amor

Turning the Unexplainable into Lullabies

The courage my mother showed opened my eyes about what it means to be courageous for her and for myself. Courage is both the innate and the learned ability to bend when all forces of gravity say you should have broken. The moment in between choosing what you think you know and what you hope will all be worth it "in the end." I do not think of courage as an everlasting resource, nor do I think of courage as having to be a constant variable in one's life. The voice of courage can be as soft and subtle as a whisper or as textured and deafening as a pounding drum. It can echo and reverberate between your skin and bones enough to make your teeth chatter or it can appear as voiceless and as faint as a muffled memory. It is as powerful as a waterfall washing over you and moves us to act, even if that act is standing still.

It is in the knowledge of the genuine conditions of our lives that we must draw our strength to live and our reason for acting.

—*Audre Lorde*

My Mother Taught Me to Be a Warrior

My mother taught me to be courageous, resilient, to defend and honor those you love and to hold on. The poetry below is a piece I wrote when thinking about my own mother, grandmother, wife, aunt and sister and all the other "Santa's, Maria's, Marcella's, Miriam's and Jeannie's in the world who firmly established in my life what it means to be a warrior woman, a loving soul, and a survivor. This piece was especially written for the daughters I hope to one day have with my beautiful wife.

We Were the Daughters

My daughter will be a warrior.
She will hunt and fish
learn how to gather and nurture
all with a spoonful of my love.
I will raise her to be strong and proud. I will teach her that self-love is preservation
and that only knowledge and wisdom will give you salvation.
I will regard her as a goddess instead of my princess.
I will teach her the beauty of her spirit will take you farther then a tight ass with
loose hips or a fake weave and liquid tips.
I will make sure she understands that love is freedom.
And peace is a revolution of the soul.
I will assure her that tears can be a catharsis and not a weakness according to
those who fear your power and want to oppress your spirit
my daughter will be sharpened for battle.
And when the time comes her eyes will be wide and alive and full of the power she
holds from the way down-inside,
all within the flowing rivers of herself.
She will take the world by storm,
and like her mothers possess the power and the form; of the wind.
My daughter will be a warrior

Birthed from my womb
With honor and sword in hand
With wisdom from those before her imprinted deep within her palms

She will walk through a blood-tainted earth remembering hymns and psalms sung
by women who have broken their hips and backs in the name of being strong.

My daughter will be a warrior.
Stronger and wiser with her-story based in the victory of the silences I have battled
She will speak it, breathe it, and live it knowing the women before her
Took up space allowing for the grace called her to exist.
My daughter will be a warrior.

—Wind Paz-Amor (2010)

Love and loss are thick areas that are major components of how I have set the guiding principles in my life that have allowed me to honor my most authentic self. How has love shaped you? How do you practice loving yourself? How do you show others you love them? I would describe love as what I strive for in every step and loss as what has guided me towards choosing the best possible next step. Love and loss allow me to remember and know where I am, where I have been, and where I want to be. Both demand of me to live my truest self. We all walk with our truths in hand and heart; love and loss are threaded throughout those truths for me. There is not much that has more meaning to me then love. It is the vessel that holds the thought that awakens in the actions of my everydays. Loss reminds me to cherish what I love, to share what I have, and to do it with both my heart and head as guides. Seeing myself and seeing others in my own life has really come down to learning how to be ourselves with each other.

Finding and Accepting Your Authentic Self

The truth is we all ache. We all have growing pains and wonder if we are okay or enough and loved. The thing is—we are, really. Without the silver shoes and leopard print sheets. We are enough without all the things we buy to make us much more than we are or need to be. We are simple and complex and rare as is.

—*Rene Brown*

Finding and accepting my authentic self, came with both "seeing me" and "seeing you." It came from self and from others. From sharing deep connection with myself and others through reciprocity, honesty and with integrity. It came with real lessons that chipped away at my guards and ego and left me pieced apart, put together and refurbished; Wind 2.0 each time. Each lesson brought about a new awareness of the world and how I choose to walk in it. "A strong belief in our worthiness doesn't just happen—it's cultivated when we understand the guideposts as choices and daily practices" (Brown, 2011, p. 11).

The following Scholarly Personal Narrative speaks about a time in my life when I had it set in my heart and head that I wanted to go to Law School. Anything but the goal signified failure to me. I would not accept anything at that time other than my getting into Law School. It was my own special recipe for disaster. How do you allow yourself to dream? How do you think about success or failure? How does it guide you? Stifle you? Free you?

Reciprocity, Honesty and Integrity

When I set a path for myself, make a commitment to something, I work hard to accomplish it. That is one of my staple motto's in life. If I want something, I just need to make it happen. It's going to take hard work, creative approaches, but I can really do anything. DANGER: APPROACHING A SETUP. LIFE MOTTOES SHOULD INCLUDE SPACE FOR MISTAKES, DETOURS. YOU ARE ONLY HUMAN. That particular rule in my life hit me like a baseball going 100 m.p.h. It happened after receiving my 30th rejection letter from Law School. Yes, I said 30th rejection letter from Law School. If you are reading this asking yourself who applies to 30 Law Schools over three years, then please know that I don't blame you.

I spent years of studying, tutors, LSAT courses, and nothing seemed to be helping. I have had my heart set on attending Law School for quite some time. I had a plan...quit my job, commit to studying every day, take two practice LSAT exams every week, and then obliterate the actual exam! Land myself into a fantastic Law School. Do "whatever" that entails, graduate, save the world, make a heap load of money and BAM! Success. Right? Well...not exactly; in fact, if that plan was a highway, let's just say I ended up an island with no roads at all.

I never got into Law School. I held onto this feeling that I had failed for a long time. I felt lost and unclear about my next steps. I'd had this plan for so long, I forgot to make a "plan b," a "get out of jail free card," options for another direction. I had the hardest time being honest with myself. I kept coming up with high-ego excuses and put-downs when the reality dawned that it wasn't my path. By holding on to what I had deemed a failure in my life, I was preventing myself from dreaming of new roads to travel. If allowing your heart to dream is a risk, then healing is in order. "Whole-hearted living is about engaging our lives from a place of worthiness. It means cultivating the courage, compassion and connection to wake up in the morning and think, No matter what gets done, and how much is left undone, I am enough. It's going to bed at night thinking, YES, I am imperfect and vulnerable and sometimes afraid, but that doesn't change the truth that I am also brave and worthy of love and belonging" (Brown, 2011, p. 11).

When I finally realized that I needed to continue to move forward, a new dream arrived—getting my master's degree in Interdisciplinary Studies in Higher Education and then going for my doctoral degree in Higher Education Leadership and Policy Studies. It took hard work, community and connection, holding my head up high, and having the honesty to name to others where I did not achieve what I had set out to do. It took great giving and receiving for me to learn how to let go and move forward. "Giving and allowing another person to penetrate our barriers and receiving helps us to enter the river of spirit that connects us to each other" (Kasl, 1999, p. 131). To give to others is to feel the joy of creation spilling from us. To receive is to be humbled, to shed our ego. Doors began to open for me and before I knew it, I was proudly walking through them. It doesn't mean I don't think about Law School now and again; it just means I think about so much more for myself in the now.

As a lesbian, Latina woman who works in a "Public-Ivy" university and is in a doctoral program in Higher Education, authenticity, although rewarding, can also look different in different environments. Remember that sharing your full self with others is a gift. Be mindful of how you share that gift. Use your voice wisely and kindly. Develop a method for yourself that will allow you to be more mindful of how you speak to yourself and others. Ask yourself questions like, Why am I saying what I am saying right now? Is this kind? What are my intentions? Remember to carry the best intentions with what you do and try not to allow that pesky, somewhat alluring ego to get in the way. Find your voice and use it!

Although I have learned of many ways to express myself to myself and others, there is no greater, more satisfying way for me to honor my most authentic and autonomous voice than through the vehicle of poetry. "…Women have survived as poets. And there are no new pains. We have felt them all already. We have hidden the fact in the same place where we have hidden our power. They surface in our dreams, and it is our dreams that point the way to freedom. Those dreams are made realizable through our poems that give us the strength and courage to see, to feel, to speak to dare" (Lorde, 1984, p. 39).

My "real" authentic voice is where I store my power. To remember it is to free the scared, doubtful ghosts that linger and make camp when enabled. The "me" that first walked into Higher Education felt tightly clasped to a narrative that said my voice, my experience could not find place or have worth in Higher Education. The me that stands here now knows that what I have to offer is a unique voice filled with compassion, love, wisdom and a deep well of knowledge. I have carved my place in Higher Education, and that means carving or digging into the earth that makes up the fullness and wholeness that is "me." The woman, the Brown, the Black, the Latina, the Lesbian, the woman of size, the Poet, the emotionally available, the Spiritual self; it is all me, and all has a place; all of my multiple intersecting identities.

In telling our stories we create opportunities for others to share theirs and find connection and understanding. If I cannot bring my full authentic self to the table in my life or in Higher Education, how can I expect my students to?

It is in sharing the vulnerability of my experience that I can help to create space for others to do the same; and it is also how I honor the life guidelines that I created for myself that allow me to live what an autonomous life means for me. My place in Higher Education lies in infusing pockets of reciprocity between educator or service provider with students as appropriate.

In doing so, I believe we can all walk away with more of a meaningful and holistic experience. It is always a risk to show your true self, but I do not have the commodity or the luxury to not, "say it like it is." The risk of losing my voice, my essence or my courage is just too great. If you risk your authenticity...what do you have left? The most important lesson I have learned about authenticity is that without love and tenderness for myself, my family, my experiences and my community, my voice falls prey to silence and inauthentic behavior—the price is too costly. "Love and belonging are irreducible needs of all men, women, and children. We're hardwired for connection—it's what gives purpose and meaning to our lives" (Brown, 2012, p. 10). It comes down to love again...figures.

A final word on authenticity and autonomy and how it connects to seeing yourself, others, and loving, living and accepting our truest selves. Having the courage to own who you are in this world will allow you to be your most empowered and powerful self. Loving yourself in a world like today is a radical notion. Instead, we are taught and encouraged to look for what will make us "whole" *outside* of ourselves. Don't believe the hype. Everything you, I, or any of us have ever been searching for, you have found, and will find within yourself. Believe it. Radical? Perhaps, but a notion I hope you fully embrace—rewind, play, and repeat again and again. Do it. I bet we change the world for the better. See me + see you = learning to see yourself in everyone you meet.

Chapter 13

Enlarging the Circle of Students' Self-Understanding Through Stories

MADELYN A. NASH

Understanding My Own Story

There is power in the story
It can teach, inspire, and guide...

When I think back to the formative stories that have been a part of my changing narrative over the years I am struck by the difference between my early experience of school and life within my large, extended Greek Armenian family. One was, early on, an alienating, scary experience; the other, one of belonging, comfort, and identity. The comparison is best captured in the figure of Miss Horn, my first-grade teacher, and my Yia Yia (Greek for grandmother) and the life she created inside our three-family home in Dorchester, a neighborhood in Boston, Massachusetts.

My Scary First-Grade Teacher

I can see Miss Horn putter about her desk and then write assignments on the board as I walk toward the classroom firmly clutching my mother's hand. The halls are empty. The walls are pale, grungy beige cement blocks and the floors, marble. Our footsteps echo in this unwelcoming place. All the other children have already found their classrooms and are quietly doing their early morning seatwork. All I can think is how I hate the smell of this school—a combination of musty wood, floor polish, assorted cleaners used by the custodians, and that awful sawdust smell that reminds me of all the times I have thrown up. Just catching a whiff of sawdust can trigger rising waves of nausea. I do not want to enter the room, but my mother kisses the top of my head, pries my hand out of hers, and gently pushes me forward as she turns to leave. The children glance up but I quickly turn my eyes away so they won't see how scared I am. I walk slowly to the back of the room and hang up my coat and put my lunchbox into the coatroom that will be covered by panels that slide down to cover our things. They don't block out the smell from everyone's lunchboxes and that smell will get increasingly stronger as the day wears on, especially the egg salad sandwiches.

I find my seat, the last one in the last row of bolted-down desks, furthest from the door, near the windows which are too high for me to see out of once I am seated. No one sits on either side of me or in the chair just in front of me. Although I am too frightened to talk to anyone there is no possibility of it easily happening. I wonder why I am seated here so far from the other children. I think it is because the teacher doesn't like me. She does not call on me or include me in the Bluebirds reading group. When it is time for my reading group to come to the front of the room I join them, sit silently waiting my turn, listening to my classmates stumble over words I can easily read. As others read I so want to read on and turn the page but we are forbidden to move ahead; those who do so are sharply disciplined. I want so desperately to be in the Bluebirds group that moves more quickly through the book. Somehow that sense of excitement I feel when I attend story hour at the public library and hear the storytellers I so love is never captured as I read these stories. Even knowing that there is a fairytale at the end of my Dick and Jane series doesn't help make the book feel special since we may not move ahead to read it even if we have finished our work. I am confused. How can stories be so engaging at the library—so full of adventure and joy, sadness and resolution—yet so deadening in school?

I forget story hours. I just need to get through the day. If only I can make it to recess and smell the air on the playground, then get through the next math drill or seatwork paper. Dear God, let her not get angry with anyone. She is so scary when she is angry. I must try very hard not to be bad. Michael was bad and she pulled him by the arm out of his seat and made him stand with his hands out in front of him while she went to get her rattan out of the bucket of water. He stared defiantly at her but I closed my eyes so I hear only the swatting sounds of the reed against the back of his hands. How many times will she do it? When I dare to peek through my fingers I can see that there are red welts beginning to raise on his hands. She pushes him toward her desk, pulls out her chair, and pushes him under her desk with the edge of her chair. He stays under there such a long time while the class continues as if nothing has happened. But I cannot forget. I see him in my mind's eye crouched in that tiny space and pray that I will not be bad. If only I can remember what he did so I won't do it by mistake. My stomach hurts so badly. What if I throw up? She will be so angry. She hates it when I get sick, but the swells of nausea will not stop.

Today she seems particularly angry with us, although I do not know what we have done to make her feel this way. But it is almost the end of the day and I am already thinking about my YiaYia and the yummy sweets she will be baking for us when I get home. Soon I will run down the street to my house out of this unfriendly place. What is she saying? I haven't been listening. She is getting on her coat. The bell for dismissal rings, but she harshly tells us to stay in our seats. We will not be going anywhere. We have been a very bad class today. "You will just have to stay here," she tells us as she walks out the door and slams it. I start to cry and so do many other children. I must go home. My mother will wonder where I am. How can she leave us here? The room is noisy with children's talk and tears. Several minutes pass but no one gets up to leave. Just then a mouse runs along the edge of the wall near the blackboard and students on that side of the room start to shriek. The door to the classroom opens and Miss Green, the second grade teacher enters. She quiets us and calmly tells us we should get on our coats and she will walk us to the front door. I can go home.

I rush out the door of the school building and hear its loud clunk as it closes behind me. Running across the empty schoolyard and out between the tall iron gates, I can hear my heart thumping in my ears. It is just down the street, past the houses of my friends, and that other one with the chain-link fence that holds the Doberman whose growl I am still afraid of, to my own three-decker house on the corner.

My Wonderful Yia Yia

I slow as I reach the garden fence lined with the lilac trees my Yia Yia has planted. My hand finds its familiar place on the wooden gate and I push it open. Once inside a comforting closeness and beauty surround me. I feel the gentle touch of the hosta leaves brushing against my ankles as my feet seek their comfortable places along the winding brick pathway that curves around our house. My eyes catch sight of the budding roses on the arbor to my right and my nose fills with the sweet scent of the peach, apple, cherry, and pear trees that are laden with blossoms. I drink in these familiar smells that are as much a part of me as this brown-shingled three-family house, the biggest on the street, the place that Papou and Yia Yia bought when they came from Armenia. It is home to my mom and dad, my two older sisters, my two aunts and uncles and their families (five cousins in all), and, of course, my Yia Yia.

I notice that this year the grape vines have grown to the second floor porch and their three-fingered leaves are already crowding the open places in the lattice work fence enclosing the bottom portion of the porch making the space a cozy play place for my cousins and me. Yia Yia will soon be picking the tender leaves to make dolmadakia with the rich lemony spiced rice filling I love. My tongue puckers as I imagine biting into one of the neatly formed rolls. Rounding the corner of the house, I quicken my pace and easily leap the three steps to the back door.

As soon as my hand pulls on the doorknob the sweet aroma fills my nostrils. Yia Yia has been baking today and the doughy scent of her deep-fried loukoumades fills my nostrils. Quickly I pass my Aunt Margie's back door and climb the well-worn wooden stairs, twelve in all, winding round in an ascending circle to the second floor. I eagerly open my Yia Yia's door that is unlocked, as usual, and find her softly rounded four-foot eight-inch body standing in front of a large black pot on the stove. Her silver hair is drawn into its customary bun on top of her head, her patterned apron dotted with flour covers the cotton dress with its lace-edged collar. She pauses briefly to turn and greet me, her round face forming a smile, as she lifts a perfectly shaped round ball of fried dough from the steaming fat and places it first on a paper bag to absorb the fat and then into the saucer of honey and cinnamon. Once it is coated, she gently paces it atop a mound of similar goodies on the blue-patterned oval platter that I know will be her gift to my family on the third floor that evening. Another platter is being prepared for my aunt on the first floor so that everyone in the house will be happily munching this doughy sweetness tonight.

She beckons me to a special place near her on a stool close to the stove and gives me a small dish containing a warm loukoumades. I pick it up, its stickiness coating my fingers, and take a big bite. The delicious sweetness fills my mouth. For now I forget my day at school and the island our family seems to be amidst the others in this Irish Catholic community—the others who seem to belong in a way that never seems possible for us. Everything about my family marks us as different—our olive skin, our dark eyes and hair, the rich tones of our Greek and Armenian conversation, the spicy food we eat, our holiday rituals, the way we celebrate birthdays with family but not friends, even our god, whom I am assured by my Catholic neighbors is not the one true god. But inside our home I can shut out these contrasts and bask in the feeling that here I belong.

Had I been able to bring the sense of connectedness I felt at home to school and share it with my classmates and, especially, with my teacher, the chasm between my school and my home life would not have loomed as large. To do that would have necessitated sharing more of my story and the strong emotions attached to it than I would ever have felt comfortable doing within Miss Horn's class. There was no opportunity to express the feelings that I, and probably many of my classmates, carried around. Perhaps if there had been we all would have been more available for learning. Jane Tompkins in her *A Life in School* reminds us that schools "instead of ignoring the strong emotions that create problems for the student, [should] admit them and offer help...." School should be a place that "accepts the importance of the inner life" (p. xiv) and "the need for purpose and connectedness to ourselves and one another. [School] would not leave us alone to wander the world armed with plenty of knowledge but lacking the skills to handle the things that are coming up in our lives" (p. xvi). And those things that come up in our lives are intimately connected to our stories. Recognizing and appreciating the story of each child that comes to school is necessary if we are to see how they shape the way each will see the world and interact with it.

Making Space for Our Students to Tell Their Stories

"There is power in the circle
In our sitting side by side."

How do we create the kind of space that invites our stories? My poem's lines hint at the symbolic power of the circle. Might the potential for community created by the circle be the place where our stories are welcome? After all, it is often in a circle where we both tell and are told stories. How different my first-grade year would have been had we had an environment that welcomed all of who we were. I might have found that sense of belonging at school as well as at home.

Classrooms that don't invite students to share their stories stand in sharp contrast to the Responsive Classroom where creating a safe and respectful community is considered the foundation for learning. The Responsive Classroom was not a part of educational theory when I was in grade school and desks were still bolted to the floor, yet in no other class that I had after first grade (including my sixth-grade teacher Miss Miller, whose demeanor had scared me as a primary student) did I experience these lonely, frightened feelings. Somehow my later teachers invited us into their lives. They shared who they were as human beings—a creative artist, a mother of a young son, a world traveler, etc. They made connections with me inquiring about my interests, calling on me, praising, encouraging, and supporting me. They did all this without a physical circle, but I felt its presence nonetheless in the way they communicated with me, taking the time to comment on my creative abilities and my love of reading. It was most evident to me in fourth grade, however, when my father died and these same teachers shared my overwhelming grief by coming to his funeral. How strange it must have seemed to them to be surrounded by people speaking two other languages, dressed completely in black, but they came and made time to talk with my mother, each of my sisters, and me. They had made the professional relationship personal in a way I will never forget.

Although each interaction, smile, question or comment these loving teachers made was not in and of itself noteworthy, it was the cumulative effect of these gestures and words that signaled my importance to them. It was abundantly clear I mattered to them and because of that I felt safe and respected for who I was. In contrast, my first-grade teacher did nothing to make me feel included in her class. Perhaps my inability to reduce my anxiety as the year progressed irritated her or made her feel unsuccessful. Whichever truth I choose to believe, her impact on me was tremendous, but perhaps not in the way she would have imagined, for I believe that my first-grade experience allowed me to be a more compassionate and sensitive educator. (Another bonus: I taught myself not to throw up and, in the process, I learned about the power of the mind!)

I remember not one academic thing this woman taught me, but who she was as a person is indelibly imprinted in my mind's eye. I never wanted to be like her. Parker Palmer was right about the lasting impression we leave on our students, not by what we teach but by who we are. And if who our students are is to be appreciated we must create an inviting space for our students' stories to be told. Just as my experience in elementary school is an essential part of my story and grounds my work with children, so too are the everyday interactions in the classroom bound to become part of our students' stories. Just as my choices about who, how, and what I will be in my role as an educator are intricately tied to my story, so too are my students' choices determined by their own stories.

Students Find Meaning in Their Stories

"Others' stories draw us inward
Yet make us open to reveal
All our struggles and confusion
All our questions and our zeal."

In my work as a school counselor I often find myself being a kind of cheerleader for my students—helping them to become aware of their own best qualities, making them aware of the ways in which those qualities invariably grow out of the stories they believe about themselves. This awareness—their belief in the story they come to accept about themselves—is hard for some of them to see, especially those that have been wounded in some way by life's circumstances or have endured too many crises in their young lives to be able to bring some larger perspective to their story on their own.

Although I have come at this topic in a variety of ways over the years it was not until I saw the impact of personal narrative in my own life that I saw how powerful this approach could be in my work with young adolescents. When we write or talk from our personal story we have the opportunity to remake the story, to play with its meaning for us at that point in our life, to reinvest it with new meaning and so be touched and changed by it on many levels. Just as we "rewrite" a favorite storybook each time we read it—investing it with our own meaning—we can rewrite our own personal stories until they work for us in some positive way. This retelling or reframing of our stories is a powerful metaphor for the change that can take place within students when they do this.

When students share their stories with each other they invite connection because what they write or talk about are things that touch our hearts. Invariably the stories must be "personal, candid, and deeply felt" as Keyes reminds us. Writing an SPN gives us the opportunity to become aware of the parts of our story that don't work for us, that keep us from moving forward. When we have this awareness we can choose to rewrite our story in a way that is more positive and helps us to grow. I want my students to understand the impact of their stories on their choices and see the myriad ways in which their stories connect with each other. In many ways, I believe SPNs might satisfy our need for transcendence—that something beyond us with which we feel connected—by providing us countless opportunities for our stories to connect. Helping my students to give voice to their stories and see how those stories connect with their classmates is what I believe my role as a school counselor should ultimately be about. For how can we hear others' stories without being touched by them in some way? What better way to build empathy and understanding between and among students?

One Strategy for Revealing Stories

"We are so rich in stories
If we but give ourselves the time
To share and hear each other
The bonds grow both strong and fine."

Jane Tompkins rightly asks, once finding her voice that speaks from the heart, if the "longest journey is from the head to the heart…who is helping our students to make this journey?" In many ways I hope I am helping my students to do this each day by asking the kinds of questions that get them thinking about what they believe and value, what is important to them. I want to do it better. I am continually struck by how fortunate I am to know many of the stories my students have to tell, and by how many more need to be told so that each child feels understood and accepted. Their stories are indeed rich in heart. I know that one way their stories will gradually unfold is by creating a space that is safe and respectful. Only then will they feel free to do so.

On this day we are working toward this goal. I have the fifth-grade class sit in double circles of eight students each, with four students sitting backs together facing outward as four more students face in, so that each student has a partner. "Often we tell others who we are by talking about the groups we belong to and why we enjoy being a part of them," I say. "Today we are going to share a bit of who we are by telling about the groups that we belong to. Let's brainstorm some of the groups that you are part of." They call out "family, friends, sports teams, our class, church, Girl Scouts or Boy Scouts, 4-H, OM, spelling bees, fifth-grade team," and more and we list them on the board. "I would like you to share with the partner you are facing right now a time when you were really proud to be a member of one of the groups that you belong to. Be sure to tell what made you proud to be part of this group."

To start them off I share with them how proud I feel when my extended family gathers to share Christmas at my house. As twenty of us sit around the big and little table the room is filled with talk and laughter and good food and Greek pastries. We spend the day together in a perpetual meal. "The person facing in should begin first. I will let you know when 2 minutes are up. If you are the listener I am going to ask you to remain silent while your partner is speaking." The room fills with quiet chatter as they animatedly tell tales of winning baseball or soccer teams, family reunions over holidays, being on the OM team, and more. When they switch the murmur of voices continues. Each time they finish a topic I ask those who would like to share to tell us some of the things that make them proud. Each time we finish a topic more and more children opt to share as they hear stories that validate their own experience. Then the outer circle moves to the left and with a new partner they share a different experience as a group member—a time when they were teased for being a member of a group, a positive time as a member of a group, a negative or embarrassing time as a group member.

We continue with this kind of sharing, changing partners and topics until everyone has moved and spoken to 4 people in the group and all have had a turn speaking about topics related to their group membership. In our processing time I hear "My family is a really important group I belong to and my favorite memory of being with my family is when we have a big family reunion in the summer and all my cousins come and we all play games and have a cookout." "One time when I went out to play soccer with kids from my class everyone chose up sides but I was last and the two captains got into a hassle about who should have to pick me this time." "Some kids made mean comments about my being Muslim but they don't even know what that is." "I thought me and my best friend were really close but now she has been hanging out with some new friends and she only talks to me when they aren't around." "When I contribute my ideas in the project group the other kids act like my ideas don't matter. They don't listen but they use everyone else's ideas." "Sometimes my friends make fun of "Nancy" because she dresses different than the other kids and I want to say something but I am afraid that they will turn on me too."

What inevitably happens is that students recognize that many of them share similar feelings and experiences—all have been both proud and discouraged as group members. When group identity is so important to us, especially at this pre-adolescent age, seeing both the positive and negative aspects of groups can give them a richer perspective from which to make decisions and rewrite their own story of group membership. It may help them to be sensitive to the role they can play when group membership turns ugly. It may also help them to redefine how they engage with the group they value and reassess how their group identity either positively or negatively affects the story they tell about themselves. Ultimately it makes them more aware of important aspects of their story and the way in which these impact how they see themselves and the decisions they make as a result.

"[E]ach one of us must someday, explain, and claim, our truths in our own voices....what makes you more than how you've been shaped by the academy to talk and write" (Nash, 2004, p. 47). Anne Lamott says, "Your anger and damage and grief are the way to the truth. We don't have much truth to express unless we have gone into those rooms and closets and woods and abysses that we were told not to go in to." Only when we spend some time exploring these places within ourselves "are we able to speak in our own voices." Using this knowledge to help my students recognize that their beliefs and experiences guide their choices and make them who they are (for better or worse) is a useful construct for me as an educator and school counselor. Often the students I work with, especially the troubled ones, see the world as acting upon them.

They blame others for who and what they experience. They often see themselves with no choices. Perhaps for them the truths they would find are too difficult to face without placing blame elsewhere. But what I want them to realize is that they can rewrite the story, find the places where they can make choices they like better, grieve what they are missing and move on. I want them to claim the truth in their own voices and recognize the power of their choices.

And this age group—early adolescence—seems particularly suited to this kind of work. Bleich reminds us that "[a]n adolescent is intensely preoccupied with their own person, physically, psychologically, and socially… these preoccupations and concerns are the key to bringing out a new serious awareness and understanding of the role of the emotional life in intellectual development." There is also much precedent for teaching from the personal. Freedman's words validate what I know to be true and seek to create: "When I invoke the personal as pedagogy, stance, or style, what I am really endorsing is connection" (Freedman, 1993).

One of the things I recognize can be tremendously helpful with my students is my own willingness to self-disclose by sharing a piece of my own story. When I can admit some of the struggles that I have dealt with, I find that students are willing to recognize and verbalize their own. I am in agreement with Nellie McKay when she says, "I am convinced that the personal voice, used seriously and responsibly, has an important role to play in the education of young people." The connections they make with other students when we do this is validating for everyone. It is a valuable way of making meaning, of finding alternative ways to deal with tough issues. Gornick tells us that it is not what happened to us that matters but what sense we make of the events. Although not all students feel comfortable sharing in this way, I believe that hearing others do it is helpful even if they ultimately choose not to share. Perhaps it gives the more reluctant speaker a safe way of doing the internal work that needs to be done before they can go public. Writing about these issues may also work better for some students because there is time to formulate what we want to communicate and the process of writing helps us to make sense of things. I believe that these experiences provide an opportunity for our stories to "transform the meaning of events" or "deliver wisdom" that others can benefit from.

Reflecting on Our Own Stories as Educators

"What a freedom to arrive here
At a place where we can be
Both vulnerable and excited
About this journey of the we."

Making this happen with students is more likely if we as teachers see the value in knowing and understanding our own story's influence on our life choices. Doing that means we will need to become more vulnerable to each other as we explore the meaning of our work and the influence of our story on our professional stance and style, much like Parker Palmer advocates in his Courage to Teach retreats for teachers. What a freeing feeling to meet with our colleagues and know that we are in this work together, struggling to improve, becoming more self-aware, sharing both our struggles and our passion.

For example, as I reflect on how my story might have meaning for myself and others, I recognize that all the choices I have made in my life are in response to the story I tell myself about who I am. My story is a function of how I process the healed childhood wounds, how I celebrate what has helped me soar or survive the hard times. For example, the reason why I became a teacher was to make sure that no other kindergartner or first grader would share that piece of my story—my horrible start to school. (I was sure I could save all children then.) Because of this experience I would become a teacher and create the kind of classroom that was safe, comfortable, and welcoming. And I consciously worked to do just that during the years I taught kindergarten in both an inner-city school and a wealthy suburb.

Embracing the Responsive Classroom philosophy is a healing result of my own early school experience. I firmly believe at a visceral level that creating a comfortable and caring community is *the* prerequisite before any learning can take place. How I wished that *my* first grade teacher had taken the time to reach out to my six-year-old self and find a way to help me make connections to her and the other students. Instead I remember her as a short, harsh woman with an unsmiling face and cold eyes that didn't seem to connect with people. Her voice seemed perpetually perturbed. Was she happy to be a teacher? Did she feel overburdened by her responsibilities? I don't know the answers to these questions but it is clear from her demeanor that she displayed no passion for her work.

Becoming a counselor after several years of teaching is also a natural extension of having lived my negative school experiences; in this role I can help many more children to have a positive school experience. My own dismal start needn't be repeated. Empathy for children who are anxious and/or fear school is extremely easy for me. They tell me their stories and I find an echo in my own early struggles. I often ask myself how might I help my students to "re-examine their own truth stories in the light of the truths that I am struggling to discern in [my]... life-story?" Will my story, as Richard Rhodes says, "enlarge the circle?" Can I help them enlarge the circle of understanding that draws us together in community. As I discern my own stories and their meanings for me, I am more able to help my students do the same. How might other teachers use their stories to make connections with students?

Pamela Gardner says "bringing narratives to consciousness and analyzing them teaches us to become better observers of ourselves and actively participate in the authoring of our lives" (as quoted in Nash, 2004, p. 145). How best to help students safely navigate this process? I have done many activities with students to get at bits and pieces of their stories similar to the activity described earlier. And at nine and ten years of age they don't always have a sense of their own efficacy. Some don't easily see how this story they tell about who they are, based on what they have experienced, influences the kinds of decisions they make and how these reaffirm their story. I want them to see that when the story they tell about themselves works well it has a positive impact for them, but when it reinforces negative images they have of themselves and furthers their helpless feelings it confines the person they might become.

Taking a Risk to Grow as Educators

Does it mean we have no struggle?
Do we reach a place of ease?
Within our circle of compassion
We feel renewed and once more see
There is power in the story…

These helpless feelings can be as true for teachers as they are for students. Today a group of us, about eleven teachers from various grade levels, met for our first ever Responsive Classroom Share. The idea for the "share" grew out of summer work many of us did at a week-long institute the Northeast Foundation for Children (R.C.'s parent organization) offered at an elementary school in state. Seven of the eleven teachers who went opted to stay overnight in a condo nearby as a way to further the conversation about R.C. begun during the workshop day. For each of us the appeal of creating a safe and respectful school community in which children feel free to risk was and is an exciting endeavor to embark on together.

And what became apparent from our discussion once back at school is that each person was eager to feel that sense of safety and perhaps redefine how she sees herself as a teacher. One teacher commented "I have such good intentions each year. I am a wonderful teacher for the first week of school but then the honeymoon ends and I find myself resorting to impatient reminders about our rules. I want all my good intentions to last. How can I do this better?" Such a revealing self-disclosure doesn't happen unless people are willing to trust that others will be accepting and nonjudgmental. I know that trust would not have been there if we had not spent time laughing, swimming, walking, eating meals together, little by little sharing more of who we are, our ideas and our struggles. We shared first within the context of the R.C. workshop classroom and then slouched on couches in our condo or on walks, while playing pool or traveling back and forth to the workshop in an ever-changing arrangement of cars and travelers.

Sharing who we are takes safety and trust, but it also takes time—a luxury teachers often feel is in short supply. What R.C. advocates is that the first six weeks of school be devoted to building community and the norms by which the class will live together. Students will not feel comfortable revealing themselves in ways that matter to their classmates if there hasn't been time devoted to doing that. They will also not feel free to risk making mistakes in order to learn. Some teachers feel that taking this time is wasteful given everything that needs to fit into an already stuffed curriculum. What we are only now taking time to recognize is the need we, as adults, have to feel that same sense of trust and safety if we are to reflect on our practices, dare to admit that we have had less than stellar results with some lesson or activity, risk to try some new ways to make our work better.

Supporting and Nurturing Each Other

Then we are more than single songbirds.
Our voices mesh and meld and grow
For we create the songs that nurture
A true community "in the flow."

This summer when I attended the Responsive Classroom workshop there was ample opportunity to hear others tell their stories as educators, to reflect on their work and help others to do the same. We sat in a circle—seventeen educators from Vermont and beyond—and learned to know and trust each other through an activity, a game, or reflections on a reading. Each day people revealed more of themselves—their hopes, their struggles, their poignant moments with their students—but always the richness of who they were as people and how that had affected who they were as educators was evident. Although total strangers at first, we quickly found trust through the skill of a talented facilitator and the willingness of our group to do the work that makes experiences like this work: we listened carefully and non-judgmentally, we took risks in our own sharing, we encouraged and supported each.

What happened and was necessary with these adults is not unlike what we each want to have happen in our own classrooms with children. I am struck by the circular nature of the process: we cannot be effective at creating this kind of learning environment for children unless we also nurture it among the adults. It is as if we have writ large the Golden Rule—when we care for and value what each adult brings to the table, we are modeling for children what it means to show acceptance and belonging and they in turn show those qualities in their relationships with their peers and the adults with whom they interact.

Our facilitator asked us to sum up what we had learned from our week together. I was struck by the simplicity and power of two constructs: the circle in which we sat each day of the workshop (simulating the daily Morning Meeting of Responsive Classroom) and the stories we shared. I hope, with the support of my colleagues, to recreate the opportunity for both in my school. The poem I wrote to capture my learning appears below only slightly changed. It represents for me another way to invite students to share their stories, feel connected, and grow.

The Story and the Circle

There is power in the story
It can teach, inspire, and guide.
There is power in the circle
In our sitting side by side.

Others' stories draw us inward
Yet make us open to reveal
All our struggles and confusion
All our questions and our zeal.

What a freedom to arrive here
At a place where we can be
Both vulnerable and excited
About this journey of the we.

For others share our passion
And see the power of these –
Both the story and the circle –
For our teaching and the peace.

We are so rich in stories
If we but give ourselves the time
To share and hear each other
The bonds grow both strong and fine.

Then we are more than single songbirds.
Our voices mesh and meld and grow
For we create the songs that nurture
A true community "in the flow."

Does it mean we have no struggle?
Do we reach a place of ease?
Within our circle of compassion
We feel renewed and once more see

That...

There is power in a story.
It can teach, inspire, and guide.
There is power in a circle
In our sitting side by side.

Chapter 14

Anybody's Fairytale

JENNIFER PRUE

Writing can be a pretty desperate endeavor, because it is about some of our deepest needs: our need to be visible, to be heard, our need to make sense of our lives, to wake up, to grow, to belong.

—Anne Lamott

Dear Reader,

I am a *university* professor. I often ask my students to think about their identity and what makes them who they are. Different activities usually yield a similar outcome: a personal inventory. My inventory reads like this: woman, mother, Jew, wife, thinker, friend, reader, sibling, daughter. Taking a page from the backward-design curricula model, I chain-backward and intellectually explore how/what and who shaped the inventory. In addition, the constructs of narrative therapy (Freedman & Combs, 1996) have guided my personal explorations. I want to own my narrative, and I want very much to share the "now whats?" (Nash, 2013).

It isn't easy to be a parent. This I know. Perfection and parenting do not, should not be coupled. D.W. Winnicot describes "good enough" parenting, and that is the model I strive to emulate. Good enough—with the caveat that the underlying anchor is good enough for the children. My parents sometimes managed to hit the bulls-eye of "good enough" at times; but very often their North Star was meeting their needs, prioritizing them ahead of the need of my sister, brother, and me. Who I am now is the result of who I was; how I made meaning out of my experiences and tried to move from wallowing in the "what?" understanding the "so what?" and finally, focusing on the "now what?" I want you to know that this SPN essay is not meant to be a "hatchet" piece bashing parents or anyone else. It is as much *because* of who my parents are as *who they weren't*, that I am who I am. I hope that what you walk away with is an understanding of who I became as a result of the experiences I lived through. Looking back, I can see a pattern: things happened, I lived through them, worked out some way to manage my experiences, looked for the meaning, and used those answers to move ahead. Now, with the lexicon of Scholarly Personal Narrative and the addenda of the typology: *what, now what* and *so what*, I have a frame for presenting my narrative. Further, because of a trusted friend and colleague's helpful suggestion about using a letter format (what he calls *epistolary Scholarly Personal Narrative*, or *eSPN*), I think I captured some important pieces of my story.

People who get to know me often ask, "how did you turn out so normal?" I suppose I was born with some genetic tools, learned things as life unfolded, and possessed some attributes that enabled me to keep looking and moving ahead. At times, my family resented this resiliency, perceived it as a threat, a rebuke of our familial status quo as in-messed up family systems that tend to try to maintain and defend themselves. But I was hard-wired to succeed whether because of, or in spite of, my upbringing. This essay then can be read more as a roadmap that explains who I am: a 47-year-old Jewish woman, mother, wife, daughter, and sister. I am a perpetual learner who believes that I should be doing something to improve the world around me. Very often, the "world" means my immediate one—the world my husband and I have created for our children, friends, and neighbors.

A wonderful friend and colleague of mine suggested that after years of self-wrangling and trying to figure out how to fit my stories into some formal, literary structure, I try letter writing. At the same time, he told me something which resonated with me—"Sometimes in writing a personal letter, you can say things in a more candid, and authentic, way, because you will be more relaxed and less prone to playing the game of academic impression management." I want you to know, dear reader, that I have been looking for you for a really long time. I have had my experiences, and maybe as a way of coping or rationalizing or what I like to call fairytale-izing, I have felt compelled to share them, compelled, driven—something along those lines. I remember even as a young child thinking, "well this isn't ok, but maybe I am meant for bigger things, maybe I am supposed to learn something to share with others." I also knew that there was someplace in me, at some point I identified it as my soul—someplace where none of the bad, scary, sad stuff could infiltrate. And because I thought this, I thought I was special.

When things would happen to me, like being bullied in school while teachers, peers, and my parents looked on passively, I would think "well, someday, you will make something out of this." Or looking back on such experiences, I would start to re-write them as life-stories (sort of like the re-authoring idea of narrative therapy), and by re-writing I do not mean airbrushing them like models in magazines—the women with no blemishes showing. As you will read, I don't airbrush; I have a tendency to look for the irony, the sardonic twist in my experiences (another coping mechanism ala Sigmund Freud), but the facts, as I remember them, remain the same.

I am not looking to forgive or forget. I am not looking to remain a victim. I knowingly gave that role up years ago, choosing the one of victor instead. I am, however, looking to explain why I made those choices that changed my life and the lives of people I love and who hurt me, and the people I love who did/do not hurt me, and most importantly I want to touch, and inspire, the lives of my children. And I want to share how writing about my experiences helped me make sense of them. In some ways, writing about my life is helping me to heal. Writing this extensive eSPN (epistolary Scholarly Personal Narrative) has also allowed me to identify what gives my life special meaning at this time. My hope is that you, my readers, find some transferable value in my stories that will help you to make sense of your own lives.

                                                                Jennifer Freifeld Prue

· ·

Dear Marie Antoinette,

You were a sitting duck. You didn't stand a chance—young, uneducated, believing in fairy tales. I know you must have been looking for all the things any high school girl is: romance, friend and someplace to belong. You thought life would be a fairy tale, but no one told you the truth. They (your family, the French advisors) wanted a brood mare. No one told you all those ribbons and bows were a façade. Poor girl, you never got it, never understood the realities that existed, and no one bothered to tell you life is never a dress rehearsal; there are no do-overs. No, they just marched you, totally unsuspecting, into a maelstrom of political intrigue and watched you vanish.

Here is the thing, Marie: nothing changes. Women are always looking for the fairytale, and I don't mean the big, over-the-top, Officer-and-a-Gentlemen kind of fairytale (although some of us do). Most ordinary women, myself included, simply want to believe there is a reason for what we experience; there will be some sort of pay-off and, if we are being honest with ourselves, we have some burden of responsibility for what occurs in our lives. The most amazing part of this is that we don't talk to each other about our fairytale-izing; and let's be honest—women talk a lot. I suspect it is because we are a little embarrassed. Would you like to admit that you were partly responsible for what happened in Versailles? Your naivete was in some part a conscious choice you made to play a certain role while history was being made outside your gates?

It comes down to choices. I have a friend, Maggie, who at one point in her life was walking through a passion-less marriage. It was more like plodding, one foot up, the other down, one after the other. It wasn't that it was a bad marriage; she and her husband were compatible as companions, but it was just not much fun. Maggie would look for her fun by buying herself extravagant jewelry as if it was a symbol of the kind of life, the kind of spur-of-the-moment, flight of passion, she didn't have or experience in her marriage. Her fairytale was the relationship she had to the jewelry and the sort of life it represented to her. Her marriage didn't smack of being fairytale-like. The good news is that she left the marriage-twenty-five years in, and found love and a life that was enough of real-life fairytale to take away the jewelry need.

One of the interesting things to me, the therapy proponent, introspective person that I am, is that she made the decision without much talk or input from others. I did point out that all women are deserving of good relationships. This was an ironic observation given the tumult of my parents' marriage, which for me, like most young women, represented the template I used for my relationships (or in my case, the inverse template as in—hell no, I will not be with a man who hits me because I like it). I also suggested at times to Maggie that it was okay to expect real warmth and intimacy with a partner. Ultimately, Maggie, unlike you, Marie, decided that 1) she had been in control of her decision to marry in the first place 2) she had experienced enough distant, less than intimate, time with a partner and 3) if all of that was true, she could damn well take control and make another decision. She could leave the marriage.

You did none of those things, Marie, and how could you? Men ruled your world. Misogyny was invasive and maybe even more destructive than today. Had you lived in another time and place—the women's movement, the advent of birth control, the slow march on economic parity that women continue on today—these events might have made you aware of choices. Today, it is all about choice—the right to make it and the responsibility to make it right. But you were enthralled with your particular fairytale and for women in your era making choices, seeing themselves as agents of control and change, were not accepted parts of fairytales. I feel bad watching Hollywood depictions of you. I think that had you been given a chance to think, explore and evaluate your life, you might have made other choices. If I could be there with you, perhaps I would have handed you paper and quill pen and asked you to write about the place where you felt most safe, most alive. Then maybe you could have taken the reins and re-written your story.

Jennifer Freifeld Prue

. . . .

Dear Aunt Julia,

I wrote this letter and then, unexpectedly, you died. So now I am re-writing it as a eulogy of sorts. This is more like a love letter to accompany you to wherever it is you are going. There is a beginning, middle, and end to our story now, and my writing to you makes your death that much more final.

Every child needs a particular someone, a touch-point, a mentor-someone that child can go to, whether literally or not, for calming, for reasoning, for support. You have been my touch-point my entire life, or as long as I have been capable of connecting with you. You gave me: Bonwit Teller's, roast duck, escargot, lovely clothing, clean-boundaried love. I think about Bowen's Family System's Theory and the idea that I played a crucial role in my parents' marriage. I was the third leg of the "stool" that represented their marriage. Anything that pulled my attention, that clouded or in reality clarified how wrong that was—my parents attacked. You showed me that there was a different world, one where children are just children without adult responsibilities; one where an adult tends to the needs of a child. And that knowledge poisoned the well so to speak. My parents couldn't just go on as if I didn't know that the reality we were living wasn't copasetic. I lied in the beginning, or rather I didn't talk about what was happening at home. I knew that to do so might upset the delicate balance of relationships between my mother, you, and grandma. I never shared details with grandma.

But as I got older and was taking care of myself, I doled out details, in bits and bites, as I thought you could handle them. Even when we were leaving for Israel and I knew that I could potentially set wheels in motion that might have kept me with you, I didn't speak out. The truth is, abused children don't run…usually. The narrative of abuse includes this reality: we stay because we can't imagine life any other way. We stay because we believe as I did that our parents are our lifeline. We stay because they are our parents, and letting go of the illusion that they will ultimately make the right or better choice is to accept that we are expendable.

Time passed, and our relationship stayed stable; over time, outside of my marriage, ours was the most stable relationship in my life. Seeing you at Christmas was sobering, a wake-up call. You looked old, no escaping it; you reminded me of that fact whenever I saw you, and then you were in pain. I hated seeing you in pain. I hated knowing that your life was constricting. I tried to stay non-emotional (overt emotionality makes you uncomfortable) and to talk pragmatically with you about what it would mean for me to lose you. I wrote this poem about the experience of seeing you in pain.

Untitled

She says pieces of her are missing
Her arm is outstretched, the skin hangs loosely
Take some of me I think, I can spare what you need
I can give you what you feel is missing

I'm not of this world anymore, she says
I wake and it feels like parts of me are gone

I'm watching her let go
I'm watching life leave her

There was so little time; I didn't know that of course. A quick visit in the spring—your face was bruised from a fall in the middle of the night, and you looked feeble, tired. I helped convince you that surgery on your failing hip would add years to your life. I could be my own person standing on principle with my parents when I knew you would always greet me with open arms. I would always be your Jenny Wren, and I could do no wrong. Who doesn't want to be loved that way? Your love allowed me to re-write the narrative of my life [poor girl with crazy hippie parents who never stood a chance], and I paid a price for loving you, openly and honestly. The fractured relationship between you and my mother haunted ours. Whatever she felt was lacking in our mother-daughter relationship, and yet working in our aunt-niece relationship, she perceived as a threat. I never revoked or gave ground. I loved you staunchly, and I refused to defend, or surrender, our relationship.

So, you remained for me the normal touch-point in my abnormal life. I have come to understand how your brand of cool, never-expecting-emotion parenting impacted your children. I understand the pain that mode of interacting can cause, but as an antidote to my mother's constant need for attention and emotional assurance, please know that it worked perfectly for me. The thought of your ceasing to be was terrifying. I explained all of this to you, as I begged you, selfishly to not let go, not yet. You had seen me through a traumatic childhood, marriage, two children, and yes, I was asking for more time. Ironic yes, because I was making an emotional request of you. And in your usual manner, you coolly promised to consider my plea.

And then you died. Others far more talented than I have written about the death of a parent. This is what I know: my world shifted, and I don't think it will ever go back to spinning on the same axis in the same way. I can't imagine that the images of you in my house will ever fade. I can still hear your voice, and I don't want those auditory memories to fade. Your voice reminds me that there are never enough tears to truly mourn the memory of a loved one. I am the best parts of myself, because you loved me. You helped right the teetering, sinking ship that I was. I thought of that line from *Philadelphia Story* while standing at your grave. The one where Cary Grant is with Katherine Hepburn. They are divorced, but they still love one another, and he buys her a model of a boat they once owned as a wedding present (she is re-marrying some bland, non-Cary Grant man). They are looking at the model float in a pool and he says "…she was yar, wasn't she, Red?" and Red/Katherine answers, "…yes, she was yar…" We both loved that movie. Looking down at the box holding your ashes I knew, for sure, that we were yar.

Jennifer Freifeld Prue

. . . .

Dear G-d,

I've known you forever. I met you when I was maybe three or four. We lived in a railroad flat on Houston Street in the city. I remember every inch of that apartment. My bedroom was at one end, there was a small mid-room (I think my father kept books and writing materials there), then the kitchen, then my parents' bedroom, and the bathroom. The door to the apartment was in the kitchen. Why did I meet you then? I wonder. I can't remember that part clearly. I know I was aware that there were two realities in that apartment. One was routine and normalcy. I went to a pre-school at some nearby Temple. My mother was home all the time. I had a friend upstairs, Danine, who had a big German Shepherd, so gentle, that let us crawl all over her. We would get take-out from Katz's Delicatessen across the street. The other reality was one that felt uncertain. I can't explain how, but I could feel the changes in energy between my parents and in the apartment. Arguments yes, but other things that maybe I couldn't consciously register but could feel. And, at those times, I went looking for something and somehow found you. I also found something inside of me. Maybe we would agree it was my soul.

I have been talking to you since then, haven't I? I worked out a system of understanding what role you played in my life. I didn't expect you to get involved in the day-to-day stuff, even when it got bad. I suppose I thought that you would keep an eye (how anthropomorphic of me to think you would have human characteristics) on me, and somehow my fate and your intervention, along with a smattering of luck, would carry me along. Do I sound glib? I don't mean to. I really think this system has worked for me. It hasn't been an easy life on certain levels—emotionally most of all. But when I needed to feel heard, I believe you listened.

When I was lying on the floor of my college apartment during my sopho-more year, just off the phone with my parents who savagely whipped me emo-tionally, I knew the edge of sanity was just at the ends of my fingertips. But I reached instead for you and that strong place inside of me. Years later, when I felt our house deck collapse under me and I knew Zoe was standing at the door watching me fall, when I came to on the ground and knew both children were okay, I let go and reached for you. I will never forget that ambulance ride. I was not alone because you came with me. As I lay there, I let go. I truly let go, and all there was was quiet, not even any pain, at least not immediately. And I felt light. Maybe that is the place people are describing when they talk about meditation.

Faith is a tricky thing. We selectively decide when to draw on it, when to rail against it, and when to eschew it as some irrational flight of imagination. People who say they don't believe in you believe, instead, in not believing in you. Humanity needs faith to survive. We simply choose what to have faith in so that we don't feel quite as alone in the universe. I chose you. I choose to have faith in your existence. I rarely ask for proof, although I will confess at times I say "see there is proof G-d exists." I said this when two healthy chil-dren emerged from my body and when neither child suffered during the deck accident. As much as people argue that faith is a matter of emotional need (I honor that idea), I assert it is also a matter of logical reasoning. I think, I feel, therefore I am; therefore, I decide to believe in you. I use the word *decide* be-cause thought goes into my faith.

Sometimes you seem to take vacations, and I don't begrudge you that at all. I just need to believe that when I feel the lowest, when one more fight with my family about my upbringing-narrative exhausts me, or when I felt my cognitive functions were chopped off after the deck-collapse accident, that you would listen. Sometimes my prayers are simple, maybe even trivial. "Please g-d, let this migraine end," or "please let me get through this family gathering without killing anyone!" But you know sometimes my prayers are ferverent and focused on bigger things: "please bring me back from this all-consuming pain." "please let my child be born healthy.

I'm sorry that I am jumping around in my life, but then again you probably don't require a linear presentation do you? So even though it felt at times like I was out of step and alone in my family, I didn't feel alone. And when we moved to Israel, I understood more about my connection to you. Placing my feet on the ground of places so ancient steadied my sense of myself as a Jewish woman with ties directly to you. So here we are: I arrived at a physical place that allowed me to connect my faith in you, to a place and a way of being which felt comfortable for me, a mixing of spirituality–temporal space–rituals and faith. Whether *you* gave me Israel or it was a *coincidence*, who knows. But pieces fell into place for me. I can't separate you from Israel, and as I moved ahead in my life, I presented to my children a conjoining of G-d and Israel.

And now…now I feel normal ebbs and flows in my spirituality, I feel alive and crackling at times with faith and a sense of clarity about it all, including an awareness of the layers of time and space that accompanies faith. And, at times, I feel that energy sliding away; who knows why…maybe sometimes I am too distracted, not plugged in enough. But, I know you are here/there, and that feeling alone steadies me.

Jennifer Freifeld Prue

. . . .

To the Anti-Semite Who Carved the Swastika on My Car,
At first, I didn't really register that it was a swastika. I looked, half perceived what was there, got into the car and drove out of the parking lot. As I drove, I kept glancing back. I could see the outline of the swatsika in my rear-view mirror. I pulled over into the parking lot of the campus gym and got out of my car. It was there—an ugly, terrifying swastika on my car. I had a fleeting moment of fear and then cold anger. I called campus police, and I made a report. Leto, the university officer, took pictures of the car, and I let my friend, Lia, hold me briefly. Fast forward: I followed the report to its demise in the bureaucracy of a university. I found safe places to talk about what had happened. And I connected to others who, like me, were outsiders. I realized that as "out" a Jew as I am (I asked for permission to use that term in this context from gay friends), I am not out enough. And, as is my pattern, I took the experience and moved forward, driving toward some change, some difference, some solution to the problem of barely hidden, just-below-the-surface anti-semitism that thrives on the campuses of innumerable institutions of higher education. That part of the story continues, but here is what I want you to know, Anti-Semite, whenever I am asked to explain what happened and how it affected me.

I have never been "on the inside looking out." I have always been on the outside looking in. Lower East Side, born Jew, to parents who originally celebrated Christmas and remembered to tell me I was Jewish on high holidays. Those same parents decided that to live off the grid in the middle-of-nowhere Vermont smacked of revolution and a way out of the city, so there I end up: a scrawny, sickly city kid in hand-me-downs, only non-Christian student, for that matter non-whatever-everyone-else-was person in any room I entered. Outside looking in. My first-grade teacher asked me where my horns were, and when I brought matzah to school for Passover I knew to hide it. And even with momentarily lapsed Jewish parents, one message got through—The Holocaust. Loud and clear, we were an endangered species. I was not to sing Christmas carols because of The Holocaust. My parents had to fight the appearance of a map in a school textbook defining the boundaries of present-day Israel incorrectly because of—The Holocaust. And when eventually my mother went from lapsed to fervor-entry Zionistic, a move to Israel became eminent, The Holocaust was a pillar upon which she built her pro-move argument. The Holocaust weighs heavily on every Jew, and I am no exception.

So, to come out of my campus office, a place I had worked in for 18 years and to see the handiwork of a cowardly Jew-Hater, I was pissed, both for myself and for my six million relatives. Had my mother not dragged me to Israel at age 15—I was convinced I would die in the desert a virgin—I might have seen that swastika, gotten scared, and run. Israel does many things to Jews. For me, it made me pick my head up, plant my feet solidly on its hallowed earth, and know myself. Because of Israel, when I saw that nightmarish symbol painted on my car, I got angry. And, as I have done countless times in my life, I used the anger as rocket fuel. I got involved in my campus Hillel organization. I shared my story and made sure students knew there was a Jewish professor who, like them, refused to take anti-semitism lying down.

In the end, Jew-Hater, all you did was push me to further define what it means to commit to *tikun olam*—healing the world. As a Jew, I have responsibilities to the world around me, and maybe I was too complacent. Maybe I thought that because it felt like I was living an observant life it was enough. Your actions pushed me to look around and get more involved. I won't say thank you, I wouldn't mean it, but I will say you taught me a lesson: anti-semitism is a many-headed dragon. I better keep a sword in hand.

Jennifer F. Prue

• •

Dear Reader,

I always tell my students that I must be able to answer their "so what..." questions; as in, "so Freud described early childhood development—so what? What does that mean for me as an emerging educator?" And I must provide an answer, or I am not doing my job. The answer: Freud explained/defined a way of discussing how prior experiences impact current functioning and how our internal processes work to protect us from trauma. And, so, dear reader, after reading my letters you have every right to ask, "so what?" Here is what I know. Writing cleanses my mind. Writing connects my thoughts and my emotions and helps clear the way toward more balanced decision-making and living. Notice I did not say "rational"—I said "balanced." I am not enamored of the rational; in fact, current brain research indicates that emotions precede, and beget, rational cognition (Damasio, 2006). But in order to work through experiences, in order to re-author my narrative as Michael White (2007) says, I write.

By writing I have been able to heal myself. Good friends, wonderful children, and a loving husband have helped my healing process. But, in the end, it has always been me, Jennifer Prue, and my struggles to put thoughts into words in order to send a message or tell a story. I have been writing poetry since childhood, and these poems have always been letters to myself. Sometimes I have shared them and, when I do, they have become messages to the outside world. All the while, I have tried to heal myself and create a new reality.

Untitled

Where is she?
little girl with a face of optimism
eyes huge with a hunger for love
where is she, did she die
did her soul crumble in to the ashes of womanhood
does she still live in the hidden caves
of a body riddled with the scars of forgetfulness

The "so what" for all my readers is this: without outside help or intervention I can, and have, re-authored my narrative—the story of who I was, who I wanted to be, and who I have become. I have authored myself. Words heal, writing heals, and, in order to go from simple survival to meaningful living, I am convinced that the way forward for each and every one of us is through honest, authentic, no-holds-barred, personal narrative writing. Try it!

—Jennifer Freifeld Prue

●

Chapter 15

A Final Letter to Our Readers
Down-to-Earth Tips for Writing Stories That Heal

SYDNEE VIRAY

Dear Readers,

Because to write healing stories in a frank, personal way can sometimes mean to suffer, it is imperative to practice a few helpful, self-confidence exercises to ensure that this process is productive. I offer you the following down-to-earth tips for getting started, sustaining, and finishing:

1. ***Believe in yourself at all costs***. I even went to the literal extreme of buying a 2" by 3" piece of canvas board and took out my colorful Sharpie to write the words *BELIEVE IN YOURSELF.* This cue card still sits near my computer whenever I write.

2. ***Become comfortable when you feel uncomfortable***. It can take me hours to get myself to sit down to really write. I will employ the most elaborate strategies to avoid writing, especially if the pages before me are blank. So I learned to make my writing space inviting and warm.

3. ***So what if you write poorly; the riches come in the editing and re-writing***. Do not, and I repeat DO NOT, obsess over your grammar errors and spelling mistakes as you write your first draft. Your work is not yet *art*; at best, it is *crafting* something that you can work on later in order to polish, burnish, and beautify it so you can turn it into art. Don't even try to make it perfect on the first try. This is a losing game. Because getting the words on paper for the first time often produces an ugly mess, trying to make it perfect will only make you feel ugly and imperfect. Immanuel Kant once said that the *best* is always and everywhere the enemy of the *good*. Settle, instead, for

writing a coherent manuscript on the first try, and, then, maybe, possibly, you can produce something fair or good on successive tries. Let's be honest: the so-called *best* manuscript is probably only a fantasy, no matter how many times you try to beautify and perfect it.

4. ***Find a friend, or two, or three, who will (even if not writing with you) help you commit to your writing practice.*** While writing my SPN thesis, I had at least two or more people I could count on to remind me that I had an important task to complete. The same is true while writing my first book. I needed my trusty cheerleaders to "celebrate me home." I needed them to remind me that I am not alone.

5. And a note on critical feedback from significant others. This will be the greatest gift someone will give you. Whether it is a publisher, editor, mentor, advisor, teacher, or your family and friends, each wants you to succeed, and they all have a stake in your persistence. So, receive the critique as a potentially golden key to open your heart so that your writing will be as good as you can make it. I encourage everyone to first learn "to be" in the criticism they receive; and then pursue the course of giving their writing to others for feedback. And, if publication is your goal, in this day and age, know that self-publishing is becoming more and more an option. So, explore all those alternative publication avenues but only after you have learned from the critiques and after you have made peace with them.

6. ***There is healing power in seeing your story's words reflect back at you on your computer monitor.*** In fact, as we have pointed out time and time again in this book, the act of writing itself can be its own healing salve. Even if you don't intend to submit your manuscript to anyone, your writing will not be in vain. Nothing written is ever wasted.

7. ***Take one writing step at a time.*** There is no need to run; as long as you have one foot in front of the other...one word after another... you are writing. Most important, don't obsess about where you need to go, or what that idea is leading to, or when the deadline will come crashing down upon you. Just write one word after the other. Voila! Sooner or later, you will cross that finish line. Think of words like passing seconds. Sooner or later the seconds become minutes, which then become hours, which then become days, which then become weeks, and on and on. And before we know it, we have lived an entire year. Or to apply the metaphor to our writing—we have produced an entire manuscript. Imagine!

8. ***Write it down seven times and edit eight.*** Write, write, write, and then improve, improve, improve when you do your editing. Celebrate both the unedited and edited writing. One is necessary in order to produce the other.

Roy Peter Clark says that every writer has to learn how to "prune the bushes," and "kill our darlings," when they don't serve the best interests of our manuscripts.

9. ***Do not fear the "I don't know where I am going" mindset.*** There is wisdom in allowing the destination to come to you. Let the writing flow. How lucky you will be when you get into the "authorial zone." Most flow-writing comes from being willing to let go of knowing beforehand what the results will be. There is wisdom in not knowing. Medieval Christian writers called this a "higher ignorance." As long as you are aware of your general themes, both personal and generalizable, seek the unpremeditated flow in your writing. "Flow, glow, and let it go," as Robert often says. And, by the way, sometimes key themes that you didn't even know about before you started writing evolve during and after the writing.

10. ***Make good use of what you might think of as being your humdrum, uninteresting, everyday experiences.*** Every experience contains a story, or, acutally, a multiplex of stories. And every story contains a theme and a possible insight for others. You and I live in our stories. We learn in our stories. We love in our stories. Our stories contain our native wisdom. Don't be afraid to return to your motherland, and native tongue, when you write. And who has the right, or the authority, to tell you that your stories are humdrum anyway?

11. ***Let go of trying to be an expert before, and during, your writing.*** Think, instead, of writing your way into some kind of expertise…or better…some kind of wisdom that you can share with others. Expertise comes during, and after, SPN writing, not before it. In fact, put yourself in a position to learn something from a so-called non-expert. Talk to those who know nothing about the content in your writing in order to get them to respond to one sentence, one paragraph, even one page or more… and see where that takes you. There is wisdom in ignorance, believe it or not, especially when you can use it to your own benefit.

12. ***Experience your writing fully.*** Don't worry about what others might think. Have you ever taken a child to the movies? Everything is amazing to children. They gaze at the bright lights in the foyer. They investigate each popcorn kernel with great concentration. They stare at everyone sitting around them. They flinch when the music starts. They scramble onto your lap when the monster appears on screen. They laugh aloud when actors do something that's funny. They live fully and uncensored in each moment. This is the way that I try to write my manuscripts. I want to be like the children who are so fully immersed in film-watching that they could care

less about what others might be thinking about them…except, of course, when they become bothersome distractions themselves. I don't ever want to become a bothersome distraction to those around me. I will, therefore, write in solitude, and seek total immersion in my work. And I will be amazed by what I am experiencing.

13. ***Don't worry about always having to express the voice of conventional academic sense in your writing.*** Think of all the great thinkers and artists out there who have stood the test of time. They are non-formulaic in their artistry. They avoid specialized jargon. They challenge the rigid conventions of their disciplines. They break new ground in their genres. They create in order to innovate, in order to come up with something fresh and insightful. If they were common or conventional, they wouldn't be great. Think of such writers as Ernest Hemingway, or Margaret Mead, or Bertrand Russell, or E. B. White, or Maya Angelou, or any number of "public intellectuals" who have successfully bridged the worlds of academia and the general public. Invite yourself into the land of creative, uncommon sense instead! Write for an enlarged audience.

14. ***Invite, and welcome, the spirit of inquiry into your writing, and don't forget to write down the questions.*** Aristotle said that all of wisdom begins in wonder. No wonder, no wisdom. No questions, no answers, no matter how tentative. A professor once visited a Japanese master to inquire about Zen. The master served tea. When the visitor's cup was full, the master kept pouring. Tea spilled out of the cup and over onto the table. "The cup is full!" said the professor. "No more will go in!" "Like this cup," said the master, "you are full of your own opinions and speculations. How can I show you Zen unless you first empty your cup?" This story applies not only to learning about Zen, but to learning about anything at all. The spirit of inquiry requires that the writer's mind be open to the unknown, and empty, as much as possible, of pre-conceived ideas. An SPN tip: Focus on the questions, not the answers. Start with innocent wonder, and be content to end up with even more wonder. Nobody that Robert and I have read on the topic of meaning-making has come up with a single reason to disavow the wonder that resides in all of us. And, in the spirit of the poet Rilke, we ask you to follow the questions wherever they might lead. Sometimes they result in answers, but most of the time they result in more questions. You might be more than pleasantly surprised where you end up.

So, dear reader, these are a few brief, simply stated, tips for writing stories that heal. These tips help me to go beyond my fears whenever I sit down to write the story of my life. Please feel free to refer to my tips during your writing or, better still, even when you are not writing. Maybe a few of these tips will get you to your writing space. Scholarly Personal Narrative writing can be very, very challenging. Each of us needs all the encouragement and help we can get to start, sustain, and finish our manuscripts. But it all starts with your motivation, and confidence, to write your life.

I urge you to add your own writing tips to the above list. Please know that neither I, nor Robert, have the final word on how to write stories that heal. Like you, we are learning each and every time we sit down in front of our computers how to write from our inside to our outside. There is no one tried-and-true formula for doing this. Feel free to experiment. Take some chances. I give you unqualified permission to write your way into healing, meaning, and wholeness in your own best manner. I know that I will learn from you.

And, if you are a first-generation, or non-traditional, college student (like myself and Robert were), who never thought that being a writer or scholar was in your future, I ask you to reconsider this assumption. Deep down, in an uncensored space, most successful people we know will acknowledge that, at one time (or even all the time) they never thought they could achieve anything truly worthwhile as writers or scholars. Believe me, dear reader, you are worthwhile. You will take SPN writing to heights it has never been before. Why? Because your story is unique. And, yet, it is also universal. As the poet said: nothing human is alien to me. Nothing. So just get started. Something wonderful will be born. Trust me on this!

Respectfully,
Sydnee

Bibliography

Abbott, H. P. (2002). *The Cambridge introduction to narrative*. New York: Cambridge University Press.

Angelou, M. (2009). "The Art of Fiction," *The Paris interviews: Vol. IV.* Ed. P. Gourevitch. New York: Picador.

Anzaldúa, G. (1987). *Borderlands/ la frontera: The new mestiza.* San Francisco: Aunt Lute Books.

Banks, J. T. (1986). *Literature and medicine.* Baltimore, MD: Johns Hopkins Press.

Becker, E. (1973, 1997). *The denial of death.* New York: Free Press.

Behar, R. (1993). *The vulnerable observer: Anthropology that breaks your heart.* Boston: Beacon Press.

Bleich, D. (2013). *The materiality of language: Gender, politics, and the university.* Bloomington, IN: Indiana University Press.

Brooks, P. (1985). *Reading for the plot.* New York: Random House.

Brown, B. (2012). *Daring greatly: How the courage to be vulnerable transforms the way we live, love, parent, and lead.* New York: Gotham Books.

Brown, B. (2007). *I thought it was just me, but it isn't.* New York: Gotham Books.

Brown, T. D. (2011). *Education through meaning-making: An artist's journey from quarterlifer to educator.* A University of Vermont Master's thesis.

Bruner, J. (2002). *Making stories: Law, literature, life.* New York: Farrar, Straus and Giroux.

Chodron, P. (1994). *Start where you are: A guide to compassionate living.* Boston, MA: Shambhala Publications.

Chua, A. (2011). *Battle hymn of the tiger mother.* New York: Penguin.

Clark, R. P. (2010). *The glamour of grammar: A guide to the magic and mystery of practical English.* New York: Little Brown.

Damasio, A. (2006). *Decartes' error: Emotion, reason, and the human brain.* New York: Penguin.

Dillard, A. (1990). *The writing life.* New York: HarperPerennial.

Ferrucci, P. (2005). *El poder de la bondad: Solo tendremos futuro si pensamos con el corazon.* Barcelona: Urano.

Frankl, V. (1959, 2006). *Man's search for meaning.* Boston: Beacon Press.

Freedman, D. P., & Frey, O. Eds. (1993). *The intimate critique: Autobiographical literary criticism.* Durham, NC: Duke University Press.

Freedman, J., & Combs, G. (1996). *Narrative therapy: The social construction of preferred realities.* New York: Norton.

Graff, G. (2003). *Clueless in academe: How schooling obscures the life of the mind.* New Haven, CT: Yale University Press.

Kabat-Zinn, J. (2005). *Wherever you go, there you are.* New York: Hyperion.

Kasl, C. (1999). *If the Buddha dated: A handbook for finding love on a spiritual path.* New York: Penguin.

Keyes, R. (1995). *The courage to write: How writers transcend fear.* New York: Henry Holt.

Lamott, A. (1994). *Bird by bird: Some instructions on life and writing.* New York: Random House.

Lorde, A. (1981). "The Master's Tools Will Never Dismantle the Master's House" in *This bridge called my back: Writings by radical women of color.* Gloria Anzaldúa, Ed. New York: Kitchen Table Women of Color Press.

Lorde, A. (1984). *Sister outsider.* Freedom, CA: The Crossing Press.

Maisel, E. (1999). *Deep writing: 7 principles that bring ideas to life.* New York: Jeremy P. Tarcher/ Putnam.

Nash, R. J., (2002). *Spirituality, ethics, religion, and teaching: A professor's journey.* New York: Peter Lang Publishing.

Nash, R. J., (2004). *Liberating scholarly writing: The power of personal narrative.* New York: Teachers College Press.

Nash, R. J. & Bradley, D. L. (2011). *Me-search and re-search: A guide for writing scholarly personal narrative manuscripts.* Charlotte, NC: Information Age Publications.

Nash, R. J. & Viray, S. (2013). *Our stories matter: Liberating the voices of marginalized students through scholarly personal narrative writing.* New York: Peter Lang.

Paz-Amor, W. (2010). *A pluralistic approach to addressing sexual and gender-based violence on college campuses.* A University of Vermont Master's thesis.

Phillips, C. (2001). *Socrates cafe: A fresh taste of philosophy.* New York: W. W. Norton.

Riley, N. S. (2011). *The faculty lounges: And other reasons why you won't get the college education you paid for.* Chicago: Ivan R. Dee.

Schucman, H. & Thetford, W. (2009). *A course in miracles: Text, workbook for students, manual for teachers.* Omaha, NE: Course in Miracles Society.

Smedes, L. (2007). *Forgive and forget: Healing the hurts we don't deserve.* New York: HarperOne.

Smiley, J. (2005). *13 ways of looking at the novel.* New York: Alfred A. Knopf.

Taylor, C. (1992). *A secular age.* Cambridge, MA: Harvard University Press.

Tolle, E. (2005). *A new earth: Awakening to your life's purpose.* London, England: Plume.

Tolstoy, L. (1879, 2009) *A confession*. New York: World Library Classics.

Vedder, R. (2004). *Going broke by degree: Why college costs too much*. New York: Aei Press.

Ward-Harrison, S. (1999). *Spilling open: The art of becoming yourself*. Novato, CA: Villard Books.

White, H. (1973). *The content of the form: Narrative discourse and historical representation*. Baltimore, MD: Johns Hopkins University Press.

White, M. (2007). *Maps of narrative practice*. New York: W. W. Norton & Company.

Zinsser, W. (2001). Ed. *On writing well: The classic guide to writing nonfiction*. New York: Quill.

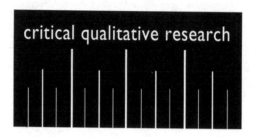

critical qualitative research

Shirley R. Steinberg & Gaile S. Cannella, *General Editors*

The Critical Qualitative Research series examines societal structures that oppress and exclude so that transformative actions can be generated. This transformed research is activist in orientation. Because the perspective accepts the notion that nothing is apolitical, research projects themselves are critically examined for power orientations, even as they are used to address curricular, educational, or societal issues.

This methodological work challenges modernist orientations and universalist impositions, asking critical questions like: Who/what is heard? Who/what is silenced? Who is privileged? Who is disqualified? How are forms of inclusion and exclusion being created? How are power relations constructed and managed? How do different forms of privilege and oppression intersect to affect educational, societal, and life possibilities for various individuals and groups?

We are particularly interested in manuscripts that offer critical examinations of curriculum, policy, public communities, and the ways in which language, discourse practices, and power relations prevent more just transformations.

For additional information about this series or for the submission of manuscripts, please contact:
  Shirley R. Steinberg and Gaile S. Cannella
  msgramsci@aol.com | Gaile.Cannella@unt.edu

To order other books in this series, please contact our Customer Service Department:
  (800) 770-LANG (within the U.S.)
  (212) 647-7706 (outside the U.S.)
  (212) 647-7707 FAX

Or browse online by series:
  www.peterlang.com